My Brother
EVELYN
and Other Portraits

Alec Waugh has written
more than forty books. They include

Novels
The Loom of Youth 1917
Kept 1925
Nor Many Waters 1928
So Lovers Dream 1931
The Balliols 1934
Jill Somerset 1936
No Truce with Time 1941
Unclouded Summer 1948
Guy Renton 1953
Island in the Sun 1956
Fuel for the Flame 1960
The Mule on the Minaret 1965

Short Stories
My Place in the Bazaar 1961

Travel
Hot Countries 1930
The Sugar Islands 1958

General
In Praise of Wine 1959
The Early Years of Alec Waugh 1962
A Family of Islands 1964

My Brother
EVELYN
and Other Portraits

by
Alec Waugh

Farrar, Straus and Giroux
New York

To the memory of my brother Evelyn
in homage and with love

Contents

Part Two

PART ONE

Foreword

In 1962 I published a partial autobiography, under the title *The Early Years of Alec Waugh*. I was born in July 1898 and the book took me up to the summer of 1930. It told how I had become the kind of person that I am, restless, rootless, eager for change, avid of the sun, finding his plots between capricorn and cancer. The year 1930 was a watershed for me. It marked the end of a major love affair, and the success in America of a travel book *Hot Countries*—which was a Literary Guild selection—introduced me to the United States. From that point on, my professional base began to shift from London to New York.

One or two of the reviewers of *The Early Years* were kind enough to express the hope that I should write a sequel. Perhaps I shall, one day. But this is not that book, although it is reminiscent and told in the first person. Its 'I' is the observer and the commentator, the *raisonneur*. This book is an attempt to present a picture of the English literary world as I have known it, through a series of portraits of some of the men and women who comprised it. Where I have been autobiographical, it is only because cer-

3

tain of my experiences as a writer illustrate my general thesis.

It is in no sense comprehensive. A number of prominent writers have been omitted, even though I may have known them; but I think that each of the portraits will be found to illustrate and interpret one aspect or another of the writer's life. It takes all sorts to make a world, and the literary world with its excitement and its monotony, its sudden changes of fortune; its rich rewards, its bitter disappointments; its salutations in the market-place, its essential loneliness; its precariousness, it penury, its deep personal satisfaction from doing in one's own time, in one's own way, what one enjoys doing most—presents an infinite scope for drama. I hope that these pages will give the reader some concept of that scope.

Most of these portraits were sketched separately at different times; some of them have appeared in magazines, some were originally intended for inclusion in *The Early Years,* but in the end did not seem to fit satisfactorily into its pattern. For the convenience of the reader one or two of the chapters have been dated.

I

Cousin Edmund

SIR EDMUND GOSSE

My first novel was published in July 1917, so that I have been part of the literary scene for half a century, but I have been an observer of it for a good deal longer, through my father, Arthur Waugh, who for forty years directed the fortunes of Chapman & Hall, Dickens's original publishers. My father has told his own story in *One Man's Road*; my brother Evelyn has told it in *A Little Learning*; I told it in my *Early Years*.

My paternal grandfather was a west country doctor, who hoped that his son would inherit his practice, but from early days it was obvious that by taste and temperament my father was unfitted for a life of medicine. He had a passion for books, for the library not the laboratory. At the age of twenty-three, having won the Newdigate Prize Poem at Oxford, he went up to London to earn his living with his pen.

He started his adventure without financial backing, but he had what was more valuable than capital, a blood relationship with Edmund Gosse. Gosse is far from forgotten, even now. Critical articles constantly refer to his writings and to his personality. His autobiography *Father and Son* is 'required reading'. For over forty years he was influential in the world of letters. Nobody could have been better fitted to give a young man like my father his first chances.

The actual degree of cousinship between the Waughs and Gosses is a little distant—my great-grandmother was the first cousin of Edmund's father—but the links

5

between the families have long been affectionate and close and they go back many years. My father's mother spent part of her childhood in the same melancholy religious atmosphere which Edmund Gosse described in *Father and Son*. 'The Plymouth Brethren of this circle were,' my father wrote, 'a desperately sincere but terribly depressing company whose principal interest was a lively and immediate expectation of the second coming.' My grandmother recalled how Philip Henry Gosse would stand in the doorway, austere, solemn, confident, unwinding an interminable worsted scarf from about his neck and saying to her mother, 'Well, Cousin Anne, still looking daily for the coming of the dear Lord Jesus. Are not all the prophecies indeed fulfilled?' The ominous decision would then go forth that the Lord would accomplish the number of his elect on Saturday afternoon at about three o'clock. When Saturday afternoon came and waned to evening, without the expected event occurring, a new text was found next morning to justify the delay.

The young Edmund was brought at the age of seven, after his mother's death, for a visit to my grandmother's home. He seemed a precocious infant but she, several years his senior, was touched by the eagerness which was one of his greatest charms and used to tell how he knelt excitedly before a case of stuffed birds exclaiming with high pitched enthusiasm, 'Cousin, you have here a remarkable specimen of the Golden Oriole.'

Max Beerbohm, in his series of cartoons, 'The young self meets the old self', drew Gosse in his last decade, surrounded by important friends, being startled by the unannounced invasion of that august assembly by a small earnest infant waving a flag and shouting 'Are you saved?'

To the reader of today, Gosse is remembered in terms of those two selves: the young evangelist of whom he

6

himself has drawn an unforgettable picture in *Father and Son*, and the doyen of letters whose legend has been enshrined in Osbert Sitwell's *Eminent Presences*, Max Beerbohm's *A Christmas Garland* and the imaginary conversations in *Avowals* with George Moore.

Gosse was the first important writer whom I met, yet it is with hesitation that I write of him. As a schoolboy I asked my father if he had ever met Oscar Wilde. He shook his head. 'No, and I only saw him twice. Once in London, when he put his head round the door at a party and said, "I have come to tell you I can't come," secondly in Paris, after the scandal.'

My father was in a café, so he told me, with Sidney Pawling, Heinemann's partner, and Peter Chalmers Mitchell who directed the London Zoo and was subsequently knighted. Wilde came in, looked round him, then went out. Mitchell said, 'That's Wilde. I'll go and speak to him.' He was away ten minutes. On his return, he said, 'I don't see why you should cut a man because he's had a scandal. I've no use for fairweather friends who drink a man's wine when he's in favour and look the other way when he's in trouble.' He was so persistent and generally self-righteous that finally Pawling said, 'What are you making all this fuss about? Waugh doesn't know him. I've scarcely met him. Don't be such an ass, Mitchell, finish up your beer.'

That was the story as my father told it me. Many years later, in his autobiography *My Fill of Days* Mitchell described how he found himself in Paris with 'two quite nice people, one a stockbroker, the other a partner in a publishing house, both what may be called "men of the world"'. On Wilde's appearance, so Mitchell said, 'my friends got up to go. "You can stay if you like," they said. "He is probably here under a false name. The hotel should be warned."' Mitchell said that he and Wilde talked for two hours.

Mitchell had the warmest affection for my father. He wrote a few pages later, 'Arthur Waugh is another of my lifelong friends for whom the years have done nothing worse than to silver his hair. By nature a poet, he is the rare combination of a man of letters and a man of business and has been one of the steady and beneficent forces in the English literature of our time.' He had clearly forgotten that my father was in his company that evening.

My father's account of the incident is far likelier to be correct. He recounted it twenty years before Mitchell wrote his book, his memory was very sound, moreover he was not the kind of man to make a scene in public, and very far from being the man to turn against anyone who was in trouble. It is clear to me that Mitchell confused what might have happened or rather what he would like to have happened with what did happen.

I recall the anecdote here because it exemplifies the danger of accepting even what is known as first-hand evidence. When we look back at our childhood it is impossible to distinguish between what we actually remember and what has been remembered for us; in later life we are often in the same predicament. However clear may be our mental picture of this episode or that personality, we can never be certain that it has been wholly painted by what we have ourselves seen and heard and not in part by what we have heard repeated, and in the case of Edmund Gosse, I am very conscious that my knowledge of him is largely based on what I have heard my father say of him. Yet even so he is as distinct to me as many men whom I have been meeting regularly over years.

As a schoolboy I saw him intermittently, when he and his wife came to lunch on Sunday. Those visits are vivid memories. My father was an excellent host, but on the eve of any occasion he was invariably nervous lest 'everything should not go off all right', and he was particularly anxious when the Gosses came. I was myself very conscious that we were receiving a visitor from a larger world, who knew personally men and women with whose faces I was familiar in the Press, Balfour and Asquith and Lord Salisbury, men whom I could not quite believe to be real people with headaches and indigestion like the rest of us.

I remember Gosse describing Queen Alexandra's lengthy visit to his library (would she never leave?) and how at length he had been driven to exclaim, 'I fear, Ma'am, that I have nothing else to show you that would be worthy of your attention.' I was very proud to have so distinguished a relative.

He had too an imposing presence with his head carried erect above a high collar, whose pointed ends were turned but not folded back. His drooping moustache was tidy; he had retained in full the hair to which Sargent in an early portrait gave a tint of lilac. Maugham described him as the most brilliant talker to whom he had ever listened. Gosse dominated but did not monopolize the talk. With memory's eye I can see him very clearly, sitting bolt upright in a hard-backed chair, clasping firmly against his waistcoat the spine of our grey-blue Persian cat while he stroked its underbelly with both hands. He professed great love of cats, but I was never convinced that our particular cat appreciated his attentions. When I attempted similar endearments, I was scratched. But perhaps his long fingers possessed a mesmeric quality that mine lacked.

In the 'twenties as a member of his own club—the Savile—I saw him oftener. He was then in full enjoyment of a mellow St Martin's summer. At the age of sixty-six he had had to retire from the Librarianship of the House of Lords. He was irritated at the time, but his release from official duties was in fact a benefit. He had more time for writing and for social activities. His links with European writers had been always close and during the war he acted as a literary ambassador between France and England, taking the chair for Frenchmen visiting London and himself addressing French audiences in Paris.

After the war honours came thick upon him. On his seventieth birthday he was presented with the bust of which a reproduction stands in the London Library. He was knighted, and as chief literary critic to the *Sunday Times* he could write within two columns' length exactly as he liked about any book he chose. Some of his best writing appeared there.

I have read recently one or two denigrating references to his qualities and capacities as a critic, and it cannot be denied that he was no more infallible in his judgement of contemporary writing than his predecessors were and his successors have proved to be. He was susceptible to personal influence. He liked to be courted, to be approached with deference. My father once asked him if he was interested in a certain young poet. 'I have not been invited to take an interest in him,' was the reply.

But the qualities that make a man a good judge of contemporary writing make him as often as not a pedestrian writer. The best poets and novelists are usually erratic judges of each other's work. Wilde's definition of criticism as 'the adventure of a soul among masterpieces' asks of the critic flashes of illuminating interpretation, and such flashes Gosse provided in full measure. He was fervent in his love of letters; widely read, he was human in his approach and he saw life itself on a broad scale. Much had he seen of men, climes, peoples, governments. He had wit and a large vocabulary. The

English language, in his hands, was a highly flexible and polished instrument. Books such as *Gossip in a Library* are very well worth re-reading. I doubt if anyone has written more readably about books and writers.

During the 1920s his many qualities had full scope. The *Sunday Times* gave him a forum. He had outlived his enemies. The young were gathered round him. He had glamour for them as the friend of Stevenson and Swinburne, of Tennyson and Hardy. They brought their books to him for his approval. Every Saturday he lunched at the same table at the Savile with old cronies, like Ray Lancaster. Against the background of his library and his pictures, in his charming house in Hanover Terrace looking over Regent's Park, he held court like royalty.

That is the Gosse whom Osbert Sitwell knew, and that is the Gosse who has found a niche in literary history. But it is a different Gosse that I remember. Through following the same profession as one's father, one acquires a panoramic outlook; one sees contemporary events and the rise and fall of reputations in the lengthened perspective of an added generation. When I think of Gosse I see him in terms of an episode largely forgotten now, which did in fact colour his later life and explains the eccentricities that marked his behaviour in his middle period. It took place in 1886 and it is worth recalling in a book which is primarily concerned with the rise and fall of literary reputations.

In the careers of most ambitious men there is a point when the formula of Greek tragedy is fulfilled and a man, through arrogance, through 'hubris', incurs the irritation of the gods. Gosse was, then, in his middle forties and his career of unbroken success was at its peak. As a poet, as an essayist, as a lecturer, he was the object of an adulation that passed in places the boundaries of idolatry. No one sets much store by his poetry nowadays, but each new volume was highly praised. He had a genius for friendship, and he was on close and affectionate terms with the best writers of his day.

Applicants for the post of Clark lecturer at Cambridge were required to support their claims with letters of recommendation from distinguished figures. There was competition to obtain as many signatures as possible. Forty or fifty was considered a modest quota. Gosse presented himself with three, Tennyson, Browning, and Matthew Arnold. He obtained the post.*

That post was the origin of his reverse. He was a great success at Cambridge. Under the aegis of his appointment, he was invited to lecture in America. It is very easy for an English visitor to have his head turned by American hospitality and American readiness to applaud success and welcome 'the new thing',† and Gosse lost momentarily his sense of focus, accepting the public's evaluation of his powers. 'He was credited,' Charteris wrote, 'with the authority of a learned scholar, a position which his knowledge, various and discriminating though it was, never really justified and at this time was far from supporting. It was assumed that anyone who wrote so well and ranged so widely must be erudite in the most specialized sense of the term. Scholarship was in fact being thrust upon him; he was driven to living beyond his intellectual capital.'

'To adjust the minute events of literary history is tedious and troublesome,' Dr Johnson wrote. 'It requires indeed no great force of understanding but often depends upon enquiries which there is no opportunity of making

---

* Sir Evan Charteris's reference to this incident does not altogether endorse the story as I had it from my father. This is one of the points where I write with hesitation.

† Gosse's mother was an American and he had a natural affinity for the country.

or to be fetched from books and pamphlets not always at hand.'

Gosse was too creative, too original a writer to possess the meticulous painstaking caution of the scholar. He needed an editor who would closely check his manuscript for inaccuracies. But he was now so self-confident that he appears to have trusted his own memory in the very kind of book where accuracy is essential. Under the imprint of the Cambridge University Press, signing himself Clark Lecturer, he published *From Shakespeare to Pope: an enquiry into the causes and phenomena of the rise of Classical Poetry in England*. A book with such a title requires to be above suspicion, but Gosse in his self-assurance allowed slip after slip to go uncorrected.

It was the opportunity for which the many who envied him had been waiting and, in October 1886, there appeared in the *Quarterly Review* one of the most virulent and sustained attacks that has been delivered against a man of letters. Forty pages long, entitled 'English Literature in the Universities', it purported to be a review of *From Shakespeare to Pope* and its opening paragraph contains the sentence: 'That such a book as this should have been permitted to go forth into the world with the Imprimatur of the University of Cambridge affords matter for very grave reflection. But it is a confirmation of what we have long suspected.'

Churton Collins, the author of the article, was everything that Gosse was not. He was a great and meticulous scholar, but he was little else. When he died in 1908, Arnold Bennett wrote that 'he was quite bereft of original taste. The root of the matter was not in him. The frowning structure of his vast knowledge overawed many people but it never overawed an artist unless the artist was excessively young and naïve . . . his essays were arid and tedious.'

13

Collins had been an unsuccessful applicant for the Merton Professorship of English at Oxford and his article was manifestly inspired by malice and ill will. At its close he wrote, 'And now we bring to a conclusion one of the most disagreeable tasks that it has ever been our lot to undertake', but it is clear that he had relished every spiteful phrase. There were many of them. 'Will our readers credit. . . .' 'This is a University lecturer. . . .' 'But this is nothing to what follows. . . .' 'Our readers will probably believe us to be jesting when we inform them. . . .' 'Not the least mischievous characteristic of the work is the skill with which its worthlessness is disguised. . . .' He compares Gosse with Mr Pecksniff. 'About the propriety of his epithets, so long as they sound well, he never troubles himself.'

In tone the article is pompous and self-righteous, but there Churton Collins was in tune with the temper of his time, and when he refers to his victim's 'habitual inaccuracy with respect to dates', he was well armed for the attack. 'Of all offences of which a writer can be guilty,' Collins was able to write, 'the most detestable is that of simulating familiarity with works which he knows only at second-hand or of which he knows nothing more than the title. That a lecturer on English Literature should not know whether the Arcadia of Sidney and the Oceana of Harrington are in prose or verse or, not knowing, should not have taken the trouble to ascertain, is discreditable enough, but that he should under the impression that they are poems, have had the effrontery to sit in judgement on them, might well in Macaulay's favourite phrase, make us ashamed of our species.

'Unless the Universities give care to the teaching of English,' the article concluded, 'so long will our presses continue to pour forth such books as the books on which we have been animadverting and so long will our leading literary journals pronounce them "volumes not to be glanced over and thrown aside but to be read twice and consulted often".'

The article caused a great sensation. Letters were written to the Press. No man knows who his friends are till he is in trouble. Gosse had always recognized the hostility of the Henley group, but many whom he had thought his friends had been secretly envious of his success and now joined the chorus of contumely. Gosse in his dismay and indignation may have exaggerated the extent of the calamity, as when a few weeks later he was bewailing to Thomas Hardy that, 'my little influence for good is almost gone', but there is small doubt that his prestige at that moment stood perilously low. His income dropped. Editors were no longer so anxious to employ his pen. At Oxford it became a stock saying for anyone who had made 'a howler' that he had made 'a Gosse of himself'. And a ludicrous sidelight on the situation is provided by his cook's giving notice because she did not like seeing 'the master's name so often in the papers'.

Gosse never got over the attack. It affected his entire conduct. He became hypersensitive to criticism. Warm-hearted and affectionate by nature he was on his guard against betrayal, considering it disloyal of a friend to praise in print someone whom he held to be an enemy. With most of his friends, during the 1890s there were periods of estrangement when something written or repeated had been misunderstood.

My father shared an experience that was nearly universal. He had written an article that rather pleased him, and in the course of casual talk mentioned it to Gosse, saying he would like him to look at it. Two days later he received a biting letter from Gosse saying that while he recognized that a working journalist had to accept what-ever commissions he was offered, he did not see why his attention should be called 'to such lucubrations'. My father had presumably written a kindly word about someone who, unknown to him, had forfeited Gosse's regard. My father hit back, and there was a two years' schism.

Gosse never overcame the sensitiveness to criticism which Collins's article created, yet he gauged correctly not only the limited extent of the damage that it could do him but the nature of his own fallibility; and later he found a parallel for his own position in Ralph Brook's attack on Camden's *Britannia*. In an essay in *Gossip in a Library* Gosse referred to the 'very hasty pamphlet which created a fine storm in an antiquarian teapot'. This attack was the work of a man who would otherwise be forgotten, who was jealous when Camden was promoted over his head to be Clarenceux King-of-Arms. Camden, like Gosse, was guilty of a number of small inaccuracies, and how accurately Gosse diagnosed his own weakness when he wrote that 'Camden had sailed too long in fair weather' and 'needed a squall to recall him to the duties of the helm'. How completely has Gosse's prophecy been fulfilled. Is Churton Collins remembered today for anything except his attack on Gosse?

The incident has its significance in literary history. It shows that attacks are soon forgotten provided the object of them continues to produce works of quality. There is only one answer to attack, to write a better book next time.

2
Authors at Underhill

E. TEMPLE THURSTON,
DESMOND COKE, ERNEST RHYS

My brother Evelyn and myself—Evelyn was born in October 1903—were brought up in an atmosphere not only of books but of professional writing. We lived in Hampstead on the edge of the Heath in a house called Underhill and our father invariably returned at the end of the day with a new book under his arm—one that he had for review or one that Chapman & Hall had published. His conversation with my mother turned on office problems, on difficulties with a bookseller or an agent, or an author's reluctance to 'tone down' a manuscript.

My father was convivial and hospitable. But he was asthmatic and in consequence reluctant to go out at night in winter. In later years his deafness made him avoid large gatherings, but he loved having his friends round him. Most Sundays there would be visitors. Occasionally one or two would stay on to supper. Most of these friends would in my father's house avail themselves of their chance of learning about this and the other authoress and author. Writers provide material for gossip. The reader forms a mental picture of his favourite author. He wants to know what So-and-so is 'really like'. He is also inquisitive about an author's earnings. 'How much did So-and-so make out of that?'

I was continually listening to literary 'shop'. I was brought up to think of literature as a profession, almost as a trade. I used to hear how this writer's stock was going up, while that other's was going down. I was clothed and fed, housed and educated by my father's pen. There did not seem to me to be anything peculiar about a man being a writer. On the contrary, it seemed to me to be a most natural occupation.

As a schoolboy I was read poetry by my father almost every evening; I have seldom heard poetry read as well, and never better; I heard much talk of publishing and the auction-room of letters, but I am surprised, in retrospect, that so few authors should have come out to Underhill. During the ten years before the war, Chapman & Hall published a number of prominent writers, H. G. Wells, Arnold Bennett—*The Old Wives' Tale* was on their list—Somerset Maugham, Sheila Kaye-Smith, but none of them ever sat in his oak-panelled book-room with its warm red lamps. This was in part because of his resolve to forget his office in his home at night, and partly in order to keep business and friendship separate. He had a great distaste for calculated hospitality. 'I know,' he would say, 'why Johnson's asking me to lunch. He wants me to send a MS. to the Ipswich Press.' Johnson was a shareholder in Chapman & Hall. The Ipswich Press, which he managed, was every bit as good and no more expensive than any other firm. There was no reason why Johnson should not have had his share of the firm's printing and several very good reasons why he should, but my father hated the idea of a lunch party having a commercial aspect; business, he felt, should be transacted in an office. He did not until his very last years have an entertainment expense account. To him the home was sacrosanct. The only two of his authors whom I remember meeting as a schoolboy were E. Temple Thurston and Desmond Coke.

Both of these had special and different reasons for making an appeal to me. Temple Thurston because he was the favourite author of a contemporary at Sherborne, two years senior to myself, in whose eyes I managed to acquire prestige as the son of his favourite's publisher, and I was at pains to return from the holidays each term with gossip-column information about Thurston's plans and movements.

This boy, whose name is Noël Whiting, and who has become one of my closer friends, though I see, alas, little of him nowadays—we rarely find ourselves at the same time in the same place—was one of the most remarkable of my contemporaries; and in retrospect I am surprised that I did not include him among the characters in my school novel; I suppose the reason is that I did not recognize then that he was remarkable. In my eyes he was no more than an agreeable and elegant eccentric. It was not till later that I came to recognize him as an insistent individualist, who got his way by passive resistance, a rebel who did not rebel, a nonconformist who did not challenge the conformity of others.

Graceful and good looking, with a gracious voice, he had the air of an Etonian; but his family had entered him for Winchester, where he failed to pass the College entrance examination, a thing that it was not difficult to do. The educational standard at Winchester has always been exceptionally high; and he had come to Sherborne because our headmaster Nowell Charles Smith was a Wykehamist. He was what was described in those days as well connected. His background was a wealthy one, but he never displayed his ampler means. He never 'dropped' important names.

He had a contented nature, because he had interior resources. He could be perfectly happy, provided that no one interfered with him. He was resolved to enjoy his five years at Sherborne, in his own way. He was physically strong and became one of the best swimmers in the school, but he did not want to play cricket or Rugby football.

Games were compulsory at Sherborne until a boy had reached the top form, the sixth, but Noël always arranged to do something in the afternoon for which it was permissible to get 'leave off games'—a music or a drawing lesson, an archaeological expedition or a game of fives. In the end, house captains ceased to post him on cricket and football sides, and he was able to spend a couple of afternoons every week reading in the library.

The O.T.C. (Officers' Training Corps) was technically voluntary, but 95 per cent of the school joined. Noël availed himself of his technical liberty and did not join it; not on pacifist, non-combatant grounds—when the war broke out, he applied immediately for a commission—but because he wanted to use his spare time in other ways. He was not a classical scholar; he never reached the sixth, but he spoke excellent French. The wife of the drawing master was a Frenchwoman, and he used to give weekly tea parties in his study where only French was spoken.

He interfered with no one and no one interfered with him. He wore his hair a little longer than was officially approved, but no one told him he must get it cut. You would have expected that such a boy would have been ragged and bullied in his early days, that there would have been an equivalent for the 'Shelley Hunts' at Eton; that tough Philistines would have insisted that his duty to the house forced him to the football field: 'get into the scrum and shove, you little scum'; but they never did. From the start his independence was respected. Many years later, as a result possibly of his experiences in India and Burma during the war, he became a Buddhist. Without knowing it, he had been a Buddhist from the start, adopting a policy of non-aggression.

He had at that time four main objects of enthusiasm—music, painting, Napoleon—the walls of his study were

covered with portraits of the Emperor—and the novels of
E. Temple Thurston. I still cannot understand why those
particular novels should have held such a strong appeal
for him. I can think of so many other novelists with
whom he might have been expected to find himself in
tune.

Temple Thurston died suddenly, when he was
apparently in good health, early in 1933. I do not suppose
that any of his books are still in print, but for twenty-five
years he was a prominent and successful author. He was
one of my father's discoveries. His first novel *The Apple
of Eden* recounted a priest's fall from grace; 'religion and
sex is an infallible mixture', my father said. Thurston
wrote two kinds of novel: the one powerful and realistic
like *The Apple of Eden*, the other sentimentally romantic
like *The City of Beautiful Nonsense*—which was a considerable best-seller. He was extremely anxious to succeed
on the stage and wrote a number of plays that had little
success, but at last, soon after the war, he had a genuine
'run' for *The Wandering Jew*—a lavish full-scale production at His Majesty's Theatre. He wrote scenarios for the
films. He made a reasonable amount of money; he was
able to finance his share of matrimonial confusion without
excessive strain. He could have looked forward to at
least another fifteen years of steady profitable production.
Yet he was very far from being a happy man.

It is possible that he was not a very pleasant one,
though, personally, I found him companionable, agreeable and encouraging. He was a great egotist, utterly
self-centred; never satisfied that his work was receiving
the attention that it deserved from publishers and critics.
He was not easy to do business with. He published for
ten years with Chapman & Hall and dedicated one of his
novels to my father, but he was never satisfied with his
books' sales. 'Hodders have offered me an advance of

£700,' he would say. 'You say that my last novel only earned £500. Perhaps Hodders with their bigger organization could push up my sales to seven hundred.' When eventually he left Chapman & Hall, he changed his publisher several times.

He made considerable demands upon his publisher. He would bring my father the first four chapters of his new novel, then eight weeks later he would arrive with the next four. My father at Underhill that night would press the back of his hand against his forehead. 'How can I be expected to remember the precise impression that was made on me by four chapters of a novel two months ago. Think of all I've read in between.' I have taken that lesson to heart and been very careful not to submit my work in short instalments. One of Thurston's agents said to me: 'I know that authors ask me out to lunch because they want to talk about their work, but I wish Thurston would wait till I have finished my first cocktail before he starts telling me the plot of his new novel.'

He was a lone wolf. I do not think that he had many men friends, though he was the kind of man whom you would have expected to have them. He was athletic and played lawn tennis well enough to compete in the opening rounds at Wimbledon. He played cricket at Lord's for the Authors against the Publishers and took three wickets. His last victim jumped out to drive him, missed the ball and was bowled. By a mistake of the scorer, the batsman appeared next morning in *The Times* as stumped. This distressed Thurston. He thought that it would look as though the batsman had held his bowling in such contempt that he had run out of his ground to swipe it.

Tall, dark, lean, photogenic, he looked both as the author of *The Apple of Eden* and *The City of Beautiful Nonsense* could have been expected to look; tough with a tender side. But he had a chip upon his shoulder.

He had not been to a university, nor to one of the recognized public schools. *Who's Who* contains no autobiographical details and that mattered quite a bit in England before World War I. His first wife came from a superior social caste. She wrote a novel, *John Chilcote M.P.*, which was a 'best-seller' and of which he was so jealous that he persuaded my father to issue one of his novels in minute editions of 250 copies so that he could claim to have sold more editions than she had. Many years later when I was myself published by Chapman & Hall, I followed his example, though for different reasons, and arranged to have one of my novels issued in small editions so that it could be advertised as 'seventh large printing exhausted before publication'. In 1957 when my brother brought a libel suit against Nancy Spain and I was one of the witnesses, the question arose of how many copies there were in an edition; the judge was highly amused when I told him of this device. 'Mr Waugh, Mr Waugh,' he admonished me, 'you are giving the whole show away.'

Thurston evaded military service on the curious medical grounds that he suffered from agrophobia—the fear of open spaces. His nerves, he claimed, would disintegrate on Salisbury Plain or on a battlefield; although, as my father remarked, he could with impunity take a cross-channel steamer to Ireland and France. Perhaps it was a pity that he did not have the opportunity that war provides of mixing in a community. It might have taken him out of himself. Instead he became more ingrown.

Though a member of the Garrick he never seemed to belong anywhere. In a sense that is an advantage for a writer. It is unhealthy for him, in the long run, to belong to a coterie. A clique becomes a *claque*. And when fashions change, a writer goes out of favour with his fellow members. But Thurston was never quite strong enough, quite

23

good enough to stand alone. He was never given more than respectful attention in the weekly reviews. He was never included in general articles on 'trends in the modern novel', although even though he was not a major novelist, he had many of the minor qualities of a major novelist. He could construct a story; he had a sense of character and of caricature. He was ambitious and hard working. His trilogy *The Achievement of Richard Furlong*, which was issued in a single volume at no great profit to Chapman & Hall, only just did not 'come off'. He wrote with feeling. He was a better writer than many of those who were reviewed at length in highbrow columns. His lack of critical acclaim did not, probably, cost him a penny in royalties, and through never having been fashionable, he was spared the chilling experience of finding himself out of fashion. But he himself was perpetually plagued by this lack of recognition. He was so desperately anxious to write 'a book that mattered'.

It is a common, a familiar plight. An agent was saying to me the other day of a mutual friend, 'Poor Jackson tortures himself because he can't produce a masterpiece. If only he would be content with the kind of work he does so well and that is in fact very profitable.' Thurston's predicament precisely. But the solution is not as easy as the agent thought. It was only because Thurston was so desperately anxious to write supremely well, that he was able to write as effectively as he did.

Though I heard more talk about Thurston than any other of Chapman & Hall's authors—how well I remember my father's dismay when Thurston wanted to call one of his novels 'The Love Story of an Ugly Man'; it was an impossible title for Thurston in 1912, but possibly it would be an enticing one in our day of the anti-hero—I did not read one of his novels until I had left school. Much of Desmond Coke's work, on the other hand, I knew by heart. He wrote school stories that could be appreciated both by a schoolboy and an adult; some of his books indeed were published simultaneously in two separate editions, one after being serialized in *The Captain*, the chief schoolboys' magazine, in a popular boys' series with lurid coloured illustrations, the other by Chapman & Hall in sober hard covers for the parents.

The Bending of a Twig was published in 1906. It was in part a satire on the conventional school story. A poet suddenly decides to send his son, who has never been away from home, to Shrewsbury, the public school to which Coke went himself. The father in order to equip his son for this new experience provides him with a collection of school stories, *Tom Brown's Schooldays*, *Eric, or Little by Little*, *Stalky & Co.*, *The Hill*, and one or two of the cheaper imitations of those classics. The poet's son derives an entirely false impression of school life; and the opening chapters describing his mistakes and his ridiculous search for the school bully are extremely funny.

The first part is satire; the last two-thirds describe with sympathetic realism how the poet's son gradually becomes the conventional school prefect, how the twig is bent in fact. At no point was the system itself criticized; it was a popular conception that was satirized. Yet in retrospect it can be seen that Coke's book was the first step in that debunking of the public school mystique, in which ten years later I was to play my part.

In 1922, in an anonymous article for *The Times* on the public school in fiction I wrote that *The Bending of a Twig* had struck the first note of rebellion. Coke thanked me for the article 'in which I recognise your Roman hand. I am having my cards changed from "the last of the Victorians" to "the first of the Georgians".'

But in fact, Coke was anything but a rebel. To him the standards of public-school life were sacrosanct. Indeed he was one of those Englishmen who remain all their lives exactly what they are at nineteen, the school prefect believing that the issues that lie outside his cloistered world will be basically the same, on a larger scale. That is no doubt why I at fifteen felt so much in tune with him. He confirmed the standards to which I was being trained; he did not raise uncomfortable doubts. He was tall, handsome, neat; unobtrusively well dressed; the man who never let down the side. The mildly disapproving letter that he wrote to my father when *The Loom of Youth* was published, is now in the Sherborne school library.

Coke wrote in addition a few unspecialized novels about adult life. One of them occupies a footnote in literary history. In 1910 he published a novel called *Beauty from Ashes*. It made little stir and Somerset Maugham had never heard of it when he planned to call his long autobiographical novel 'Beauty from Ashes'. When he found that the title had already been used, he switched to *Of Human Bondage*. He was possibly irritated at the time; there was a view then that a positive was preferable to a negative title. When Geoffrey Moss's *Defeat* appeared, W. L. George said, 'What a pity he couldn't have called it "Victory".' In terms of his sequence of comedy successes on the stage, Maugham may have thought *Of Human Bondage* too drab, too depressing a title for a popular success; but how well it fitted that majestic, sombre epic. How finicky in comparison is 'Beauty from Ashes'. Perhaps under that title, the novel would not have been the abiding success it has.

Inevitably Coke in 1914 was one of the first to hurry into khaki, and within a few months was with the B.E.F. in France. He was mentioned in dispatches, but trench fever combined with a heart-attack invalided him from the service, and in the lieu of war work, he enrolled on the teaching staff of Clayesmore School. He must at times have looked forward with some anxiety to peace conditions. He had only moderate private means, his books had never earned large sums, and he could scarcely anticipate, in that direction, a sudden change of fortune; but fate 'turned its wheel'. An uncle who lived in Australia whom he had scarcely seen, who was childless and had taken great pride in having a nephew who wrote books, made him his sole heir. Coke, a rich man now, returned to the staff at Clayesmore and became one of the school's chief benefactors. He showed, unobtrusively, great generosity to many friends. He indulged his hobby as a collector of eighteenth-century silhouettes and Rowlandson drawings. He wrote a few books, which received kindly reviews, without having to worry whether they sold more than moderately well. His last years (he died in 1931) were apart from his bad health among his happiest.

I have used the general outline of Coke's career in lectures that I have given on the problems of the modern novelist, altering the facts to suit my purpose. This is the story as I have told it to my audiences. An adaptation that provides a pertinent example of the way in which novelists make copy out of their friends.

In the anecdote as I have recounted it, I have turned Coke into an elegant young man of fashion, a Londoner who wrote round about 1910 rather precious novels that were well reviewed in the exclusive weeklies. He averaged a novel a year, and usually a few months before he was due to deliver his manuscript, he paid my father a Sunday afternoon visit to discuss it. He had, he would say, a problem. It was invariably the same problem. He was two-thirds of the way through his book, and had got his characters involved into a confusion from which he could not extricate them. The situation in which they were involved never seemed particularly original or obscure. Those were the days, morally, of the double standard, and a young woman with a past had become engaged to be married and was wondering whether or not she should confess her misdemeanour. Could she act a lie; would she imperil her marriage if she told the truth?

My father who had encountered many similar situations in the novels that he had published and reviewed, suggested a conventional solution. 'Why not,' he said, 'have the girl confess, and then have the man say, "Well my dear, I'm very glad you've told me this, but in point of fact I've known it all along."'

The novelist shook his head sadly. Those were the days when plots were out of fashion, when the traffic of humanity was compared to the Heraclitan river, that changed from second to second, but continued to appear the same. All things were in a state of flux. Novels in those days did not finish. They stopped. 'No, no,' said the novelist, 'you can't have things being "known all along". That's a cliché; the kind of thing that only happens in third-rate novels.' The novel, he explained, should end in a compromise, showing how one incident flowed into another; with nothing beginning and nothing ending; a continuing process of effect and cause.

And that was how he ended his own novels, in a compromise that was a kind of fog, with nothing clearly resolved and the reader in some doubt as to what had actually happened to the various characters in whose fortunes he had been invited to be concerned; and as that is really the one thing that the reader does need to know—how it eventually works out for Jack and Jill—his novels were far from being 'best-sellers', yet equally they were very far from being failures. He had genuine merits. He had a knack of narrative; he could make a reader want to turn the page and see what was on the

next; he led a brisk social life; he had interesting settings
to describe; his work had a literary quality. He deserved
the critical recognition that he received. His books lay
on the table of the drawing-rooms he frequented. And
as he drew a reasonable private income from Russian oil
fields, he could accept with equanimity the small royalties
from his books. He reminded himself that Henry James
had never attracted a large public. His day would come.
In the meantime, the present was extremely pleasant. In
that last high rich summer of 1914, he was as happy as
any mortal can expect to be in this imperfect world.

Then the war came, changing everything. He was one
of the first into khaki, and he was gassed in the first
attack at Ypres; his health was permanently ruined. The
Russian Revolution followed and with it the confiscation
of private property and the end of his private income. His
future had suddenly become shadowed. He came out to
Underhill one Sunday, early in 1918, when I was home
on leave, in a despondent mood. 'I don't know how it's all
going to work out,' he said. He began to talk about his
private life in the same way that five years earlier he had
talked about his novels. He could see no solution to a
confused situation.

My father did his best to be encouraging. My father
had a Pickwickian manner. 'It'll turn out better than you
expect,' he prophesied. 'Those White Russian generals
have a trick or two up their sleeves. Your oil shares will
be paying dividends before very long. And after the squalor
of the trenches, the public will be wanting to read books
like yours, dignified, restrained, classical: your innings is
going to begin.'

But he did not believe it would. He had no faith in the
White Russian generals, nor did he expect that a war-
weary, but ruthless generation would have much use for
remote, austere stories about idle worldlings. A new lean

day would create its own idiom of self-expression. Yet at the same time he did not think the future was too dark. Our friend would have a disability pension; probably the Bolsheviks, once the Revolution was established, would pay some token recompense to former shareholders, so as to earn the goodwill of other governments. He would live economically on the Riviera, cherishing his health, which was in itself an occupation. His pen would still earn him something. Every so often he would address to one of the highbrow weeklies a captious complaint on the shortcomings of the latest school of novelists. 'In fact,' said my father, 'it'll end like one of his own novels, in a compromise.' But fate had a last trump in its hand.

Early in 1921 he again invited himself to tea. My father had not seen him for three years and was curious and a little apprehensive. It might be an embarrassing situation. Far from it. Punctually at half past four a long, low, shining car drew up outside my father's modest residence. The door of the car was opened by a trim chauffeur. The novelist had always been unobtrusively well dressed: dark well-cut suits and stiff starched linen. But today there was a definite gloss about him. There was also a conspiratorial twinkle in his eye.

'Now what does all this mean?' my father asked. The author laughed. This, he explained, was how it had all come about. He had had in Australia a widowed and childless cousin whom he had never seen and of whom he had scarcely heard. His novels were this cousin's sole family link with England. He bought each novel as it appeared. He had them bound in leather and arranged under glass. When one of his friends came down from one of the stations for a week-end, he would lend him one of these novels to take up to bed with him. He was delighted next morning when his friend said that he could not make head or tail of it. He was proud to have a cousin who wrote novels; he was even prouder that they were novels his friends could not understand, so that when he died, he left his entire fortune to his cousin.

The novelist paused. His smile became a grin. He had a sense of humour. 'It's the kind of thing,' he said, 'that only happens in third-rate novels and real life.'

One other writer was a constant visitor at Underhill, though he was not a Chapman & Hall author. His name is well remembered and he is held in respect today, as a poet and as the original editor of the Everyman Library.

I think that my father had first met Ernest Rhys at Gosse's; or it may have been through Richard Le Gallienne. But our two families as far back as I can remember lived on terms of close and affectionate cordiality. Rhys was married to a minor Irish essayist, and the name Grace Rhys during the 'nineties and before the First War, appeared on several charming volumes of belles-lettres. The Rhyses lived near to us, in Hampstead, we were 'in-and-out of each other's houses' and they always came to our tree on Christmas Eve. They had three children, a boy and a girl several years older than myself and a daughter Stella who was Evelyn's age, who did nursery lessons with him, and of whom he has written in *A Little Learning*. I, in terms of age, fell between the two groups. Brian, the eldest, when I was a preparatory schoolboy was an undergraduate at Oxford, and Megan was an art student at the Slade. She was handsome and dynamic, and wore loose Liberty silk blouses. For those days she was considered wild and it was whispered that she had anticipated the marriage ceremony with the man who eventually became her husband. She inspired in me an awed and breathless curiosity.

31

Rhys himself, in those early days, seemed to me colourless and ineffective. I judged him by the narrow standards of a public schoolboy. He was tall, moustached, deliberate in walk and speech. He was not untidily but loosely dressed; the equivalent in tweeds for his daughter's Liberty silk draperies. He was clearly not particularly well off. Old Dent, the publisher of Everyman, was a difficult man to work with: parsimonious and dilatory in his payments; and I often heard Rhys describe, amusingly, without self-pity, the devices to which he was driven to extract his periodic pittances. Schoolboys set high store by success and they gauge it by a very narrow standard. Ostensibly, on the surface the Waughs were doing better than the Rhyses. At the same time I thought Rhys a sport. My father told me of how at a children's party at their house, Rhys had come up to him in agitation. 'This party isn't going well,' he said, 'I'd better black my face.' I admired a grown man who was prepared to make himself ridiculous for the benefit of kids.

It was not till I began to read the minor poets of the 'nineties that I came to appreciate what he stood for. He had been a member of the Rhymers' Club of which Arthur Symons had written in his preface to Ernest Dowson's poems. He had sat in the Cheshire Cheese, with Yeats, Davidson, Le Gallienne, Lionel Johnson, listening to their poems, privileged to read his own. The Rhymers published two collections of their poems; as the sum earned in royalties was too small to be divided among the contributors, it was devoted to a dinner in a Soho restaurant. Each contributor was allowed to bring one guest. My father went as Rhys's. I could not ask Rhys too many questions about the men who had become my heroes. He had some excellent stories to tell, many of which he has included in his reminiscences.

Nor were his anecdotes confined to the poets of the

'nineties. He had kept in touch with the young, in a way
that my father had been prevented from doing by his
asthma. He knew many of the young Georgians. He was
particularly amusing about Ezra Pound. Whenever I
came home on army leave during 1915–17 I managed to
see the Rhyses. It was Grace Rhys who first took me to
the Poetry Bookshop in the late autumn of 1915 to hear
a reading of Gordon Bottomley's *King Lear's Wife*.

At that time I was interested in Rhys because he had
known writers in whom I was interested. It was not till
a good deal later that I came to realize what he was
himself. The creation of 'Everyman' was a definite
achievement, but he was much more than the founder of
a library. He was a genuine man of letters. As a critic
and a poet he had earned the respect of his contemporaries; of his elders when he was young, and of his
juniors when he was old. He had held his pen in trust.
His gift for writing poetry was a slender one, but he had
worked on it steadily, had developed it so that when a
powerful idea struck him, he was on two or three occasions
able to write a memorable poem. He often read his poems
at Underhill. I remember him on a summer evening in
1916, reading a poem which he had just written called
'The Leaf Burners'. It was rhythmed, without a marked
metre. It was alliterative. 'The rhymes,' he explained,
'come at the beginning of the words instead of at the end.'
I was moved. Later I said to my father, 'Surely that was
very good.' My father nodded. 'It is hard to tell when
you hear a poem for the first time. But I think it was.'
'The Leaf Burners' was the title poem of his next book
of poems, and it has been included in a number of
anthologies.

At his memorial service in June 1946, two of his
poems were read by Richard Church, 'The Old Men'
and 'Autobiography'.

Wales England wed; so I was bred,
'twas merry London gave me breath.
I dreamt of love—and fame: I strove:
But Ireland taught me love was best.
And Irish eyes and London cries,
And streams of Wales may tell the rest;
What more than these I asked of life,
I am content to have from Death.

Three or four poems may not seem a very substantial harvest from a lifetime's sowing, but it was only by careful assiduous husbandry that his small plot of land was able to yield those few faultless flowers. If he had not written three hundred negligible poems, he would not have been able to write those three.

A luncheon was given for him in London on his seventy-fifth birthday. Not many of his contemporaries were still alive. Yeats and Ernest Radford were the only Rhymers left, but his juniors were there to pay him honour. He had never made very much money. He had never been 'in the news'. He had never been able to entertain on a large scale, but many of us remember gratefully the small Sunday tea-parties where friends who had much in common met to exchange opinions and to read their poems. He had led a full and happy life. And he is remembered today, whereas so many who seemed so much more important during their brief, bright hour of prominence, are forgotten.

3
My First Publisher

GRANT RICHARDS

My first novel was accepted by Grant Richards in January 1917. I was then a cadet at Sandhurst. On my next leave, I called on him in his offices near Leicester Square, across the way from Ciro's. I knew more or less what to expect. 'Grant Richards', my father told me, 'is the best-dressed publisher in London and he wears an eyeglass.'

He was then in his middle forties and certainly an impressive person. He was the first 'man of the world' that I had met, and today, fifty years later, I have not met anyone who fits that role more effectively. He looked and behaved as the young Arnold Bennett from the Potteries dreamed of looking and behaving. He was supremely knowledgeable about food and wine and clothes and travel, about the practical ordering of existence. He had in a high degree what the Edwardians called 'style'.

Five years earlier he had escorted Theodore Dreiser across the Atlantic, to London and the English country-side, to Paris and the South of France. He described the trip in his autobiography *Author Hunting*. Dreiser also described it in *A Traveller at Forty*. The rough-grained Bohemian, hardened by reverse, embittered by opposition and neglect, had met no equivalent for the polished, assured cosmopolitan. Barfleur is Dreiser's *nom de plume* for Richards, and the first chapter is called 'Barfleur Takes Me in Hand'.

Richards was at that time, to employ a current American phrase, 'between wives'. He was free to concentrate his entire energies upon his guest. He stage-managed everything. He told Dreiser what to wear and what not to wear. It was, Dreiser learnt, 'not quite good form to wear a heavy striped tie with a frock coat', and 'We never tie them in that fashion, always a simple knot'.

Dreiser spent at Dover the eve of their trip to Paris and went on board before the train from London got in. Richards arrived by it, 'as usual very brisk, a porter carrying four or five pieces of luggage and his fur coat over his arm, his monocle gleaming as though it had been freshly polished, a cane and an umbrella in hand, and enquiring crisply whether everything was in order. If it were raining, according to a strip of paper on which he had written instructions days before I left London, I was to enter the cabin on the vessel which crossed the Channel; pre-empt a section of seat along the side by putting all my baggage there and bribe a porter to place two chairs in a comfortable windless position on deck, to which we could repair in case it should clear up on the way over.'

A Traveller at Forty has long been out of print. It is unlikely to be reissued; it is very long. Dreiser was diffuse; it is not easy to cut his work; its bulk can only be reduced by a process of compression. Much of this particular book is dated and a great deal of its interest is lost by its author's habit of giving his characters pseudonyms or of referring to them as Miss E and Mr G. But anyone who finds a copy on a library shelf can be recommended to give up a couple of hours to it. It has many passages on the differences between Europe and the United States that make nostalgic reading now and it presents a full-length and sympathetic portrait of Grant Richards.

The preceding paragraphs may have given the impression that Grant was managing and 'bossy' but that was not the case. It was a sense of assurance, of self-confidence, that he diffused. He was never in a hurry, he was never flustered, his voice was warm, his manner suave. His bearing suggested that the present was agreeable and, that no matter what the past had been, the future would be better still. His monocle heightened this atmosphere of well-being. It was not attached to a cord; it had no frame; it stayed in place. Only a very composed man can wear a monocle.

This air of prosperity was one of his great assets as a publisher. He restored and sustained an author's confidence. If your books were issued under his aegis, everything must, you felt, come right in the long run. He was always buoyant, always encouraging. He never interfered with a writer, never tried to edit his manuscript. He assumed that the author knew best what he wanted to say and how to say it. I published seven books with him; he only twice asked me to make an alteration. He suggested that one or two Greek phrases in *The Loom of Youth* might put off potential readers, making them suspect something over-scholarly. He was quite right. On the title page of *The Loom of Youth* I had included my middle initial, 'R'— Alec R. Waugh. He asked me to drop the 'R'. What sound advice that was.

The Loom of Youth, published in July 1917, was a considerable success. It was not for eight years that another book of mine sold well. My second and third novels, published in 1922 and 1924, sold barely two thousand copies each and created no stir of critical interest. A book of reminiscences sold seven hundred copies. I imagine that by the end of 1924 most people had dismissed me as a 'one-book man'. Perhaps Grant himself had his doubts, but he never let me suspect he had. I was welcomed with the same warmth when I called at St Martin's Street. He would enquire about my new novel, wonder whether it would be ready for the autumn season,

37

discuss who should design the wrapper. Then he would take out his pocket diary. 'Now, which Sunday are you coming down to lunch?'

He had a charming house at Cookham Dean; it was an easy excursion and a pleasant one. One was met at Maidenhead and driven, very likely in a pony trap, through a country-side that was still unspoilt. There would be other guests gathered on the lawn. It was unlikely that any of them would be writers. He liked to make his authors feel separate, distinct, apart. Grant was never the kind of man who wore open-necked shirts or high-necked sweaters. He would look countrified in tweeds or flannels. His wife, a Hungarian, beautiful and very many years younger than himself, was a gracious hostess. The food and the wine were good, but there was no excess. 'Sybarite is a mild expression for your character,' Dreiser said to Richards. But Grant was a gourmet, not a gourmand. He never overate or overdrank. I have the warmest memories of that dining-room, designed by Heal in terms of the fashion of the hour, with its bright blue walls, orange curtains and chair covers, its black carpet and cushions and black line below the ceiling. And always at some time during the meal he would find the right occasion to say something encouraging about the work of the author who was his guest. I would return to London resolved to make my new book better. I have been very lucky in my publishers, in London with Cassell's, in New York with John Farrar, Doubleday, the Rineharts and Roger Straus, but I know their feelings will not be hurt if I say that there was something special, something very special about the attention that Grant Richards gave his authors.

What a flair he had for publishing, how much of himself he gave, how much of himself he threw into it. *Author Hunting* was published in 1934. It was reissued in 1960, and it seemed to me when I re-read it that it had, like certain wines, improved with age. A few of the authors about whom he wrote are half-forgotten now, but many have increased their stature, have become more interesting because we can see them and their work in focus. They are established figures now, but Richards knew them before they were established. He recognized their qualities before the world did. He was the first publisher of G. K. Chesterton, Alfred Noyes, John Masefield. Laurence Binyon was on his list, so were Katherine Tynan, John Davidson, William Watson, Frank Norris, George Bernard Shaw, Sir Hugh Clifford, Richard Le Gallienne, Alice Meynell, E. V. Lucas, Thomas Burke, Ronald Firbank, the Sitwells, Neville Cardus, Ernest Bramah—what a list of authors!

How Grant loved books and the whole world of books. He knew that each book was personal, and, in consequence, just as each man evolves for himself a certain style of dress, so each book needs a certain format, a certain arrangement of type and binding. He was concerned with the machinery through which books are issued. He visited the big bookshops personally and made friends with the booksellers, not only in London but the provinces. He was never an extravagant advertiser, he had not the means to be, but he was a skilful one.

In the summer of 1917 he invented a new style of advertising, and I was lucky in having this innovation coincide with the publication of *The Loom of Youth*. He took every week a half-column in the *Times Literary Supplement* which he filled with gossip about his books and their authors. It was set in heavy small black type. He was a good writer and it was very readable. He was the first publisher to quote the unfavourable comments on a book. He stimulated controversy. He was unique. That was the thing about him.

After the title-page of *Author Hunting* he printed a quotation from a letter to him by Shaw: 'You should call your book,' Shaw said, "The Tragedy of a Publisher who Allowed Himself to Fall in Love with Literature...." A certain connoisseurship in the public taste is indispensable; but the slightest uncommercial bias in choosing between, say, Bridges' "Testament of Beauty" and a telephone directory, is fatal.'

This may puzzle the modern reader of *Author Hunting*. 'Tragedy? Where is the tragedy?' he may well ask. Here is the story of a man who loved books, who spent his life among books and bookmen, who published many of the best authors of his day over a period of thirty years. What a full, successful, happy life! Where does the tragedy come in? *Author Hunting* gives no answer to that question.

In an earlier book, *Memoirs of a Misspent Youth*, he covered the first twenty-four years of his life; he wrote of his boyhood as the son of an Oxford don of frugal tastes who did not provide the mental and social stimulus that an imaginative boy needed. Grant was sent as a dayboy to the City of London School, staying in lodgings with a schoolmaster near the Crystal Palace. It was a dreary boyhood from which he broke loose at the age of sixteen to work as a junior clerk with a firm of wholesale booksellers in Paternoster Row, at a wage of twenty pounds a year. Within a few months, however, he was congenially employed under W. T. Stead on the staff of the *Review of Reviews*. He gives a lively account of his experiences and of the men and women whom he met there and of his times in Paris with Phil May and William Rothenstein. His association with painters was always close, and his publication of C. R. W. Nevinson's war pictures was as important an event in 1916 as that in the following year of Siegfried Sassoon's poems.

Author Hunting is not, however, autobiographical. He

has little to say in it about himself, except in relation to the books he published and the authors who were his friends. He only once refers, indirectly, to the financial difficulties in which he found himself, and no memoir of him would be complete, would give a true picture of him, that did not refer to his two bankruptcies and to the final reorganization of his business in 1927 that left him with so little control over the fortunes of the Richards Press that he resigned his chairmanship.

His two bankruptcies came early in his career. The bibliophile will note that some of his publications appear under the imprint E. Grant Richards; that is because for a time he was unable to conduct a business under his own name and used that of his first wife. Those two bankruptcies were considerable reverses. Most of his authors went to other houses, he damaged his credit with the trade, and he lost his 'list'. By 'list' a publisher designates those books five, ten, twenty years old which sell without advertising their fifty, two hundred or a thousand copies every year, that are his 'bread and butter', and which pay his overhead expenses. Richards had in the beginning a number of such books, the World's Classics for example, and several excellent anthologies. He lost them all. Each time he had to start again from scratch.

It was an immense handicap, too big a handicap. Shaw attributes his difficulties to his having fallen in love with literature, but that was a bad diagnosis. I heard a member of his family assert that his readiness to publish poetry at his own expense in the end proved fatal, but I should doubt if on the whole he lost money upon poetry. He made a great deal out of A. E. Housman. He was a good judge of poetry and good poetry eventually finds a public. He was always prepared to run a risk, but it was not because he ran risks with unestablished authors that he ran into difficulties. It was something much simpler than that. He wanted more out of life than publishing could give him; a trait that Shaw, temperamentally, could not understand, because he had not the clue to it inside himself; but Dreiser understood it, very well. To him Richards was a character out of Balzac, a middle-aged Rubempré. 'Towards gambling, show, romance, a delicious scene, he carries a special mood. Life is only significant because of these things. His great struggle is to avoid the dingy and the dull and to escape if possible the penalties of encroaching age. . . . Just one hour of beauty is his private cry. One more day of delight, let the future take care of itself. . . . He had a delicious vivacity which acted on me like wine.' With that kind of nature he inevitably took more out of the business than it could afford.

When I first met him in the spring of 1917, he was probably as happy as he had ever been, happier than he was to be again. He was healthy, handsome, he was just too old for military service; his sons were just too young. He had remarried a year and a half before. He was in love. Books were booming. He had had the previous autumn a spectacular success with Bruce Bairnsfather's *Bullets and Billets*. Thomas Burke's *Limehouse Nights* was on its way to best-sellerdom. There was a glow about him.

In a certain sense that glow never left him. He enjoyed the adventure of living to the end, but that particular high-summer radiance was short-lived. By the spring of 1922 the chill wind of a depression had begun to blow. I was working then in publishing in a part-time capacity for my father with Chapman & Hall and I was astonished at the pace with which the depression struck. In 1919 we were paying bonuses to the staff, in 1924 we were facing angry shareholders. It was hard to see how it had happened: the annual turnover was as high, our list seemed as good, books were selling well, but increased costs and high taxation cut profits to a minimum. And if Chapman & Hall, a ninety-year-old house with a long back list, its Dickens plates and a highly profitable technical department, was threatened, how desperate was the state of an orphan firm like Richards's.

It was an awkward time for Richards's authors. He had never been a prompt settler of his royalty accounts and the delays now became exceedingly inconvenient to a race that lives upon a shoestring. I learnt from another of his authors that he preferred to settle his accounts with acceptances at six months. That seemed in keeping with his optimistic, improvident temperament, and I accepted the solution. 'Grant,' I would say, 'it looks as though my next royalty account which is due in November will total about eighty pounds. I'm short of money. Do you think you could let me have a bill at six months that I can discount?' He would stand against the light, benign and bland. He would nod his head. Yes, he thought he could manage that. He was generous, always anxious to help a friend. He might not be in a position to cash a cheque for twenty pounds but he would always sign a bill for fifty. And he looked so sleek, so prosperous; his manner was so assured, so reassuring that it was impossible not to believe that the situation was sound at base. For a year, two years, it went on like that. Then the day came when a bill was not honoured.

It was a major shock to me. I was young and selfish, ambitious and self-absorbed. I thought of my own temporary embarrassment, not of the permanent predicament in which the man who had launched and befriended me now found himself. A sheltering presence had dissolved. I shivered. 'You now go out into the wind,' I told myself. During those months I was one of many, very many.

Richards was then in his middle fifties. It was too late to make a third come-back.

Author Hunting seemed to me in 1960 a better book than it had in 1934. It was also a different book. It had had on its first appearance a melancholy quality. Everyone knew about his difficulties, of his attempt to come back with insufficient backing and the public's faith in him diminished. It was hard not to think, reading it, 'Poor Grant, why couldn't he have pulled it off?' He was not, let it be understood, in a desperate position. He returned to authorship. He was far from being negligible as a novelist and a reprint company might well do worse than reissue *Bittersweet. The Coast of Pleasure*, about the Riviera, is far more than a guide-book. Max Beerbohm in his preface to *Memoirs of a Misspent Youth*, wrote of him as an author who 'knows just what he wants to say and can say it—always lightly, firmly, vividly, amusingly, endearingly'.

I often saw Grant during the 1930s. His wife had a flat in Monte Carlo. He never forfeited her devotion. His zest for life was unabated. He still added to the enjoyment of any party he attended. He was still, moreover, operating as a publisher, in a restricted way. I remember a party in 1930 which Betty Askwith and Theodora Benson gave to celebrate their *Lobster Quadrille* of which Richards was the publisher, and how we lingered long into the morning at Cadogan Gardens with Grant not seeming by any means the eldest. But the big days were over. A curtain fell in 1927.

Reading *Author Hunting* in 1934 one felt one was following the story of a failure. But in 1960, ten years after Grant's own death, I felt that I was reading the story of a success. Events have fallen into focus. We can see the literary history of an era in perspective. We can see how much Grant achieved.

The small magazines and the small publishing houses —how would authorship fare without them? The big firms—the Heinemanns, the Cassells, the Macmillans —are on the look-out for budding talent. But they cannot devote to apprentice work the attention which the young writer needs. A writer is self-taught. He teaches himself by writing. He needs to see himself in print. Until he does, he cannot judge himself, cannot assess himself. He needs to talk his work over with his contemporaries. The young must have something in print to show each other. That is how they become writers. And how can they do that without the small magazines, without the small publishers? Literature stands in the debt of those who give the young that opportunity. They do not, the men who fulfil that function, finish rich, with titles and large houses in the country. But they have their reward, in the history of their country's literature.

We make and pass and our place knows us no more. Nothing is more dead, nine times in ten, than the last decade's best-seller. But there are those who do not 'all glut the devouring grave'. There are those who set their names as publishers on books which are part of our eternal heritage; men who enrich the world by the work they do in it. Who can think of the eighteen-nineties without remembering Elkin Mathews, John Lane and Leonard Smithers? Who could write of the years 1910 to 1925 without paying tribute to Martin Secker? And the name Grant Richards will be always honoured on account of the authors that he sponsored.

4
Frank Swinnerton's
Nocturne

I told in my autobiography of the lucky concatenation of circumstances that made a best-seller of *The Loom of Youth*. The timing was lucky and 1917 was a lean year for novels. Nineteen-sixteen had been a very good year, and 1918 was to be, but when I read after Christmas, in my dug-out, north of Arras, the various estimates of the year's books, I recognized how little competition I had had to face.

The year's best-seller was H. G. Wells's *Mr Britling Sees It Through* which had been published in the preceding autumn; Stephen McKenna's *Sonia* came second and that too had been published in 1916. Arnold Bennett had not published a novel, one of the few years in which he had not; Galsworthy had published an astonishingly poor book. J. C. Squire, reviewing it in *Land and Water* under the heading 'Galsworthy gives them Gyp', started with a quotation, then went on: 'you recognise the style? It is the Family Herald, it is Mrs Barclay, no, you are wrong. It is Mr John Galsworthy in his novel which for some reason that is beyond me, he calls "Beyond".' Conrad was silent. None of the younger novelists, Hugh Walpole, Compton Mackenzie, Gilbert Cannan, D. H. Lawrence, W. L. George, was represented. Gilbert Frankau, who up to then had been known as a writer of light Kipling-esque verses, began his career as a novelist with *The Woman of the Horizon*; it sold fairly well, but was not accorded much critical attention. Norman Douglas's *South Wind* had, indeed, come out during the spring, but that kind of book does not create an immediate stir, in war-time. I did not myself order a copy until January. It was a lean, lean year and as I read the various critics' assessments of the year's output, I could myself recall only one novel that had struck me as important; a book that had been highly praised but had had little public success—Frank Swinnerton's *Nocturne*.

Today that book is an established classic. It holds a unique position. It stands in a field of its own. It is under fifty thousand words long; which is an admirable length by artistic standards; since such a book can be read in a single evening and the author can impose and maintain his hold upon the reader through its entire course, but it is a bad length commercially. It was, then, too long for a magazine, and circulating libraries do not like it; subscribers need a book long enough to last them over a week-end. A novelist faced with a subject suitable to such a length preferred to compress it into a long short story or enlarge it into a 75,000-word novel. *Nocturne* was, so it seemed to me, an exceptional example of literary integrity. Swinnerton had felt that this particular story could be told only in this way, and had eschewed the possibility of greater emoluments in the resolve to make his book as good as possible.

On my return to England, when I spoke of this to Gilbert Cannan, I was greeted with a smile.

'There was a sound commercial reason for *Nocturne*,' I was informed. 'Swinnerton had one more novel to deliver under an old contract with Martin Secker. He had been offered a very much better contract by Methuen; he wanted his next major novel to be published by them, so he decided to polish off his Secker contract with a short novel.'

That story had always seemed to be an excellent example of the fortuitous nature of creation. Great books often are produced by a fluke. I had meant to quote *Nocturne* as an example. Before I did, however, I took the precaution of writing to Frank Swinnerton to ask if the story was true. In return I received the following letter, which he has been kind enough to allow me to quote.

What a good job I'm still alive to tell you the true story of *Nocturne*! What you were told was, as they say in *Alice in Wonderland*, 'all wrong from beginning to end'. All the same, I think the true story is just as illuminating of the casualness of events. What happened was this. In 1911 or so Algernon Methuen, hearing that Arnold Bennett thought well of my prentice work, made a contract for two books with an option on a third. The second of these books, *On the Staircase*, was published in the Spring of 1914 and pleased old Methuen (whose wife apparently read it to him in bed) so much that he took up his option on the third book and made a contract for 3 more books. I was thus bound to him, when the 1914 War broke out, for no fewer than 4 books.

Methuen, as you remember, thought books would be absolutely ruined; so he wrote to his famous authors, Wells, Bennett, &c., offering ½ advances, while to me he suggested that a suspension of authorship for the duration would be desirable. This must have been in 1915; and I had written or was writing a novel called *The Chaste Wife*. Not to have published it would have been a financial embarrassment, as I had relied on advances of £75 apiece from England and the U.S. At this point Secker, who had published my much decried book on Stevenson in 1914, said 'I'll publish it'. So he did, by arrangement with Methuen, who allowed this one book to be interposed without regarding it as a breach of their contract.

Then, one day, Secker and I were lunching with Nigel de Grey, who remarked incidentally 'I wonder nobody has ever written a novel about the events of a single evening'. We couldn't remember that anybody had done this: & I said it wouldn't be easy to do it. As Secker and I walked away after lunch, he said (I think with a memory of Oliver Onions's *In Accordance with the Evidence*) 'I wish you'd write me a novel *under* the Methuen contract length—say fifty thousand words'. I said 'I will. I'll write one about the events of a single evening.'

I can't remember how soon I began the book; but it was being set up from my MS. while I was still writing it; and I think Secker brought me the first galleys the day after I had delivered the last chapter. He said 'It begins well.' When he brought the second batch of galleys he said 'I think

48

it's very good.' And when he brought the end he said 'I think it's a master-piece.'

I have never thought much of it myself; but of course I'm much obliged to it. I'm also much obliged to you for your praise of it. Thank you. I am delighted that it should still please.

Yes, I'm very well, thank you. Rather overworked at the moment, as Penguins are bringing out half a dozen Arnold Bennetts next year (including the O.W.T.) and I have been writing introductions to the books and making a frightful butchery of the Journal to make a single volume. I have mentioned that the publishers were rather horrified by the O.W.T.'s [*Old Wives' Tale*] length; but the Journal makes it clear that your Father soon realised its virtue. I think one always has to remember that the publisher sees a book as typescript, with no aura of prestige; and in 1908 Bennett, though recognised as a clever fellow, had never had any sale. In fact he had just left Chatto & Windus for Chapman & Hall because he was not (I think I am right in saying) earning the small advances Chatto's gave him.

With all good wishes
Yours sincerely
(signed) Frank Swinnerton

A postscript about *Nocturne*. I offered our then maid the MS. for fire-lighting. She said the paper was too stiff. I told Secker, who said 'Oh, give it to me!' I did so; he had it bound, and kept it. When he was terribly hard up he sold it to Hugh Walpole, along with the MS. of 'Sinister Street' and perhaps others. Walpole gave his collection of MSS., I believe, to King's School, Canterbury. Secker could tell you about this. He could also confirm what I have said about the writing of *Nocturne*. The book sold 1500 copies; was then out of print for a year owing to Secker's absence from the office; and was later reprinted several times. Then it was put into 'The World's Classics'. Then Hutchinsons, by their marvellous mass salesmanship, sold enormous numbers at 6d or 1/6d. The result of this is that the book has lost all computation. Rather an amusing history.

In the New Year Honours list appeared the names of several men of letters. Anthony Hope was honoured with a knighthood, so was John Galsworthy. Next day it was announced that Galsworthy had declined the honour but that his letter had not reached the appropriate authorities in time. The *New Statesman* on the following Saturday

FRANK SWINNERTON'S *Nocturne*

devoted its entire 'Books in General' page to the subject. It opened with the following three paragraphs:

The posthumous honours bestowed upon Mr. Anthony Hope and Mr. John Galsworthy are ... Thus had I begun when I opened another paper and learnt that Mr. Galsworthy's knighthood had been refused. The conferments, intended and achieved, are of the usual sort. Mr. Galsworthy's best work was done years ago, and Mr. Anthony Hope ought to have received a knighthood from Queen Victoria or not at all. I remember him with affection which has not been dimmed by the long lapse of years since I last heard of him. Up to the time of 'Sophy of Kravonia' he amused and moved me more than most. His defects are obvious, and it is too late to discuss them; but he only narrowly missed being a very good novelist.

The usual thing has happened. When every honours list is being compiled some responsible jack-in-office remembers that 'we must give a knighthood or two to literature and art'. Out of some Panjandrum's stagnant and cobwebbed mind emerge names from the past, names which were much talked of when last the dignitary read a book. I wonder how often they have to make researches to find out whether the objects of their esteem are really still above ground. I wonder whether this year, or last year, they wrote to Wilkie Collins or George Gissing offering a knighthood and received no reply. They are obviously running fearful risks; for the Galsworthy episode shows that proposed names sometimes slip into the definitive lists when answers have either not been received or have not been properly docketed.

Mr. John Galsworthy did himself credit, and his craft justice, in electing to remain a gentleman—even though on this occasion he would have had the distinction of climbing the honorific ladder in company with, though below and behind, that illustrious man, who has become a baronet, and Marmaduke, Lord Furness, who has been made a Viscount, shortly after complaining bitterly about the taxes at a company meeting whereat he also declared a dividend of 30 per cent. One cannot too often repeat that these titles, as a body, never have been any test or token of merit or service and are to-day less than ever so. Consequently, they are wasted on men of conspicuous genius or virtue unless they are given sufficiently early to be —the world being what it is—a real help in the man's career. A good artist who has not yet arrived at financial security could certainly be assisted by a knighthood, which would convince the sheep and the slowcoaches that he really was a person of importance. But to a man who has reached fame and a competence the thing has no uses at all.

This article had two amusing sequels. Galsworthy far from having 'done his best work years ago', completed *The Forsyte Saga* with *In Chancery* and *To Let* and wrote two of his best plays, *The Skin Game* and *Loyalties* during the next five years.

The article was signed Solomon Eagle, the pseudonym of J. C. Squire, who became Sir John Squire in 1933.

5
The Soldier Poets

ROBERT NICHOLS, ROBERT GRAVES,
SIEGFRIED SASSOON,
RICHARD ALDINGTON

Nineteen-seventeen, though a meagre year for novels, was a vintage one for poetry, and saw the emergence of a new group of soldier poets. The Rupert Brooke wave of enthusiasm which had welcomed the declaration of war, had not survived the slaughter of the Somme. In France, Henri Barbusse's novel *Le Feu* had struck a note of outraged indignation that was repeated by several of the younger English poets.

The third volume of *Georgian Poetry* was issued in the autumn and E. M. wrote in his foreword, 'Of the eighteen writers included, nine appear in the series for the first time. The representation of the older inhabitants has in most cases been restricted in order to allow full space for the newcomers; and the alphabetical order of the names has been reversed, so as to bring more of these into prominence than would otherwise have been done.' The newcomers were W. J. Turner, J. C. Squire, Siegfried Sassoon, I. Rosenberg, Robert Nichols, Robert Graves, John Freeman, Maurice Baring and Herbert Asquith.

The three war poets, Nichols, Graves and Sassoon, were at that time treated as a team in the same way that Cecil Day Lewis, W. H. Auden and Stephen Spender were in the 1930s. In both instances the differences between the three were far greater than the resemblances, but the fact that the poets of the 1930s had left-wing affinities and that the soldier poets of 1917 were brother officers made their linking convenient and inevitable.

Graves, Nichols and Sassoon were all highly praised, and the order in which their qualities were assessed often depended less on the intrinsic merits of their poetry than on the political slant of the reviewer. Sassoon has told in his Sherston trilogy the story of his revolt against what he held to be the imperialist conduct of the war, and he was a useful weapon with which a left-wing writer could attack the Government. He had moreover a concentrated satiric strain, a journalist's eye for the telling phrase. The poems that were most quoted were those in which this strain was most pronounced.

'Blighters'
I'd like to see a Tank come down the stalls.

'In the Pink'
To-night he's in the pink; but soon he'll die.
And still the war goes on—*he* don't know why.

'The General'
'He's a cheery old card,' grunted Harry to Jack
As they slogged up to Arras with rifle and pack.
. . . .
But he did for them both by his plan of attack.

Less attention was paid then to the tragic, tender poem 'The Death Bed' by which today he is more often represented in anthologies.

For an imperialist, of the 'my country right or wrong' type, like E. B. Osborn, Robert Nichols was the favourite. Nichols struck the heroic note:

Arms to have and to use them,
And a Soul to be made
Worthy if unworthy;
If afraid, unafraid!

Nichols's poetry could be used effectively, as Rupert Brooke's, in the peroration of a sermon. This is not said in disparagement of Nichols's poetry; what seemed good in it then, seems good today. He was a genuine poet, but he appealed to a different public. He was in tune with the loyalties of a larger audience; *Ardours and Endurances* was the best-selling book of poetry since *1914 and Other Poems*, and he was sent to America on a propaganda mission.

Robert Graves was, I fancy, the least immediately successful of the three. He stood outside the conflict. He was wistful, witty, sentimental, regarding the war as an intrusion on his private world of childhood memories. He did not provide quotable material for the pacifist or for the home-front patriot. On his marriage to Nancy Nicolson in January 1918 Sydney Pawling remarked, 'Heaven knows what they are going to live on, even if they roof their bungalow with the unsold copies of *Fairies and Fusiliers*.'

Graves sent me a copy of *Fairies and Fusiliers* inscribed 'in hope of friendship', accompanied by a letter which I treasure. Reading it in my dug-out, I looked forward to the day when I should be back in London, when I could meet and become friends with him and with Sassoon and Nichols. I cherished, as every other soldier, the pipe dream of an easy wound that would send me back to London with a thin gold stripe upon my sleeve.

But I did not meet Graves till the autumn of 1963. We corresponded, we tried to arrange a meeting in 1919, but he was little in London, and our private lives took us on different roads. I have followed his career with the friendliest well-wishing. He has stayed the course and it is good to see that the youngest poets are reading him with respect.

Siegfried Sassoon was the only one of the three whom I met with any frequency; not nearly as often as I would have liked. Our meetings were so few that we can scarcely describe ourselves as being friends, but our meetings were so pleasant that acquaintanceship is too cold a word.

When the *Herald* became a weekly paper, Sassoon was appointed Literary Editor and I was one of his reviewers. I persuaded him to play in a cricket match against Clayesmore School; Gilbert Cannan was one of the other players. He and Sassoon had the same type of good looks, tall, thin, blondish, with Roman noses. They were both excellent company when they were in the mood, but they could both be very silent. We travelled down, ten of us, in a third-class carriage; Cannan and Sassoon sat opposite each other, in the centre. They did not speak a word the whole way to Winchester, and their barrier of silence divided the team into two quartets.

Sassoon has had a curious career. He started melodramatically, with questions being asked about him in the House of Commons. He was the rallying point both for the extreme left-wing pacifists, and for the men in khaki who suspected that the war was being unduly prolonged by interested parties, by the old men who were doing well out of it. It seemed to us desperately important that the realities of the war should be brought home to the civilian population. No one was bringing it home with the force and vividness that Sassoon did. He was the perfect person to argue our case for us. He was not a weak-kneed, long-haired neurotic. He was strong, handsome, vigorous, an athelete; there was no question of his courage, he had been awarded the M.C., his reckless feats in the line had become a legend. He was a case against whom it was very hard for 'old men sitting in their clubs' to argue.

His start was meteoric. He stood on the threshold of infinite possibilities, and then quietly, undramatically, he left the stage. There are many poets who concentrate the essence of their work into a few years of intense production; Wordsworth was one them, Swinburne was another, though each went on writing into late old age. Poetry is the wind that bloweth where it listeth; it visits certain people for a few years and then abandons them. The fires blaze high and then subside.

During the early 'twenties and possibly afterwards, Sassoon had a house in Westminster which he shared with W. J. Turner. Turner was a good friend of mine. What was Sassoon doing, I would ask him? 'I never see him about anywhere.'

'He's in the country,' Turner would reply. 'He doesn't like London. He only comes up to listen to concerts.'

After the publication of the fifth volume of *Georgian Poetry 1920–1922*, E. M. considered that the series had served its purpose. In that last volume Sassoon was not represented. There was no means of guessing into what new directions he had developed. I presumed that he was passing through a fallow season. Then in 1928 there appeared quietly and unobtrusively *Memoirs of a Fox-hunting Man*. It was published anonymously. I have no idea why; not, I am very sure, to stimulate conjecture. That kind of thing would not appeal to a man so reserved and dignified. Perhaps he wanted to avoid the legend that had gathered round his name. He wanted his book to be reviewed on its own merits. He did not want to read review after review beginning: 'How little one suspected in 1918 when *Counter-Attack* fluttered so many dovecotes that ten years later we should be considering such a book as this, yet it must not be forgotten that his previous book published a year earlier was entitled *The Old Huntsman*. What a change, though, from that high, fierce temper of revolt.'

When the book proved a success he made no attempt to make a mystery about its authorship. The secret was out within a few weeks. It was followed by a series of further memoirs and the Sherston trilogy is today an established classic. But he did not write about anything that had happened after 1922.

For the majority of writers there comes a time when they lose interest in the future, swing round in their tracks and start a second voyage 'à la recherche du temps perdu'. A capacity to develop, to remain contemporary, to keep pace with the present and scan the horizon eagerly, is not necessarily a test of quality.

I met Sassoon for the first time in the spring of 1919. He lunched with me at the Savage Club and brought E. M. Forster with him. There are points of resemblance between their careers. Writing in the *New Age* in January 1911, Arnold Bennett said that 'no novel for very many years has been so discussed by the critics as Mr Forster's *Howard's End*. . . . Mr Forster is a young man. I believe he is still under thirty if not under twenty-nine. If he continues to write one book a year regularly, to be discreet, to refrain absolutely from certain themes, and to avoid a too marked tendency to humour, he will be the most fashionable novelist in England in ten years' time. His worldly prospects are very brilliant indeed. If, on the other hand, he writes solely to please himself, forgetting utterly the existence of the elite, he may produce some first class literature. The responsibilities lying upon him at this crisis of his career are terrific. And he so young too!'

Forster's reply to that prophecy was to make only one further appearance as a novelist, fourteen years later, with *A Passage to India*. In close upon half a century he has produced in addition to that one novel, a collection of short stories and a few volumes of belles-lettres.

Both he and Sassoon have, I imagine, adequate private incomes. A novelist is rarely able to retire before his talent has declined; I fancy there comes to most writers that period in mid-career when they feel written out, and would give anything to be Civil Servants, to have a steady job with a pension at the end of it. Because they cannot afford to retire, they force themselves to go on writing and eventually get their second wind.

It may be that 'autumn laurels wreathe for them' and they write one of their best books in their last decade. But it does not happen very often. Most writers who develop early have done their best work before they are fifty. Who will say that Forster was not wise since fate gave him the opportunity of doing so, to stand upon his achievement, in the belief that he could only smudge his record? Few names are more honoured today in English letters.

As the 'thirties drew to their close and the threat of war became insistent, I wondered what Sassoon was thinking. Was he oppressed by a feeling of frustration? His protest had been in vain and the world had not learnt its lesson. In 1938 he published a book of poems that did not attract very much attention but had a new quality of wistful resignation. He seemed to have accepted the inevitable. Perhaps he had come to feel as many others had, that no compromise was possible with the Germany that Hitler had created. The world might be in a better position today if we had made peace as we could have done in December 1916, before the Russian Revolution, before America had entered the war, before the collapse of social life in Germany and Austria had paved the way for Hitler, and before all those hundreds of thousands of young men had been slaughtered in the mud of Passchendaele. It may be that a chance was missed then. But by 1939 it was too late, Hitler had to be brought to book. The Second War had to be carried through to 'unconditional surrender'. The first need not have been.

I last saw Sassoon in October 1940 under ironically appropriate circumstances.

A few weeks earlier I had been posted as staff-captain to the Petroleum Warfare Department, a branch of the Ministry of Mines, that under the dynamic inspiration of Geoffrey Lloyd made a considerable contribution to the war effort. The full story of the department has been told by its D.G., Major-General Sir Donald Banks in a book called *Flame over Britain*. At that time we were chiefly concerned with the defensive uses to which oil might be put, flame-throwers, tank traps, flame on water. In mid-October we went down into the country to give a demonstration.

It was what is called a typical, which is to say it was an exceptional, late autumn day; a day that started with mist and a chill in the air, a mist through which the sunlight began to break about eleven. By noon it was summer hot. It was the perfect day to drive down into the country with a team of cameramen to film the demonstration and it was a perfect picnic site that had been chosen for the demonstration, at the head of a valley, with the grass very green with dew and the trees red and brown and yellow and the spire of a church showing between the branches of an orchard.

We got down early, set out our cameras and waited. The blitz had been heavy on the previous night. It was a relief to lie out in the grass, with the sun warm upon our faces, in a countryside untouched by war. The valley was quiet and deserted: nothing dramatic in the country's history had happened here. It was strange to reflect that within an hour its slopes would be lined with red-hatted officers; a whistle would blow, the handles of the cameras would turn, explosion would follow on explosion, the soft greensward would be scorched and ripped and scattered into a desert of smouldering fires and scarred iron.

The demonstration started at two o'clock. Within a quarter of an hour the beauty of the valley was destroyed and it was just as the high grade staff officers were moving to their cars, as the final informal conferences were breaking up, that a horseman, a civilian, came trotting by. This was, no doubt, a favourite ride of his. He had had no idea that this demonstration was to be held. It could scarcely be a pleasant surprise for him. I looked up, to note with a start of surprise that it was Sassoon.

My first instinct was to run across and greet him: but a second, wiser instinct checked me. There was an inscrutable expression on that drawn, handsome face as it looked down on the charred and littered grass.

What thoughts, I wondered, were moving behind that mask: how many different thoughts must be creating a mixed mood—memories of the last war and his revolt against it, his contempt for 'scarlet majors at the base', his poems that had seemed then and later the battle call to a crusade; the sacrifice of his generation that had failed to prevent this second war, whose intensified horror was exemplified by these new engines of destruction, with himself a quarter of a century later, in his fifties and too old for service?

It was kinder to leave him to that mood, those memories.

Two soldier poets, now generally recognized as two of the most important, were not included in the December 1917 reviews of the year's poetry—Wilfred Owen and Richard Aldington. Owen's story has been told once and for all in Osbert Sitwell's *Eminent Presences*. To Richard Aldington's story, I can add a footnote.

The story is peculiar, and its peculiarity lies in this. That we know almost nothing of his background. He was born in 1891. He was educated at Dover College, and afterwards in France. But he has told us nothing about his home, his family, his upbringing. He was so anxious to attribute T. E. Lawrence's ideas of grandeur to his illegitimacy, that one wonders whether the vein of bitterness that marked and in my opinion marred so much of his prose writing may not be due to some kind of an unhappy home. That is conjecture. I have no means of knowing. He has told us nothing. Nor has anybody else. At this late day it is unlikely that anybody will —or can.

Almost the first thing we know of him is that by January 1914 he was one of a group of poets who paid tribute to Wilfrid Scawen Blunt. His companions were W. B. Yeats, T. Sturge Moore, F. S. Flint and Ezra Pound. He was then moving in high company. But during the war, he was never in the news. He was absorbed in the anonymity of army life. He served in the ranks. He was posted to an officer cadet training unit. He fought as an infantry subaltern in France. He wrote poetry in his dug-out. He was an 'Imagist' not a 'Georgian' and was represented in the *Imagist Anthology* of 1917, but not in the *Catholic Anthology* of 1915. He was never publicized as a 'soldier poet'.

He married H. D. (Hilda Doolittle) the Imagist poetess. An American. It was a short-lived and must have been an unusual marriage. In 1952 I met their daughter who told me that she had no recollection of either of her parents. Aldington, on the very rare occasions when he mentioned H. D., spoke with warm appreciation of her poetry; he never spoke about her as a woman. I never met her.

Aldington matured young. Nichols, Sassoon and Graves had not reached a position in January 1914 when they would have been invited by Yeats and Sturge Moore and Pound to present a tribute to Scawen Blunt. Moreover Aldington had spent his maturing years in France. Englishmen of the late Victorian, Edwardian and

Georgian periods, because of the public school system, sexually developed late. Graves has in his maturity written a number of deeply intimate love poems. But there is no evidence of that intimacy in *Over the Brazier* and *Fairies and Fusiliers*; nor is there in the poetry of Nichols or Sassoon. Aldington, on the other hand, through his years in France was sexually mature when the war broke out. He is essentially a love poet. He saw war in terms of his exile from love. No other English poet did. 'Reverie', 'Meditation', 'Epilogue' may not be greater poems than Graves's, Sassoon's, Nichols's and Wilfred Owen's. But they are different, in that profound respect.

I met Aldington for the first time at one of Harold Monro's Poetry Bookshop parties in the early spring of 1919. There was a difference of seven years between us, but we met on equal terms, as subalterns 'home from the wars' who had won their spurs as writers and now had to come to terms with a post-war world. There was an instantaneous affinity. A few weeks later I read his poem 'Reverie' in the *English Review*. I thought, I still think, that it is a very lovely poem. My appreciation of his poetry was an added bond between us. I wrote an article about him in Holbrook Jackson's magazine *Today* which he carried round in his pocket for so long that it became dog-eared, with the creases split.

How many times did we meet in the next twenty years? Not so very often in actual fact. But when I read of his death in 1961, I felt that I had lost one of my closest friends. It is not the quantity but the quality of the meetings that count. I always met him under intimate conditions, often with Harold Monro. I remember in particular a dinner just the three of us at the Poetry Bookshop, and a summer evening when Monro and I were on a cricket tour that was based on Newbury.

Aldington had a small cottage then at Bucklebury; he came over to watch the game and took us back with him for dinner. He was living alone and cooked the meal himself. He came little to London then. He could not afford to, he explained. He needed peace of mind to follow his own thoughts through; he was reviewing French books for the *Times Literary Supplement*, on which he could support himself as long as he avoided London. He lived simply, but not austerely. He enjoyed the pleasures of the table, of wine particularly. It was a solitary existence, but he was a dedicated man. His work came first. He was resolved to make the most of his talent. There was an air of reality about him; of putting first things first. There was also an air of warmth. In personal relations he was the same person that he was in his poetry.

He lived in Bucklebury for several years (later it gave him the material for *The Colonel's Daughter*). Once when I was playing cricket at Aldermaston, with J. C. Squire's XI, he came over to watch the game. He was wearing a beret and a beard. He was with an attractive female who was his companion for quite a while. His beard gave him a foreign air; before he had looked like an army officer in mufti. I did not think that the beard suited him. I mentioned this to Monro. Monro shrugged. 'It is a symbol of emancipation. I grew one myself when I first went to live in Italy.'

In 1926 I began to travel and I lost touch with Aldington, as I did with many other friends. He was still, I gathered, living quietly, mainly in Europe now. Then in the autumn of 1929 *All Quiet on the Western Front* started a boom in war books. It had been taken as axiomatic in the trade that war books did not sell; though one or two good books had had large sales, Gilbert Frankau's *Peter Jackson, Cigar Merchant* and Wilfred Ewart's *Way of*

Revelation while the American play *What Price Glory?* had a long run in the U.S.A. It would be truer to say, not that war books were not being read, but that they were not being written. Writers like readers wanted to forget the war. Then suddenly a mood of nostalgia forced upon both writers and readers a need to relive their past; there was a flood of war books, most of them of high quality, *Goodbye to All That*, *All our Yesterdays*; Richard Aldington's *Death of a Hero* and the play *Journey's End*.

The obvious and superficial comment on this flood of war books would be that all over the world a number of writers decided to cash in on the success of *All Quiet*. But that is not the way good books are written. A good book is written when a good writer feels a need for self-expression, and a moment's thought will show that a book takes a year to write and several months to publish. Even if a number of publishers in Europe and the U.S.A. had said to those of their authors who had seen war service, 'Now's the time, now's your chance. Get cracking', there would not have been the time to catch the market. Clearly what happened is this: all over Europe a number of writers felt simultaneously and independently a need to relive their war experiences, anticipating by eighteen months or so the public's need to relive those same experiences. That is what timing is. No author can tell in 1927 what the public will want to read in 1929, but the novelist who is in tune with his time is ahead of his time, and anticipates intuitively the public's need without knowing that he is doing so. As long as he can do that, he is a best-seller. The moment he loses that subconscious power of divination, he drops out of the race. Richard Aldington, who of all writers was the very last to write with his eye on the main chance, and also the last of all writers, leading as he did a secluded and solitary life, to have expected to find himself in tune with his hour, had the deserved good fortune to hit the market with a first-class book. He became overnight one of the most popular novelists of the decade. A string of novels all of which did well, followed on one another: *The Colonel's Daughter*, *All Men are Enemies*, *Seven against Reeves*. He could live now in relatively affluent circumstances. He was free to travel as he chose. And all the time he was producing a body of, in my opinion, superb poetry.

At that time, travelling as I was, I missed *A Dream in the Luxemburg*, the beginning of this recrudescence. But in 1934, Beachcomber's column in the *Daily Express* contained a contemptuous reference to his latest poem 'The Eaten Heart'. Beachcomber, though himself a man of scholarship and taste, is in his column resolutely, obstinately 'lowbrow'. He quoted from 'The Eaten Heart'. 'This is what they call poetry nowadays,' he scoffed. I read and re-read the extract. It seemed to be what I called poetry. I immediately bought 'The Eaten Heart'; and when I had read it, I bought *A Dream in the Luxemburg*. Then I wrote to Aldington. During the next four years I kept seeing him, off and on in London and at my home in Silchester.

In retrospect I realize that I never during those four years saw him against the background of his personal life. He was either my guest, or the guest of someone else, of Douglas Goldring, at least once. The only time that I was ever his guest was on that distant occasion when Monro and I dined with him in Bucklebury. It is possible that never having seen more than one of his various homes, I have missed the clue to him. But it is my belief that he was one of those men who cannot be bothered to organize a social life, who socially live from hand to mouth, making the most of what happens to be around. This view is strengthened by the picture that he gives of himself, without knowing that he is doing so, in his book on

Norman Douglas and Orioli. He was seeing a lot of the two of them and of Reggie Turner in Florence in the late 'thirties. He had gone to Florence, because he liked the place, because he had a book to write and, since he needed conviviality, he accepted what lay to hand. This is said neither in disparagement nor approval. Some novelists feel that it is necessary for their work to organize their private lives in such a way that they can obtain the widest view of the world around them.

Aldington was not that kind of novelist, and it was because he left things to chance, that he found confusion in his private life. It is surprising that it is the poets who have been basically the purest, such as Shelley, who have landed themselves into 'the most impossible situations'.

There has been enough 'chatter about Harriet', but Aldington is an example of that particular confusion. When I re-met him in 1934, he was living with a widow rather older than himself. She was red-haired, and extremely handsome; it was obvious that she had been a very great beauty in her youth. She was still most attractive. They were not married, though she was introduced as Mrs Aldington. She had inspired *A Dream in the Luxemburg*. Hers and Aldington's had clearly been a high romance. One said to oneself, 'The disparity of age. How long will it last?'

No romance could have collapsed more disastrously. And I think the nature of that collapse was determined by Aldington's indifference to the organization of a personal life. Most men, *l'homme moyen sensual*, manage to conduct their *passades* so that they do not impair irretrievably the fabric of their domesticity. They do not make love to their wife's best friend. They maintain appearances. I do not say that this is an admirable characteristic, but it is a social lubricant. Aldington, like Shelley, within the narrow limits of his domestic circle, stumbled, unknowing, unwittingly into confusion. He fell in love with his consort's daughter-in-law. Could anything be more humiliating for a woman than to have a lover younger than herself desert her for her son's wife: and to become the father of that woman's daughter. Yet let any one who feels censorious read Aldington's 'The Crystal World'. It is a fine and noble poem. It is not an apologia. It says quite simply, 'When this happens, when this ultimate mystery is revealed, there is no alternative but to accept it.' All this happened just before the outbreak of the Second War.

Aldington died in 1961, shortly after his seventieth birthday which he had celebrated in Moscow and where he had been given a hero's welcome. A few weeks later I received a letter in faulty English from a Frenchman, Fréderic-Jacques Temple, who asked me if I would contribute to a 'Homage' to Richard Aldington. I exchanged a couple of letters with him without getting a clear idea of what form the testimonial would take, but eventually, feeling that Aldington would have been hurt if there were to be a publication of some kind in which I was not represented, I wrote a five-hundred-word pen-picture, and suggested to Monsieur Temple that he should get in touch with Richard Church who had, I knew, seen something of Aldington in recent years. I also wrote to Church telling him that I had given Temple his address.

My contribution to the 'Homage' was not acknowledged and as I heard nothing more from Monsieur Temple, I presumed that the plan, like so many other pious projects, had been abandoned. I was considerably surprised, therefore, to receive in November 1965, a bound volume, two hundred pages long, called *Richard Aldington*, edited by Fréderic-Jacques Temple and Alister Kershaw, an Australian journalist with whom Aldington had lived during his last years in France.

The book had been published by the Syracuse University Press. It contained contributions from a number of Aldington's early friends, Richard Church, Sir Herbert Read, Henry Williamson, T. S. Eliot, John Gawsworth, Roy Campbell. It had an extract from C. P. Snow's brochure *Richard Aldington, an Appreciation*—I suspect that Lord Snow scarcely knew him—a long panegyric from a Japanese student, high praise from two of the Russians who had honoured him on his seventieth birthday: and two long pieces of reminiscence, by Temple and Alister Kershaw.

Oliver Edwardes reviewing it in *The Times* said that he found Sir Herbert Read's contribution the most interesting because it told him about Aldington's early years when he was a subaltern in France; and as writing, Read's contribution, along with a thumb-nail sketch by Henry Miller is, I think, the best; but to me Alister Kershaw's article was the most interesting because it told me a great deal that I did not know about Aldington's last years, and explained in considerable part, the resentful state of mind in which he found himself: in particular his anglophobia.

I had heard something of this from Richard Church, and Church refers to it in his own essay. What had happened was, so I have gathered, this. In August 1939, Aldington was over forty-nine years old; he had had, a few years earlier, a serious motor smash. He was unfit for military service and it is hard to see what part he could have played in the general war effort. Not unnaturally, since he had spent little time in recent years in England, he went to the U.S.A. and stayed there throughout the war: some of the time in Hollywood. Presumably he made a comfortable amount of money, most of which he spent. At that time there was no double tax relief agreement between Britain and the U.S.A. so that Aldington as a

British subject was liable to taxes in England on his American earnings. He could not in consequence afford to return to England and was forced to exile himself in France. He resented this strongly; at least that is the impression that I got from Richard Church. But I had not realized how resentful he was towards the lack of critical attention that he was receiving in England, till I read Kershaw's article.

He considered himself, so I gathered from it, 'despised and rejected'; he fancied that a conspiracy of denigration was at work against him and he attributed this in large part to his attack on Lawrence of Arabia; he believed that the admirers of Lawrence and a whole group of interested and influential people were in league against him. I had heard, of course, that his book on Lawrence had been received with a good deal of indignation by T. E.'s friends. I had not read it when it came out. I am an admirer of Lawrence. I did not believe that Aldington knew anything about the Middle East. I imagined that the writing of the book was a symptom of his anglophobia. I suspected that the book would annoy me. And I did not want to be annoyed by Aldington. But after I had read Kershaw's essay, I got hold both of *Lawrence of Arabia* and Aldington's book on Norman Douglas that published a few years earlier had been considered to be in exceedingly bad taste. The standards of taste have changed considerably in the last dozen years, and I do not think that if the book on Douglas were to be published for the first time today, it would cause much offence. But *Lawrence of Arabia* is a different matter.

In his dedicatory letter to Alister Kershaw, Aldington explains that it was Kershaw who suggested that 'I should gratify your admiration for a hero by writing a life of Lawrence of Arabia.' Aldington started with the hope of investigating a hero and his deeds. But when he discovered that there was no truth in Lawrence's assertion that he had been offered the post of High Commissioner for Egypt in 1922 and 1925, he felt suspicious. He began to sift the evidence; and decided to write not a biography but a biographical enquiry. His investigations led him 'to find proof after proof that much he reports of himself, including and especially his Arabian experiences, was heightened, exaggerated, faked, boastful and sometimes entirely without foundation. . . . The national hero turned out at least half a fraud. My book is a criticism of those writings which have fostered the Lawrence legend. . . . I have tried but perhaps not always successfully to give the evidence in the whole of this book fairly and in such a way that it can be instantly unified, though not without some indignation that such a man should have been given the fame and glory of the real heroes of 1914–1918.'

Aldington's investigations revealed that Lawrence's birth was illegitimate and to this fact he attributes 'the systematic falsification and overvaluing of himself and his achievements which Lawrence practised from a very early date.' He acts throughout as the prosecuting counsel. Admitting, though reluctantly, 'the difficulty of finding any adequate means of verifying Lawrence's statements and one danger is that his unsupported testimony may be doubted when it is in fact as reasonably true as human tendency to error permits,' he assumed Lawrence to be guilty where he could not be proved innocent.

The attack was delivered with spleen and venom; a sustained sneer; and it is hard not to feel that Aldington was trying to get his own back at the country that had failed to appreciate him, by destroying a national idol, 'These be your Gods, O Israel'. He must, when he corrected the final proofs, have thought, 'Well, that'll show them'. Surely he must have known that those whom he had attacked would hit back with vigour? Yet he appears to have been indignant.

Most writers who have enjoyed a measure of popular favour have a difficult time when they are forced to realize that they are no longer 'the new thing', that they have become back numbers. They feel that they are writing as well as ever, yet their books sell fewer copies, editors no longer want their articles. Because of the war, this period came for Aldington sooner than it should. He had cut himself off from English life. He had not been a part of England's life during its period of greatest stress. The English are in part isolationist: there are two kinds of Englishman, those who won the Empire on the high seas and those who administered it from Whitehall offices. During the war they were imprisoned within a beleaguered fortress and after the war they were fettered by currency controls and austerity conditions. For a dozen years they were forced back upon themselves. Aldington had no longer a point of communication with his fellow countrymen. He had nothing to say to them. And is it surprising that the English should lose interest in a writer who had shown no interest in them during their hardest and 'their finest hour', any more than that the Russians should suddenly have begun to take notice of a writer who was in conflict with the country of his birth. In the 'thirties, a few of his novels had been published in Russia in small editions, but now *Death of a Hero* and *All Men are Enemies* became best-sellers. Aldington was saying there precisely what the Russians wanted to hear and believe about and against England. His stud of novels were for them fine debating points. They were also fine novels: they had everything to recommend them.

Aldington's last years cannot have been happy. He was

in poor health. He had not a great deal of money. He was dependent on Alister Kershaw's generosity. His second marriage had broken up soon after the war. His emotional nature was concentrated entirely on his daughter, and she had now started a life of her own. He was as a writer at the end of his material. He had no more to say. He concentrated on translations. But at the very end he had the excitement and gratification of his visit to Russia where he was welcomed with adulation. He ended on a high note.

Death of a Hero is considered his best novel, but *All Men are Enemies* is his most revealing, because in it the two sides of his nature are most markedly contrasted. There is the poetic side of him, and the angry aggressive side. They are not allowed to mix. They are kept separate. When he is writing of love he is tender, wistful, passionate: the same man who wrote *A Dream in the Luxemburg* and *The Crystal World*; when he is concerned with social satire, he is the man who wrote *Lawrence of Arabia*.

6

The University of Mainz

HUGH KINGSMILL,
GERARD HOPKINS, MILTON HAYES,
J. F. HOLMS

'The Lost Generation' is a cliché; it has been claimed that Gertrude Stein used it first in reference to Hemingway and Scott Fitzgerald, but it was in general currency earlier than that. I met it myself for the first time in 1920 when Douglas Jerrold, for many years a prominent London journalist and the author of several substantial books, in particular the autobiographical *Georgian Adventure*, offered Chapman & Hall a novel with that title. There was a very small market then for war books, Jerrold's novel was not particularly good and we declined it. As far as I know, it never found a publisher. All that I can remember about it is the title.

There were in fact a number of lost generations, each being lost in a different way: my own was lost in this, that it never became a generation.

A generation is formed when a group of young contemporaries, on the brink of their careers, meet and exchange ideas either on a college campus or in a sidewalk café. They are ruthless, intolerant, generous and self-assured: they are impatient to beat down the doors of middle-aged complacence and remould the world nearer to their heart's desire. As the years go by they watch each other, forging ahead or lagging in the race, failures, successes, or half-successes, most of them compromising with necessity, but remaining, in sympathy and heart, members of their own generation: serving the same shrines.

73

An Oxford contemporary of my brother, who spent the greater part of the Second War and the first two years of peace in Egypt, finally decided to return to his base in London on these grounds. 'After all,' he said, 'nearly all the people one really wants to see still live in England.' He was able to say that because he was part of a generation. I never could. I was twenty and a half when the war ended. I was engaged to be married. I had started a career. It seemed too late to go up to Oxford.

Yet even so I had my university.

I was captured in the big retreat in March 1918. Louis Napoleon, who was a prisoner for three years, spoke of himself as a graduate of the University of Ham. The seven months I spent in the Citadel at Mainz were my equivalent for a university. A high barbed-wire fence was patrolled by sentries, but mentally my freedom was complete. I had no duties, no responsibilities. My time was my own, to read, write, talk, play bridge or chess as I chose. In the elaborate educational programme that was organized by a camp committee, one small narrow room opening off the main dining-hall was reserved for 'authors, architects and other students'. A long table ran down its centre. It was called 'the Alcove', and here I spent my mornings and late afternoons.

I was lucky in my fellow captives; in Sir Henry Lunn's second son Hugh who later wrote under the name Hugh Kingsmill, in Gerard Hopkins who is better known as the translator of François Mauriac than he is as a novelist, good though those novels are in their careful studied way, and in Milton Hayes, the music-hall artist, creator of the *Monologues of Monty* and the author of 'The Green Eye of the Little Yellow God'. I also had my first experience, in the person of J. F. Holms, of the negative, uncreating artist, who is always going to write a book, but never does, and who is intolerantly critical of those who do. I did not then recognize Holms as a familiar type in half a hundred novels. How could I have? He was young and hopeful; strong and handsome, a fine athlete at Rugby, who had won the M.C., and a brilliant talker. His fits of brooding melancholy, his dark alcoholic bouts seemed the inevitable dark shadows in a portrait.

Morning after morning we assembled the five of us in the Alcove, with our books and pens and papers. There was no privacy and no attempt was made to impose silence. We talked to each other as we wrote, consulting Roget's *Thesaurus* for a synonym, reading out loud a passage from a book that struck us. Holms in particular provided interruptions. He always carried a school exercise book, a number of whose pages were covered with illegible pencil-inscribed sentences. I never saw him write anything in it, and he refused to read us what he had written, but he was never without that notebook. Occasionally he would pick it up and read a page or two, nod approvingly, lay it down and take up a book; after a few pages he would emit a snort of disgust and turn to Kingsmill. 'Listen to this, old man, isn't it revolting.' It was in the Alcove that I acquired the useful habit of working in public. Some of my pleasantest writing hours have been on the terrace of the Welcome Hotel in Ville-franche, at a round blue-topped table with friends break-fasting all round me.

Kingsmill was then working upon a novel *The Will to Love*. He had been captured a year earlier than I and by the time I arrived it was a third finished. In appearance he was an untidy man; loosely built, stocky rather than fat, with his short hair half brushed; he walked with a lurching gait. On his arrival at the Alcove he would take off his tie and collar and wrap round his neck a thin dark green velvet scarf. One needed to be physically at ease, he explained, if one's mind was to function freely. But though he was untidy in his personal appearance, he was punctilious in his habits. He would arrange neatly in front of him his pipe and tobacco pouch, his dictionary and *Thesaurus* and write his story in a clear, open script, keeping an exact tally of his words and averaging three hundred words a day. He copied each chapter as he finished it into another notebook, but he made few revisions.

He was equally precise in the arrangement of his day's routine. He drew up a time-table; so many hours for reading, so many for chess, so many for exercise: he allotted himself four pipes a day; the half-hour between 2 and 2.30 was devoted to sensual reverie.

He was then twenty-eight years old, and fourteen months' captivity had not damped his spirits. He had a basically sunny nature. He was warmhearted and affectionate. He had a great booming laugh. It is not easy to convey in writing the quality of conversational humour. You need the look, the gesture, the pitch of voice. Kingsmill's sallies were spiced with bawdy. 'Matthew Arnold,' he once flashed out, 'grew sidewhiskers to intimidate his J.T.'

His parody of 'A Shropshire Lad'—which Housman himself is said to have approved—is an example of his written wit. It begins,

> What, still alive at twenty-two
> A fine upstanding lad like you

and contains the couplet,

> Bacon's not the only thing
> That's cured by hanging from a string.

During the early post-war years we saw a lot of one another, Hopkins, Holms, Hayes, Kingsmill and myself.

Hopkins had a place waiting for him with the Oxford University Press. Kingsmill returned to his father's travel agency. Holms prepared—if prepared is the right word —to produce a masterpiece. He had by birth well-placed connections; he was never completely without money; he was strong, and with his vivid red hair and striking appearance, those women to whom he appealed found him irresistible; his fortunes may be said to have risen and fallen in accordance with the financial status of the particular woman of whom he was the consort.

During the early 'twenties his fortunes ebbed. In January 1919 I saw him for the first time in civilian clothes. He had been to a good tailor and looked very smart. Up to then I had only seen him collarless in ragged khaki. He was full of confidence: he was in love—'a sultry, savage passion after the long Sahara of captivity'.

'I shall soon be ready,' he informed us, 'to start on the works of my immaturity.' He always saw himself in terms of his future biographers.

The spring of 1919 was a boom period with war gratuities in the bank. They were soon spent, however, and Holms found himself with negligible resources. Kingsmill was at his side. Kingsmill had no doubt that Holms would produce a series of masterpieces one day. The problem was to find the right conditions for their creation. Kingsmill had through his family firm many facilities for finding his friends jobs. But Holms considered such employment menial. At least that was what he appeared to be telling us but it is possible that Sir Henry had doubts about his suitability as a courier. By the autumn of 1919 Holms was wearing pre-war shabby clothes, but he wore them with an air. He had grown a short pointed beard and looked like a Spanish grandee. People stared at him when he came into a room. His manner became more sombre; he was clearly the prey of intense and violent emotions. He was how I expected a genius to look before he had found his medium.

In the spring of 1920 he fell in love with a young woman who had once worked in Chapman & Hall. She was slim, very pale, with bright red hair. W. L. Courtney had once when walking through the counting house, held his hands suspended in benediction above her head, murmuring, 'I warmed both hands before the fire of life.' Her association with the firm was brief and marked by absences.

Holms was in an ecstatic trance. 'She has the most wonderful hair,' he droned. 'Even more wonderful than mine'—he had little sense of humour—then he would quote in his sing-song voice:

> Why liked me thy yellow hair to see
> More than the boundaries of mine honesty?
> Why liked me thy youth and thy fairness
> And of thy tongue the infinite gentleness?

It was a tempestuous romance. They had very little money and when they were turned out of their flat Holms was in difficulties.

He sought my assistance. I could not follow the story in exact detail, his account was so peppered with quotations, but I gathered that the final provocation had been a revolver discharged at midnight. At length, at long length, the purpose of the visit became plain. I had a small bungalow in Sussex and Holms considered the easiest solution for his problem would be for me to come up to London and stay in my father's house while he and his lady moved out to Ditchling. In the quiet of the country he would start upon his novel. London, that was the cancer eating at his heart. Oh, to escape from London.

I had no doubts about Holms's genius. I held it to be my duty to do anything within my power to smooth the path of genius, but the bungalow was a small frame construction that I had bought as a unit and had had fitted by a local builder. Its walls were very thin. 'That revolver,' I objected.

'But that's all over long ago,' he said.

'You said it was last Friday.'

He shrugged, despairingly, at my obtuseness. 'Time, time, old man, eternity within an hour.' And he was off on a quotation-punctuated discourse on the infinite divisibility of time; different parts of your life moved at very different paces, you travelled in so many different trains along parallel tracks, some were non-stop expresses, some dawdled, stopping at every halt—one's friendship with men, for instance, but love, how could you measure love in minutes, who could compute in seconds the agonies, the anxieties of a day-long separation. Yesterday was a century ago. This little moment mercifully given.

It wandered on, a trailing anapaestic anacoluthon. There was no doubt that he was a genius. But common sense counselled me to retain my bungalow.

Holms died in October 1934. I cannot remember when I saw him last. I lost touch with many friends when I began to travel, and Holms was not the man to send Christmas cards or change-of-address notes.

In *Memoirs of a Polyglot*, William Gerhardi described his first meeting with Holms, whom Kingsmill had sent down to him as a herald in the South of France, 'a gaunt redbearded young man who had never published a book but accepted the description of him as a genius without a wink or smile'. Gerhardi, who was enchanted and impressed by his conversation, and was at that time writing for *T.P.'s Weekly*, suggested that he should introduce Holms to the editor. Holms looked at him with pity. 'T.P.'s,' he murmured with infinite sadness, 'T.P.'s'.

Holms left behind with Gerhardi a battered copy of *The Calendar of Modern Letters* which contained his one short story, but Gerhardi never finished the reading of it as a telegram demanded its return. Holms needed it as a proof that he was a writer in order to obtain a *carte d'identité*.

This must have been around 1927. In the long two-column obituary essay that he contributed to the *Daily Express*, Gerhardi said that Holms spent his last five years in affluence. Brian Lunn, describing this period in his autobiography *Switchback*, wrote, 'He had settled down in a house near the Parc Montsouris with an American woman slightly younger than himself, dark haired and of a pleasant figure. She had plenty of money but he had a sufficient personal income and a nature which easily accepted affluent surroundings without imposing a sense of obligation upon the person who provided them; and besides he was very fond of her.' The lady was Peggy Guggenheim.

Usually the unproductive man grows bitter, but Holms, I think, never did. He believed in himself. He argued that when a man had a great deal in him, it took a long time to boil. 'Though he displayed' (I quote Gerhardi), 'an unnatural assertiveness that was like the exaggerated masculinity of a weak man, the protest of an inveterate passivity.' In his obituary article Gerhardi quoted Lord Beaverbrook's phrase 'the genius of the untried'. "In every age, Goethe says," so Gerhardi continued, "there are men who while achieving nothing give an impression of greater genius than the acknowledged masters of the day."'

Holms's death was in keeping with his life. It was the question of a minor operation on his wrist. He consented to chloroform though he dreaded it. He went under with remarkable ease, but he never recovered consciousness. 'He had disdained to come back,' Gerhardi said.

Milton Hayes was the complete opposite of Holms in every way. He was a North Country man; he was nearly forty; he was brisk, assured, purposeful, with his eye on the main chance. He was the first person I had heard analyse success. I had thought of success as a capricious goddess whom you could not court, who gave and withheld her favours according to her changing moods. But Milton Hayes had his theories cut and dried.

'I wrote "The Green Eye of the Little Yellow God" in five hours,' he said, 'but I had it all planned out. It isn't poetry and it does not pretend to be, but it does what it sets out to do. It appeals to the imagination from the start: those colours, green and yellow, create an atmosphere. Then India, everyone has his own idea of India. Don't tell the public too much. Strike chords. It's no good describing a house; the reader will fix the scene in some spot he knows himself. All you've got to say is "India" and a man sees something. Then play on his susceptibilities.

'"His name was Mad Carew." You've got the whole man there. The public will fill in the picture for you. And then the mystery. Leave enough unsaid to make pater-familias pat himself on the back, "I've spotted it, he can't fool me. I'm up to that dodge. I know where he went." No need to explain. Then that final ending where you began. It carries people back. You've got a compact whole. "A broken-hearted woman tends the grave of Mad Carew." They'll weave a whole story round that woman's life. Every man's a novelist at heart. We all tell ourselves stories. That's what you've got to play on.'

There was nothing particularly original in these

theories, but I was hearing them for the first time. He spoke as an actor rather than as a writer. He worked not at a reader in a study but at an audience in a theatre.

'People don't go to shows by themselves,' he would say. 'A thing that sounds silly to a man when he's by himself sounds very different when he's beside a pretty girl. Create a mood where a boy wants to squeeze the hand of the girl he's sitting next and the old married couple simper and think they've not had such a bad time together, after all.'

He talked about Edward Sheldon's play *Romance* which ran for two years during the war with Doris Keane in the lead. 'The critics thought nothing of it,' he said. 'But then they went there by themselves. They should have gone with a girl. *Romance* has everything, it's steeped in amber, the hidden sigh, the one passion, the woman who never marries. But it's not a show to go to by yourself.'

After the war Milton Hayes put his theories into practice. He was a great success on the halls with his *Monologues of Monty*. When he eventually retired to the South of France, it was with a large bank balance.

During the early years after the war, Gerard Hopkins and I lunched together regularly at each other's clubs. Though he worked for the Oxford University Press all his life, Hopkins is now primarily known as a translator, in particular of François Mauriac. I have had the good fortune to have been a close friend of C. K. Scott-Moncrieff, and to be a very close friend of Vyvyan Holland, two supremely good translators. The same criticism has been made of both—what a pity they did no creative work.

It is a short-sighted criticism. To recreate a masterpiece in another language, so that it remains, though told in idiomatic English, a French, Russian or a German novel, needs high creative capacity coupled with a high degree of scholarship. To translate Proust and Mauriac and Morand in such a way that an English reader can get the sense, the particular individuality of the writer, is performing a great service to literature.

That particular criticism was not made of Gerard Hopkins, because he did during the 'twenties write several novels. They were not sensational in subject or in treatment; a problem was set and it was resolved. There was no straining for effect. They were novels of under-tones and understatement. Those who knew the author were inclined to say, 'It's what you would expect of Gerard Hopkins. He's a man who can't let himself go.' Later when Hopkins began to make a reputation as a trans-lator those same people said, 'He's found his niche, at last. He would never have been a novelist. He's too held-in.'

The first part of that second comment states a fact, the second is a superficial criticism, based upon appear-ance. Hopkins had a foreign-office air. The Oxford University Press had an official status. Its representatives must be presentable. Hopkins was tall, impressive, tidily dressed, urbane. He looked a scholar. But though he was always the kind of man on whose behaviour even a Bohemian hostess of the 1920s could rely, he was very far from being conventional. Two incidents from Mainz will illustrate that point. Milton Hayes produced a camp revue which contained a number of *risqué* jokes and one suggestive scene, to which a padre objected. The non-conformist conscience of a section, a very small section, of the camp was roused. In a prisoner-of-war camp where everyone is under-occupied, storms can be quickly brewed in teacups. Opinions became violent. There was a general need for drama and a meeting was arranged in the theatre, at which each side could argue its own case.

83

It was important that the case for freedom should be handled with tact and skill, otherwise a censorship might have been imposed and the standard of entertainment would have slumped; it may be added that the scene to which objection was taken was very mild and could have been shown even then without offence at the Coliseum. Gerard Hopkins was chosen as the spokesman. It was felt that if he with his calm decorous manner had seen no occasion for complaint there could be none. His arguments prevailed.

But that, it may be argued, is not evidence of unconventionality. The incident does no more than indicate that Hopkins had a presence and a manner, a capacity for debate and a readiness to use it in defence of liberty of speech. All of which might be expected of a scholar and a man of letters. That is perhaps true, but the other incident does show a considerable degree of moral courage.

There was a canteen in the billiard room where you could buy wine and cigarettes. Wine cost a pound a bottle. It was a sour casual hock and we grumbled at having to pay so much for it, but we had so little on which to spend our money that before food parcels arrived, when we were very hungry, some officers devoted nine-tenths of their pay to the purchasing of bread from sentries. The standard black-market price was two pounds a loaf, but it went higher. Milton Hayes once paid three pounds fifteen shillings. When parcels arrived and we were no longer hungry, most of us welcomed an opportunity to split a bottle in congenial company once a week.

A senior officer discovered, however, that the wine for which we paid a pound could be bought in the town for six shillings; representations were made to the authorities that the profit was excessive. The authorities blandly replied that that happened to be their price. The senior officer was indignant and summoned a conclave of his

84

peers. It was agreed that the Germans must be brought to heel and a boycott of the canteen was announced. It was believed that the profits on the canteen were the private perquisite of the officer in charge. Had we been in a French camp, this would have been a natural assumption. But the Germans have a regard for correct behaviour. I imagine that the profits on the bar went to some welfare fund and the individual officer could not have cared less whether British officers drank wine or not. He had fulfilled his duty by making wine available to British officers at a price that lay within their means. But the boycott was installed and an officers' picket was posted to see that it was not broken.

Many of us were indignant; the posting of the picket was the final outrage; we might be in a preparatory school. But though many of us grumbled, none of us made any protest, none except Gerard Hopkins, and he was one of the ones who had grumbled least.

On a hot July afternoon he walked alone to the canteen. No one was playing billiards and the room was empty except for a somnolent German sentry at the bar and a bored British subaltern on picket duty. Hopkins ordered a bottle and sat down to drink it. Hopkins was a captain; the startled subaltern respectfully reminded him of the boycott. Hopkins courteously assured him that he was well aware of it and offered the subaltern a glass of wine. The picket was nonplussed and embarrassed. He would have to report the matter to a senior officer, but at half past two on a hot afternoon, senior officers were likely to be taking a siesta; they would not appreciate being disturbed. He hoped Hopkins would finish his bottle quickly and get out; but it takes a long time for one person to drink a whole bottle of wine and Hopkins was in no hurry to finish it. He had a book to read and he wished to make his gesture.

The afternoon wore on, siestas ended and the billiard table was again in use. The picket officer was relieved and sought out a senior officer. Presently a colonel came across. He sat down at Hopkins's table and Hopkins offered him a glass. The colonel began his remonstrance, at a disadvantage. Hopkins was the kind of person whom even an irate colonel had to treat with deference; he wore the Military Cross, and the colonel suspected that Hopkins had a nimbler wit than his. He made some derogatory remarks about 'letting down the side' and went away. Hopkins resumed his reading.

He made his bottle last four hours; everyone who came into the room stared at him, but he ignored them. By the late afternoon the rumour had got round the camp that the boycott was either over or being broken. Several captives came across to ascertain the facts. The picket assured them that the boycott was still in force. It did not look as though it was, they told him. One or two groups gathering courage from Hopkins's example ordered wine themselves. By the time Hopkins had finished his bottle, the boycott had been broken.

That now was a courageous act. Hopkins was under military discipline and ran the risk of putting himself in serious trouble, moreover he was very far from having public opinion on his side. Many members of the camp were in favour of 'teaching the Boche a lesson' and quite a number of them were teetotallers. Hopkins made his protest in the interests of a minority. He was far from being a conventionally-minded respecter of authority. It was not on that account that his novels had little popular appeal. He was a man who did not recognize at first the true direction in which his talents pointed.

Hugh Kingsmill's story was a very different one. On our return to England after the Armistice, I persuaded him to offer his novel *The Will to Love* to Chapman & Hall. My father was pleased with it and published it, but it was scantily reviewed and sold under a thousand copies.

A novel without a hero, in which Frank Harris, very thinly disguised, was the central character, it came out at the wrong time. Few people in April 1919 were interested in Harris. Discredited socially and financially by 1914, he had spent the war obscurely in the United States indulging in anti-British propaganda. He had yet to earn a dubious prominence as the biographer of Oscar Wilde and as a scabrous, mendacious auto-biographist.

Kingsmill's novel described how Harris seduced the daughter of a schoolmaster and blackmailed her father for two thousand pounds. It was told lightly and ironically, but the character of the girl was drawn with warmth and sympathy. Had the book been published in 1927, in the days of the Bright Young People, when domestic suceptibilities had been hardened and sharpened by Aldous Huxley and Michael Arlen, and when Harris as the author of *My Life and Loves* was 'in the news', it might have caught the popular fancy. But the public was not ready for it in 1919.

Kingsmill was disappointed but not discouraged. He had a sunny, resilient nature.

During the next few years he led an itinerant existence. Though he was married with, at that time, one child, he had no settled home. But his father owned a number of hotels, the Flandre in Bruges, the Albany in Hastings, the Hotel des Alpes in Mürren, in Scotland the Bridge of Allan, so that Kingsmill had access to a suite of rooms in half a dozen places.

I never met his first wife. She was pretty, attractive, vivacious but did not, I have been told, encourage his literary ambitions and was jealous of interests that she could not share.

On his return from captivity he took Holms down for a visit at the hotel where she was staying. Holms had some ideas on Pascal which he wanted to express. When he found that Mrs Kingsmill thought Pascal had been a doctor, he turned his back on her and addressed his conversation to her husband. He drank too much, drifted into gloom and delivered a long brooding soliloquy on suicide and Schopenhauer. Next day Mrs Kingsmill suggested that it would be more convenient if Hugh saw his 'literary friends' in London. He would have been wise, I think, to have broken the ice gently with Hopkins or myself but when I expressed a hope that one day soon I should be meeting her, he shook his head. 'Keep things in their frame, old man, keep things in their frame.'

The framework which he adopted—a wife in the country and his friends in London—may not have been the best formula for a successful marriage, and that first marriage did not survive the 'twenties, but it suited his friends admirably. He would arrive in London every three weeks, in a holiday mood, released from discipline, happy to be among us, anxious to exchange gossip and to hear our news. His exuberance was a keen and salutary stimulus; he stirred us out of a rut. If you are professionally employed in literature in a metropolis, it is very easy to be absorbed by the latest best-seller and by current gossip. It was refreshing to find Kingsmill excited over a new interpretation of *The Brothers Karamazov* and perplexed about the exact function of a minor character in *Eugénie Grandet*. There was no voice during those years that I was more glad to hear unexpectedly over the telephone.

At that time he was supremely confident in his powers

as a writer and he had a good-natured contempt for most of the idols of contemporary esteem. When such trivial fellows were admired, he should not find it difficult to carve his own career. He was impatient for the day when he would be free from the irksome routine of a hotelier. 'When I'm in the very middle of a paragraph, old man, I'm called away to inspect the roof of the maids' lavatory.' Actually he was writing under ideal conditions. When *Horizon* organized a symposium on how a writer could best supplement his earnings from his books, most contributors agreed that he needed a job unconnected with literature, that he should not be a publisher's reader, write scripts for the B.B.C. or copy for an advertising agency; he must be able to come fresh to his creative work.

Kingsmill's job was from that point of view ideal. He had warm and comfortable quarters. He was well-fed. He could travel. He was in touch with human administrative problems. He was meeting new people, and different kinds of people. His routine offered him constant copy and he was not overworked. He had responsibilities and he had to be on the spot, but he could have devised a programme, as he had at Mainz, which would have allowed him a regular undisturbed period. It was a pity he did not remain in his father's business. But he left it in the later 'twenties, when his marriage broke, and the new life which he began with his habitual confidence and high spirits was to prove a harder conflict than he had expected.

His first book after *The Will to Love* contained three long short stories and was entitled *The Dawn's Delay*. It was published in 1924 and bore the name Hugh Kingsmill. At that time his brother Arnold was editing for Chapman & Hall a yearly series called *Georgian*

Stories. The 1925 volume included a story from *The Dawn's Delay—W.J.* It was the last number that Lunn edited; next year I took it over and William Gerhardi was one of the writers whom I asked for a contribution. I sent him a copy of the 1925 volume to show what kind of company I was inviting him to join. In his letter of acceptance, he expressed such enthusiasm for *W.J.*— 'who was this genius? did I know him?'—that I sent his letter on to Kingsmill, who promptly responded by sending Gerhardi a copy of *The Dawn's Delay.*

'This,' Gerhardi wrote in *Memoirs of a Polyglot,* 'was the beginning of a friendship that has not been uneventful. It has survived two storms, which so dislocated our lives that each of us remains to this day, to the other's mother, a sinister influence in the career of her son. Kingsmill's habit, I regret to say, is to abscond and set up house with somebody in whom I have invested a good deal of emotion and then to defend the purity of their hearth against my visits, though indulgent enough to consent to meet me outside his new home.'

Kingsmill is the hero of Gerhardi's novel *Pending Heaven* and there is an excellent description of him in *Memoirs of a Polyglot.* Gerhardi never lost faith in his friend's talent. There were those, he complained, who thought that his 'literary enthusiasm for his writings are biased by friendship. The truth is my literary enthusiasm for him has inveigled me into a precarious friendship. I feel in regard to Hugh Kingsmill the satisfaction of a man who backs an outsider knowing him to be a "dead cert".'

But it did not turn out that way. I would not say that Kingsmill was a failure. He published a number of biographies on which his publishers did not lose money and which were well reviewed; his two anthologies of Abuse are classics; he was literary editor of the *English Review*;

during the war he was on *Punch*'s reviewing staff. In any
other walk of life he would have seemed successful. A
soldier who retires as a Brigadier would not be considered
a failure because he did not finish as a Lieutenant-General
and a K.B.E., but for authors the gap is immense in
terms of tangible reward between a best-seller and an
author whom a publisher is glad to have upon his list. It
is not surprising that an author should grow bitter. Why
should his books sell less well than those of a man who
is less well read than he, a less sound judge of values,
with a less concise command of English, a man who has
seen less, done less, who conversationally is less effective?
It is very easy to attribute that other man's success to
backstairs influence, a capacity to play cards cunningly
or to the low standard of public taste. And Hugh Kingsmill was one of the unlucky ones who never hit the jackpot.

All his friends thought he would; as a biographer
if not as a novelist; if not with this book, then with the
next. He had so many qualifications; he had humour and
warmth, a human approach to his subject: he wrote well;
he was widely read; he worked hard; he was ambitious.
There is a big market for the topical biography. It was
surely only a question of time before he hit on the right
subject. But he never did, and the demands upon his
purse were heavy; he was in constant financial difficulties;
and he was a generous openhearted man who needed good
fellowship and wine. If a man is tidy and goes to a good
tailor, he can look smart when his clothes are threadbare.
But Kingsmill had never been tidy. He went to a run-of-
the-mill tailor; he began to look shabby, and he was
conscious of it. Douglas Goldring described him in his
autobiography as being 'A shade embittered by the trials
and tribulations of the literary life'. 'Shade' is an understatement. As the 'thirties ran their course, he became
quick to take offence. I once asked him to dinner without

inviting any other guests. It was some time since we had seen each other and I wanted to have a gossip. His feelings were hurt. He was not good enough, he supposed, for my smart, successful friends. I found that I had to be on my guard with him, the very last thing I should have expected.

We met for the last time in September 1941 at a large cocktail party at which Hamish Hamilton was celebrating his tenth year in publishing. On the following day I was sailing for the Middle East. It was for me an occasion of dramatic irony. I was certain to be away for a long time, but I could not, owing to military security, make an occasion of my sailing. There were a hundred people there, several of them friends I had not seen since the war began; we welcomed each other warmly. I took their telephone numbers. We agreed that we must get together soon. I would write to them from the ship, I told myself.

Hugh Kingsmill was the one I was most glad to see there. He was his buoyant, warmhearted self again. Things were going reasonably well for him. He had as much journalism as he could find the time for. Paper was rationed and books were selling as many copies as the publisher was in a position to print. The 1930s bally-hoo of publishing with its high-pressure methods and double-column advertisements across the Sunday papers was at an end. When the country's existence was in peril, professional jealousies had no place. As Kingsmill's great laugh boomed across the room, I could fancy myself back at Mainz.

I heard of him several times during the war, in my father's letters. I promised myself that on my return he would be one of the first people with whom I would get in touch. But that was the kind of promise that it was easy to make three thousand miles away.

Only Londoners know how hard it was immediately after the war to keep in touch with friends; there was rationing both of food and petrol; everything you did involved an effort; you had to queue for this and fill out forms for that and await priorities. You did one thing at a time, and you concentrated upon seeing the very few friends who were special to you and relied upon running into the other ones by chance; which you rarely did, unless you belonged to the same club. Rarely have London clubs been such a refuge and a home as they were during the war and the immediate post-war years, but I did not belong to the same club as Kingsmill.

I saw him once from the top of a Number 11 bus. He was hatless, walking with his familiar roll along the Strand, a pile of books under his arm. It sent a nostalgic wave along my nerves. I *must* get in touch with him; but I was going abroad in a few days.

He died before I returned.

Whenever I hear it argued that sooner or later a good writer must strike the public fancy, if only with a single book, I have my answer ready—Hugh Kingsmill never did.

What went wrong? Was he without that point of timing that is so essential an ingredient to success or did his books lack in their actual composition that sense of moving towards a climax that carries the reader along from page to page? Had he, as a writer, the complementary defects of his qualities as a conversationalist so that he visualized his books in terms of *mots* and repartees; writing in terms of sentences and paragraphs instead of chapters building to a final chapter? In his company it was impossible not to believe that he was a person of high consequence. Did he express himself so completely in conversation that only a pallid residue was left to him at his desk?

After his death Malcolm Muggeridge and Hesketh Pearson, with each of whom he had collaborated, wrote one another a series of letters about him which they published under the title *Hughie*. It is a volume that any friend of Kingsmill's would welcome upon his shelves, but the average reader might well have asked why he was being asked to accept with such veneration and without supporting evidence the opinions of a man of whom he had scarcely heard.

The other day I re-read *The Dawn's Delay*. It has not worn well. When Kingsmill was writing through the mind of a man in liquor or half-asleep or on the verge of a mental breakdown, he could produce an occasional flash of wit, such as Polmont's: '"A good fellow," he remarked, as Glayde left the room. "A good fellow. Kind hearts are more than coronets. More numerous or more valuable? Tennyson is not explicit on this point."' But the stories have no particular point; there is no originality of plot, character or treatment. Why was Gerhardi so impressed by 'W. J.'? Is it too fanciful to suggest that by a process of telepathetic divination he recognized, turning its pages, that here was the friend whom he had missed. 'Although I had had school friends in my time and was in the army and at Oxford, Hugh Kingsmill I realized was the first whose mind exhilarated my mind and exercised it to the full; that is, a being to merit the term "friend".'

I had said very much the same thing about him in a book I published in 1932. 'Gerhardi,' I wrote, 'maintains that he is a genius. Certainly he has genius. I have liked only two men as much. I have never been so stimulated by any company. He is like the sun shining on you. You become happy. The present is rich. The future radiant. You talk well. He has the supreme gift in personal contact not only of entertaining you but making you entertain him. You find yourself talking as fast though not as loudly as he does. He envelops you with warmth and friendliness.'

I closed the section with this paragraph.

'I do not know if he will ever write a great book. Gerhardi maintains that he already has. But, myself, I feel that a man who expresses himself with such abundance in the ordinary contacts of life does not need the substitute of writing. I feel that writing is for him what living is, for Gerhardi probably, for most big writers certainly, a side show.'

7
Ralph Straus

In January 1919 I started adult civilian life with a minute nucleus of friends, but by the end of the year I had assembled quite a number; most of them men older than myself. The success of *The Loom of Youth* placed me at the age of twenty in a position that most writers do not reach till they are thirty. My opposite numbers at the Savage were all several years my senior. Ralph Straus, the first professional writer to become a personal friend of mine, was at least twenty years older than myself.

I met him first in March 1917, through Ian Mackenzie, a fellow cadet at Sandhurst who died of Spanish flu on Armistice night. He might have been a considerable poet had fate spared him. Between us there had sprang up one of those quick eager friendships that are only possible between two young men of high ambitions. We were without rivalry and jealousy as we declaimed our poems to one another, knowing there were ample kingdoms for each to conquer. We shared everything; not without boastfulness we produced our separate friends. Gilbert Cannan and S. P. B. Mais were my contributions, Harold Monro and Ralph Straus were his.

There was an outbreak of mumps that spring at Sandhurst and the college closed down for three weeks. Much of the time Ian spent at Underhill, and he arranged a meeting with Ralph Straus, at a lunch given for us by Ralph's uncle, an M.P.

Ralph was then in officer's uniform, of a kind; with a red cross instead of a star upon his shoulder. He was employed in some administrative capacity in a hospital. He walked with a stick and a limp and his leg was bent. He was clearly unfit for military service. It was a curious complaint. Before the war he had played fives for Harrow; as soon as the war was over his knee straightened so that he could play cricket, of a casual nature, regularly, and court tennis with some skill. His limp was a strictly war-time liability. We are now assured that all illnesses, except appendicitis, are mental.

In 1917 Strauss was living with his parents in an ample house in Craven Road, near Paddington. He had a large study booklined to the ceiling, with a high rounded window. He took us back to this room after lunch. He walked round his shelves, taking down book after book; he had an anecdote to tell about each one. Many had been signed by their authors and the title pages of H. G. Wells's were decorated with amusing drawings. Straus seemed to know everybody.

Before the war Straus had led the life of an industrious dilettante. He had had a private printing press on which he had published an edition of Petronius, with the Latin text facing a translation and with a number of illustrations by Norman Lindsay. It was a subject particularly suited to Lindsay's talent. I have never seen obesity portrayed more faithfully and more revoltingly than in his picture of middle-aged patricians standing round a swimming pool. He wrote a weekly bookpage for the *Bystander*. He was not highly paid for it, but the sale of the review books was his perquisite. Every other year he published a novel, on both sides of the Atlantic, that received good reviews and respectable sales. He did occasionally a specialist's book; there was one on Baskerville, the printer, another on stage coaches. He made possibly eight hundred pounds a year and that sum went a long way in 1913. Living with his parents, he had no overhead expenses.

He could travel, he could entertain and he was a generous and skilful host.

Straus was small, stocky, bald, with a thick short black moustache. He was unmistakably a Jew. Anti-Semitism is, in England, practically non-existent, but it was one of Ralph's idiosyncrasies to deny his race. His family, he explained, had backed the Young Pretender and after Culloden had deemed it prudent to change its name. Many affectionate jokes centred round 'the Straus tartan'.

His novel *The Unseemly Adventure* was dramatized. One of the characters was a duke. The part was taken by a somewhat common actor who objected to one of the phrases that was put into his mouth. 'Dukes don't talk like that. I know dukes,' he said. 'As though I didn't,' was Straus's comment, in repeating the episode.

It was amusing to watch the devious route by which he would inform his friends that he played squash racquets with the Prince of Wales.

'You know more than I do about the prices newspapers are paying now. What should I get for seven hundred words on "The Game the Prince Plays"?'

'Five, six guineas. What is it by the way?'

'Squash racquets.'

'Is he any good?'

'Not bad, not bad at all.' Then after a pause, 'I can give him three points but not five.'

Court tennis is, I am assured, one of the finest hard-ball games in the world, but I am sure that it was not the game's intrinsic quality but its aristocratic connections that made Straus take it up. He had an invariable ploy, as Stephen Potter would put it, when a man mentioned that his game was tennis. His face would light with interest. 'Indeed. Where do you play—Lord's, Prince's, Queen's?'

On learning that his friend played on grass with a soft

ball, his features would register a superior disappointment. 'Oh, you mean *lawn* tennis.'

In 1919 psychoanalysis became news in London. I heard about it first from Straus. He claimed to take private patients, unprofessionally. He talked with oracular solemnity on the interpretation of dreams. 'I was staying in a country house, the other week-end. As a matter of fact it was at Willie Mount's—you know who I mean of course, Lord Arthur Mount. A young girl came down to breakfast and described in complete innocence a dream that made me blush. I took her aside afterwards and warned her, "Never tell your dreams, my dear. Someone may know what you are talking about."' I pressed him to tell me what the dreams had been but he shook his head. 'No,' he said, 'no. I really couldn't. The subconscious plays strange and rather terrible tricks at times.'

Where psychoanalysis was concerned he had little sense of humour. Describing an occasion on which he had found himself in medical disagreement with a stranger, 'Little did he guess,' he said, 'that he was arguing with the greatest living authority on masturbation.'

We all made gentle fun of him but always unmaliciously. I have never heard anybody speak against him, just as I never heard him say a mean, unkind, or spiteful word. He liked in conversation to hold the stage, he was a snob and he allowed distinguished names to drift into his talk, but he never betrayed a confidence. If I had ever found myself in a trouble that required discretion, he was the first person to whom I would have turned.

He seemed a fate-favoured mortal in 1919 when he left the hospital at Tunbridge Wells, returned to his booklined study, resumed his literary career with a psychoanalytical novel *Pengard Awake* and became again a dilettante. As president of the Sette of Odde Volumes he brought to its monthly dinners half a dozen guests. His favourite wine, he explained to them, did happen to be champagne, but of course if they preferred burgundy or claret. . . . Many of us envied him, but not in an envious way. He was not overbearing: he did not flaunt his fortune; nobody grudged it him. Then the blow fell.

In the course of 1920, or it may have been 1921, his father, whom I had assumed to be a person of consequence in business, had a stroke. He was helpless and speechless. After a few days Ralph's mother, on going down to her husband's office to negotiate a cheque with which to meet the expenses of her household, learned that for many years her husband had been cutting into capital and that there was no money left. There had been no need for him to do so. If he had told his family fifteen years before that a need for economy had arisen, economies could have been effected without discomfort. It was a cruel blow for Straus and he took it with courage, dignity and common sense. After a couple of bewildered days, he settled down to see what could be rescued from the ruin. The house in Craven Road was given up; he sold his library and he moved his mother into his uncle's flat, occupying there himself a minute room which was both his study and his bedroom, and set about increasing his income.

In many ways it was easier then than it is now for a writer to earn a living. The B.B.C. did not provide a market, but there were many more newspapers, sixpenny weeklies and magazines. Hutchinson had a large group of magazines, so had Cassell's. A boy-meets-girl story had to be quite bad not to find a purchaser. At the same time the prices paid in 1920 were very low. Five guineas a thousand was a satisfactory price for a featured article. The *Daily Mail* paid three guineas for signed three-hundred-word articles on its leader page and advertised itself as paying the highest standard rates in contemporary journalism.

If you were to live by your pen, you had to rely on
output. Into this jungle was launched at the age of forty
Ralph Straus, who up to then had been able to write the
kinds of article he liked, at his own pace, for papers of
his own choice.

He showed great character during those next years.
He never grumbled, never displayed self-pity, never
talked nostalgically of 'my affluent days'. No one who
did not know him well would have been aware that he
had suffered a reverse. He played tennis at Prince's,
entertained at the Odde Volumes and the Omar Khayyam,
played cricket for J. C. Squire's Invalids; he was always
well dressed, he drove a Morris Cowley; he economized
in ways which were not obvious and he worked extremely
hard.

Many novelists in such a predicament would have
added to their income by writing detective or historical
novels under a pseudonym, but Straus concentrated on
journalism, particularly in the *Daily Chronicle*, adopting
a female pseudonym—Gertrude Belt, a character from
one of his novels—to increase his output; it was thus that
he acquired his nickname among the members of Clifford
Bax's annual cricket tour. One morning when we were
on tour an article signed by Gertrude Belt opened with
the line 'We women, and particularly those of us who are
blessed with nephews and nieces . . .' When Straus came
down to breakfast, he was greeted with a guffaw from
Eric Gillett. 'Well, Auntie, and how are your little ones
this morning?'

The nickname stuck and he was always known afterwards as 'Auntie'—but only upon cricket tours. A junior
member of the side who addressed him as 'Auntie' at a
London cocktail party was reminded that there was a
place for all things. He was, however, known to many as
'Uncle Ralph'. This was due to his style of reviewing in

the *Sunday Times*. At that time the paper was able to devote several pages to books. The editor, Leonard Rees, took a special pride in them. He was a good editor to work for, making his contributors feel that they were members of a family. He gave large men's dinners for them at the Savile and also entertained them—in mixed company—in his own house. He liked at the end of a dinner to send away his guests in a good temper with a commission to contribute to his columns.

Rees took a personal interest in each individual contribution and he built up Ralph Straus into an influential figure in the world of letters. To begin with he gave Straus a half-column of novels; not the most important ones and not at the top of the page. But within a year or two the half-column had become a column.

Gerald Gould reviewed novels for the *Observer* and no two men could have approached the same task more differently. Gould was enthusiastic and romantic. He was criticized for being over ready to praise, but that is a fault on the credit side. He looked for the merits in a book and the readers of his column felt on a Sunday morning that a week of enjoyment lay ahead of them. Next day they hurried expectantly to their branch of Boot's or Smith's.

Straus's approach was altogether different. He was a slippered writer. This was against him as a novelist. He liked to tell his stories through the eyes of the kind of man that he would have liked to be, a scholar and a recluse, moneyed and worldly-wise, who regards the traffic of human beings with benevolent, amused detachment. This limited his range, only a certain kind of action came within the scrutiny of his narrator. His most successful novel was entitled *The Unseemly Adventure*, but nothing indecorous occurred in it. Horace Lorrimer said that he did not mind what the characters in a *Saturday Evening*

Post serial did between instalments, but I cannot recall any character of Straus's committing an act of fornication at any point of his or her life.

The characteristics which made Straus often an ineffective novelist helped him, however, as a reviewer. He talked across a fire-place, reasonably and quietly, telling his reader the kind of novel it was and whether it was good of that kind. He was even-tempered, he was never flustered. The readers of his column could rely upon his advice, and authors found him kind, helpful, encouraging; he explained them to their public. He claimed that he could read any novel within two hours, but he always knew what the book in consideration was about. He never missed its point. His manner was avuncular. It is not surprising that he was known affectionately as 'Uncle Ralph'.

He had a happy life and very possibly in the long run he was made the happier by the reversal of his family fortune. He was brought through it into closer touch with his friends and when the Second War brought its restrictions and its burden of taxation, he was already inoculated against that kind of shock.

His writing career was exposed to the same vicissitudes as that of most of us. He had his strokes of bad luck and his strokes of good, a marked piece of good fortune coming at a time when he desperately needed money.

A. P. Herbert was complaining, I believe during one of J. C. Squire's cricket matches, that he had thought of a fine title but could not devise a book to fit it. 'What was the title?' he was asked.

'"Married Alive."'

'I wish you'd give it to me,' said Straus.

'Very well, I will.'

It was an excellent title, but it was not Straus's subject either and the book which he attached to it was feeble.

But Hollywood was so attracted by the title that it bought it for £700. The film that starred Lew Cody bore no resemblance to Straus's plot. The two words 'Married Alive' were all Hollywood needed. It had no use for the other hundred thousand. A. P. H. had virtually made Straus a present of £700.

He died in the early summer of 1950. His home in east Kent had been badly bombed during the war and on my return from the Middle East I had noticed that his right hand trembled, but he had seemed well enough during the preceding autumn and I had been seeing him constantly at the Savile Club, and at the three dining clubs of which we were both members, and for which he had proposed my candidature, the Odde Volumes, the Saintsbury and the Omar Khayyam. He was an excellent after-dinner speaker in his own flippant and facetious style and the last speech I heard him make when he proposed the toast of the guests at the Omar was one of his wittiest. I saw him for the last time as I had seen Hugh Kingsmill, from the top of a bus. He was walking slowly on the arm of a friend past the Café Royal. I had known that he had been ill, but the news of his death was as much a surprise as a blow. For me and for many others those three clubs have not been the same since.

8

W. L. George

Another novelist, also a man twice my age who was to become a close friend in the post-war period, was W. L. George. He died young, in January 1926, and it is now many years since a book bearing his name has figured upon a bookstall. A new generation has probably never heard of him, but he was a remarkable man and his name often appears in contemporary autobiographies. 'Prolific, tough, ambitious and capable' are the adjectives with which Ivor Brown describes him in *The Way of My World* and between 1910 and 1926 he was much discussed in London.

I met him at the first adult dinner party that I went to, in January 1919, at the Ford Madox Hueffers—as Violet Hunt and Ford Madox Ford were, at that time, known.* George was then forty-two years old. He was short, dapper, nearly bald, with prominent eyes and a short clipped dark moustache. He spoke with a French accent. He had been brought up in France and had done his military service there. I am not sure whether he had any English blood. His wife, Russet, was handsome and well dressed, with a great graciousness of manner.

At that time, among his male contemporaries and seniors George was by no means popular; for several reasons. In the first place he had specialized in sex. His first novel *A Bed of Roses*, a serious sociological study, showed how a well brought up woman became a prostitute. With a lurid jacket it was displayed in a shilling

---

* The story of their involved relationship has been entertainingly and fully told by Douglas Goldring in *South Lodge*.

edition in Villiers Street beside damaroids and contra-
ceptives. He wrote articles about sex, he lectured on sex;
though he did not boast of his conquests, he did not conceal that the pursuit of women was his chief preoccupation.
That in itself would not have stood against him. Few
writers have been more popular with their fellows than
H. G. Wells. But George was a Frenchman. That made
a difference. Xenophobia is easily excited where sex is
concerned. Masculine resentment is usually aroused when
a foreigner attracts feminine attention.

In the second place his methods of self-advertisement
were ostentatious; he had a facetious entry in *Who's
Who*. He was always being referred to in the gossip
columns. Clifford Bax, who disliked personal publicity,
noticed that whenever he gave a party and George was
at it, there would be a paragraph in the Press within a
week.

Thirdly, George made a substantial income out of
writing. That would not have put his contemporaries
against him. Writers usually are pleased by the successes
of their friends, because it reminds them that money can
be made out of writing. Nor do they object to a writer
stage-managing his career. Arnold Bennett was a much
loved man. But much of George's journalism was cheap,
unworthy of his own high talents and lowering to the
dignity of authorship.

Politically, he was on the left of left. He had been very
near to pacifism during the war. In view of his age
and the imminent breakdown of his health, it is doubtful
if he would have been accepted for active service, but he
is reported to have said that he had no intention of joining
the army; he did not mind being killed, but he could not
bear the risk of disfigurement and becoming repulsive
to women. He did not conceal his minority opinions, and
was nearly expelled from the Savile Club for taking

Ramsay MacDonald there to lunch. In September 1919 when there was a railway strike, he advocated in the then extremely left wing *Daily Herald* the setting up of Soviets throughout the country.

Socialism alone would not have put his fellows against him. Bertrand Russell had served a prison sentence as a pacifist. But George's urge to make money by almost any means was an inappropriate companion to his socialism, and revolutionary behaviour did not come well from a rich man who had been brought up in France. He was un-English, that was what it all came down to.

This let it be remembered was in 1919; opinions changed towards him during his last two years, and even in 1919 he had many loyal friends, women especially. He was a literary uncle to a number of young women writers, to Sheila Kaye-Smith and G. B. Stern in particular. He discussed their contracts with them and their relations with editors and agents. He helped them plot the graphs of their careers. His advice was sound commercially and it was wise in a larger literary sense. He enjoyed talking 'shop' but at the same time he never lost sight of the writer's proper goal—the writing of a masterpiece.

He was also helpful to young men. Douglas Jerrold pays a deserved tribute to him in *Georgian Adventure*. He never forced his good services upon you, he was never officious, but he was always ready to put you in touch with an editor to whom your work might appeal. He did not waste the time of busy men with pointless introductions, but where he could put the right people in touch with one another, he did. I had good reason to be grateful to him on several counts.

George was a generous host. He lived on the north side of the Park, in Albion Street, and I have the happiest memories of his parties. I noted with admiration the way he organized them; he always had his eye upon his guests; he was quick to observe when a conversation had begun to flag and he would separate the two, moving another guest across. It was annoying sometimes to be interrupted in the middle of a conversation, but more often than not the change was welcomed. You were given a chance of talking to everybody in the room. I have often thought of George in later days when I have found myself saying at the end of an evening, to a fellow guest, 'It's too bad, but we haven't had one word together.' I learnt from George one very valuable social lesson, not to be a guest at your own party.

George was, naturally, an author whom I was anxious to get onto Chapman & Hall's list, but there seemed little likelihood that I should succeed as he had recently signed a three-novel contract with Methuen, with good advances. It was through chance we got him. Lunching at the Savage with C. S. Evans and myself, he mentioned that *A Bed of Roses* was out of print. I told my father this. We were not likely, I said, to make real money from a cheap edition, but it would be good window-dressing to have George's name upon our list, and when the Methuen contract expired, he might think of us. We had better move fast, I added, or Charlie Evans would be on to it. Within a week a contract for the cheap rights of *A Bed of Roses* had been signed. A little later Eric Pinker rang me up to say that Methuen's were complaining that W. L. George's new book was obscene. Would we be interested?

The book was *The Confession of Ursula Trent*; it told the story of a girl of county family, who makes no particular resistance to a seducer in the private room of a London restaurant, becomes a manicurist and has a long illicit love affair before she finds happiness in marriage. That in itself was not very shocking at that time, but told in the first person, through the woman's eye, it had a cogent intimacy. A young woman reading it would feel that all this was happening to herself and that she was approving it. That was why Methuen's objected. But even so, even in 1921 it seemed surprising that a publisher who had signed a three-novel contract with the author of *A Bed of Roses*—knowing the kind of book that he was likely to write—should have objected to *Ursula Trent*.

George himself was of the opinion that Methuen's reaction was determined, subconsciously if not actually, by their having lost money on his previous book, a not very exciting story about a newspaper proprietor, through paying a too high advance. George's book before it, *Blind Alley*, one of his best and published during a boom, had sold very well. Methuen had expected his sales to go up but they went down instead. They perhaps welcomed an opportunity to cut their losses.

'It's always best,' George would say, 'to ask for a high royalty rather than a high advance. A publisher hates over-advances. He's always happy when an advance has been earned, even though, through a high royalty, it has been earned by the sale of fewer copies. I'd never have had that trouble with Methuen if I'd remembered that.'

Luckily for us, he had not remembered it, and luckily for himself, too, in the long run. He was as happy at Henrietta Street as we were to see him there. He became one of the easiest authors on our list. He never bothered us with suggestions or enquiries, did not ask for daily accounts of how the book was selling or with complaints that the librarian of the Smith's branch at Notting Hill had never heard of it. When he delivered the manuscript, he considered that his job was done and that it was now up to the publisher to sell it. He wrote a publicity handout for the Press and he gave his opinion on the jacket if it was invited. But that was all. He never interfered. If a book did not sell as well as he had hoped, he did not necessarily blame the publisher.

He published all his subsequent books through us. For his novels he accepted an advance of £300. This may seem very small but only authors and publishers know how little money an author can make out of a book that appears to be successful.

George gave me this advice, 'Never confess your sales as a novelist. If you tell the truth, people will be astonished and think you are unsuccessful. It harms you to have them thinking that.

'On the other hand you can safely discuss the prices you receive from American magazines. What, they will exclaim, a thousand dollars just for that!'

The Confession of Ursula Trent was published in the early autumn of 1921. It sold quite well, and a number of men, Clifford Bax among them, considered it remarkable that George should have been able to enter a woman's mind so convincingly, but it had a bad press and it was during that autumn that George's stock in terms of social popularity touched its lowest level.

In the previous autumn he and his wife had gone to America on a lecture tour. In January Russet died. She was very popular, George was devoted to her, and genuine sympathy was felt. That sympathy diminished when *Ursula Trent* appeared. A heartbroken widower should not, it was felt, have been writing at that time, that kind of book. Then in the late autumn his engagement to be remarried was announced.

The engagement, like everything to do with George, was widely publicized. His fiancée had a Spanish background and distinguished antecedents. Her photographs showed her as dark, not very tall, slight, with an exceptionally good figure, pale skinned, and with a Southern air. It was rumoured that she was rich. After the honeymoon, they were to sail for America, for a lecture tour. The general reaction was a 'Well now, really'.

That was at Christmas, 1921; within three years that estimate had been reconsidered. A great deal was to happen in that short time. In the first place his new wife, Kathleen, was to make herself greatly liked, as a friend, a hostess and a wife. She had a difficult task, following upon Russet, under such conditions, and with two step-children, the elder, a boy, by a first marriage. She displayed poise and tact and friendliness. Yet she was never not a person in her own right. She was fourteen years younger than George and in a number of slight ways his life altered to meet her tastes; they became regular first-nighters, they gave bridge parties, he took up golf. His income had increased as a result of his American trips and they moved into a larger house, in Hyde Park Terrace. Their dinner parties were more elaborate but no less enjoyable. A new marriage that is going well has a contagious, cheerful atmosphere. It is a fire at which friends warm their hands. People were soon saying, 'Kathleen is very nice. Let's hope that it works out.' Because of Kathleen, there was a sudden burgeoning of well-wishing towards George. During his previous marriage, devoted though he had been to Russet, he had never concealed that, while other men might hunt and fish and play golf, his sport was women. He never gave that impression after he married Kathleen.

In the early spring of 1924 he joined the board of Chapman & Hall. To our deliberations at Henrietta Street, he brought a fresh and practical point of view. He could on occasions act as an advocate for a refractory author, but he recognized that a publisher must make money. He also brought into the boardroom the sense of a larger world. On sunny days after the meetings I used to walk back with him across the park. Those walks in retrospect are the pleasantest feature of my years at Henrietta Street.

His wit and quickness of mind and general zest for life were never as keen as they were during that summer. Yet it was in the course of it that we became aware that there was something very wrong with him. His eyes had always been prominent, now they were protuberant. He had lost weight, yet the colour of his cheeks had heightened. He had shaved his moustache which gave him a naked look. He had difficulty with his speech; there seemed something odd about his hands. By the end of the summer his friends were beginning to be shocked by the change in him.

In September he published *The Triumph of Gallio*. It is a powerful, uncompromising novel, the story of a man who came to believe that nothing mattered, who was equally ruthless and ultimately indifferent towards success and failure, who valued nothing but his own independence. It was the best book that he had written since *The Second Blooming*, ten years before.

In England George now acted without an agent. He could do his own business as well himself, he said, and thus, save ten per cent, but in America he worked through Carl Brandt. Many years later I wrote to ask Brandt if he could throw any light on this sudden change in the quality of George's writing. 'As it happened,' he answered, 'I had a good deal to do with his later writing. Out of the air one day he came in to see me. I had always been an admirer of his work, except in the later years. I finally dug out of him what was the trouble. While at that time he did not disclose to me that he feared or knew of the disease he had, he did tell me that it had seemed necessary for him to make as much money as he could as quickly as he could. He therefore, quite cold-bloodedly, decided that sex paid off best, and had cheapened his work.

I think I was able to prove to him that it cheapened it to the point where it had no value even in return to himself. Even at that late date he was sufficiently an artist to turn in his tracks and I think you would find in his last two, possibly three, books he was again setting sail on the course which he should have followed from the beginning.

'It is to me interesting that this should have been a thought-out thing rather than a temperamental one. I've always tried to correct the impression that people had of him during the latter part of his career. He didn't have time enough to re-establish himself in the echelon to which he belonged by right of gift and craftsmanship.'

The Triumph of Gallio made many of those who had before been hostile change their attitude; it aroused admiration where *Ursula Trent* had aroused irritation and contempt. His illness made him an object of sympathy.

That autumn I gave a lecture at the Lyceum Club. George who was an able speaker was invited to join in the subsequent discussion. He was at the back of the room and I could barely follow what he said. The words seemed to be sticking in his throat. The next day I met him in the Savile. He asked me if I had had any difficulty in hearing him. I told him that I had, a little. 'I supposed so,' he said. 'We must regard it as my swan song.' Each week the effort of articulation became more marked. It was painful to see him struggling for his words.

His hands also began to be affected. The top joints of his fingers turned inwards; they became claws. After the board meetings, tea was served and it was pathetic to watch him trying to double over the slices of bread and butter with his knuckles. The upper half of the door to the boardroom was composed of frosted glass. It was gruesome to hear him fumbling at the door knob, to see his shadow through the glass and to wonder what manner of spectre would appear when the door opened.

By the summer he could scarcely make himself understood. At the end of the last meeting he attended I went with him to the stairs. The stairs were steep and I wondered if he could get down them safely. I put my hand on his arm. There was scarcely any flesh, just bone within the sleeve. I started to lead him down the stairs, but he began to choke; he seemed to shrink into my arms. He cannot have weighed six stone. I led him back into the room and a chair was brought for him. He tried to say something, but only a gargle came out of his throat. He sat there for two or three moments, then he got up and made his own way to the stairs.

Next day he wrote to explain that he had not fainted but that he had been laughing because he had not been able to make me understand that he wanted me to stand on the other side of him. I never saw him again. He died in the following February, a few days before the publication of *Gifts of Sheba*—another fine uncompromising novel that left little doubt with critical opinion that he had returned to his best form.

It was, I believe, Parkinson's disease that killed him. The stoicism with which he faced that illness, and the brave devotion which Kathleen showed—her black hair went white during that year—made many who had been hostile once, respect him. It was ironic that during the war he had said, even if he said it flippantly, that while he would not mind being killed, he could not face disfigurement. It was that very poison that fate chose to hand to him. He drank it unflinchingly, like an antique Roman, and left an honoured name.

9

The Bad Boy in the Georgian Nursery

GILBERT CANNAN, W. W. JACOBS

In March 1914 Henry James contributed two long signed articles to the English *Times Literary Supplement* on the younger novelists. The four on whom he concentrated were Compton Mackenzie, Hugh Walpole, Gilbert Cannan and D. H. Lawrence. These articles appeared on the front page, and completely filled it. James in them was at his most involved, his most diffuse. It was difficult to discover what he was trying to say, except that he appeared to discern least promise in Lawrence, whom he described as 'hanging in the dusty rear'. On the whole his articles were welcoming and enthusiastic. It is doubtful if in the history of letters so tremendous a tribute had been paid to four young men. All except Lawrence—and he was to be later—were sponsored by the youngest and the most enterprising of London publishers, Martin Secker. There was much talk of Secker's young men. The world's prizes must have seemed to them ripe for gathering but the war intervened with its consequent reappraisal and reversal of reputations.

In the autumn of 1918 W. L. George published a book entitled *A Novelist on Novels*. It was very obviously the gleanings of a desk; the kind of book that gets compiled when a publisher says to an author, 'I'd so like to have your name on our list. Isn't there anything that you could let us have? Haven't you got some magazine pieces that have never appeared in book form that you could write a preface to, so as to give some kind of cohesion to the whole. Do think about it.'

A Novelist on Novels is no more than that, yet I should not be surprised if more references have been made to it during the last forty-five years than any prose book, except *Eminent Victorians*, published during 1918. It contained a section called 'Who is the man?' which propounded the question 'Who in twenty years time will occupy the position at present held by Conrad, Wells and Bennett?' For thirty years now that section has provided a convenient lead for anyone writing an obituary of or tribute to an elder writer. 'In 1918,' the piece begins. 'W. L. George was wondering. . . . Today, quarter of a century later, we can assess the accuracy of his judgment.' If the lead is right, the other problems of an article fall into place, and George has immeasurably smoothed the path of his successors.

The seven contestants for the laurels were Compton Mackenzie, Hugh Walpole, J. D. Beresford, E. M. Forster, Gilbert Cannan, Oliver Onions, Frank Swinnerton. A section was devoted to D. H. Lawrence but he was not one of the seven.

I never met Lawrence, but I have been on friendly terms with the other seven. Oliver Onions's wife, Berta Ruck, has been for many years one of my dearest friends; the only one, however, whom I knew on any terms of intimacy—by that I mean spent a certain amount of time alone with, entertained or been entertained by—was Gilbert Cannan.

His name is rarely mentioned nowadays, but like George's it occasionally appears in current autobiographies. Ivor Brown calling him 'the comet of a few seasons' reminded his readers that in Shaw's preface to *Fanny's First Play* Cannan was the supercilious critic, Gunn. In the early 'twenties his nerves gave way; he suddenly became violent and in, I believe, a transatlantic liner, seized Horace Liveright by the throat, forced him to his knees and exhorted him to prepare to meet his maker. Kindly hands led him to a sanatorium where he spent the last thirty years of his life; contentedly, believing that he was a guest in a country house, and relieving his literary needs by inditing to politicians long letters that were never posted.

Cannan was raised in Manchester, under squalid conditions; then a rich cousin adopted him, and sent him to Cambridge, where he was at King's, one of that brilliant many-sided group that included Rupert Brooke, Lytton Strachey, E. M. Forster, John Maynard Keynes. His early novels had a sombre Manchester background. He translated Artzibasheff's *Sanine*—presumably from the French—and his first successful novel *Round the Corner* was greatly influenced by *Sanine*.

Mendel—my own favourite of his novels—is quite separate from the main current of his work. It is the story of Mark Gertler, a young Jewish painter—his parents had brought him over from Austria at the age of three—of great charm and of good looks, who earned a startling early success, was befriended by Edward Marsh, and whose portrait of his mother, painted when he was still a boy, hangs in the Tate. His success was too meteoric not to be followed by a reverse of fortune, and he died by his own hand in 1939, at the very moment, so some critics maintained, that he was evolving a style of painting that would have justified and fulfilled his promise.

Gertler when still quite young became a close friend of Cannan, stayed with him in the country and told him the story of his early years. *Mendel* is a direct transcription of those confidences. The book contains portraits of

Augustus John, C. R. W. Nevinson, Sir William Rothenstein and Dora Carrington, later Lytton Strachey's
consort, with whom Gertler was in love for many years.
Recently Carrington's brother Noel edited Gertler's
letters. There were constant references to Cannan, and
Oliver Edwardes reviewing it in the London *Times*
suggested that *Mendel* might be well worth reissuing. I
myself re-read it recently and was held and moved, but
it is difficult when one re-reads a novel to know whether
one is moved by the book itself or by the memory of
oneself reading it in one's teens.

At the time, because of its portraits of living people,
it did not add to Cannan's popularity. And Sir William
Rothenstein was deeply offended not with Cannan but
with Gertler. How could Cannan have known those
things unless Gertler had told him?

Cannan's obituary in *The Times* was headed 'Promise
unfulfilled', but in several ways he was the most gifted
of the Georgians. Henry James said in his *Times* article,
'The charm of Mr Cannan is that we can take him at his
word. His guarantee, his straight communication of his
general truth is a value and values are rare.'

Douglas Goldring described him in *Reputations* as
'the bad boy in the Georgian nursery' and by the time I
met him in January 1917, he had done much to deserve
that label. As a young man he had been befriended by
J. M. Barrie, but later Barrie was forced to divorce his
wife on his account. Mrs Barrie was many years older
than Cannan and the marriage soon broke up. When
conscription was introduced in 1916, he registered as a
conscientious objector. In the last year of the war, he
fell in love with a very attractive young South African,
of good family, with whom he set up house.

In youth one needs an unpopular cause to champion.

Cannan was mine. I fought many verbal battles on his account. I championed his pacifism. I championed his advocacy of free love. They were the easier to champion, because I sincerely admired his novels and because he lent a glamour to misdemeanour. 'What a world, what a set!' Matthew Arnold exclaimed in an amusing if priggish passage about Shelley's London group of Hunt and Hogg 'with Godwin preaching and holding the hat . . . one gets sickened for ever of the subject of irregular relationships', and it must be conceded that the inward eye's contemplation of certain advocates of licence practising any form of active love evokes discomfort, but Cannan was tall and young and handsome and the lady with whom he shared a studio in Elm Tree Road was as radiant as a bird of Paradise.

Theirs was the first big evening party that I went to. It was given in December 1918, in honour of Mark Gertler. The studio was large, with a stairway leading up to a balcony from which the bedrooms opened. I shall never forget my first sight of her, standing at the stairway's head; she was fragile and pale-cheeked and small, with blonde hair, cut below the ears, so that it swung loosely like a bell; she was wearing a tight bodice and a terraced skirt, three-layered in pink and mauve and white; her legs were very slim and she wore pink shoes. I shall never forget the timbre in her voice as she waltzed past Cannan who was in a group of talkers, 'Dance, darling, dance.'

For me she symbolized all that *vie de Bohème* I had dreamed of in a prison camp. Cannan had met her in the Charing Cross Road, in the Bomb Shop—it is called Collet's bookshop now—where old Henderson, with his red tie and red beard dispensed revolutionary literature as well as the best *avant-garde* plays and novels. In addition he published an occasional volume of belles-lettres. His shop was a kind of club. His son Frank was one of Michael Arlen's first friends in London. It was in the Bomb Shop that Arlen read the volumes of modern poetry that he could not afford to buy. Gilbert Cannan was there, with Miles Malleson, when 'she' arrived. As the story has it, they stood there incredulous and dazed, then emerging simultaneously from their trance, they hurried to opposite corners of the shop and, taking down copies of their own books, signed them for her.

I had noticed as I arrived, outside the studio, a very young couple standing in a coign of the wall, enlaced in decorous courtship. Other guests had remarked upon their presence. They were always there, Cannan said, no matter what the weather. On subsequent visits throughout that winter I saw them still, in rain and frost. They seemed like protective spirits, guarding the fortunes of the house. How long did they stay, I wonder? As long as romance itself did, possibly, for so rare a bird was unlikely to remain perched for long on so precarious a bough. Within two years 'she' had winged towards wider meadows. I have not met her since, but I have watched with affectionate well-wishing her passage in a larger world.

I met Cannan through my former schoolmaster, S. P. B. Mais. Mais used to write to authors he admired, telling them that he had read their poems and novels to his pupils. Little pleases a writer more than to be told that he is read by the young generation; such letters led to friendship; they did in Cannan's case.

Mais was staying with my parents over Christmas, and I cajoled him into including me in an invitation. I can remember little of what was said that evening. Cannan was a silent man. I presume that Mais did all the talking. We went on to the Café Royal afterwards. It was my first time there and the Domino Room was crowded with men back on leave; several groups were in fancy dress and the party at the next table wanted us to go on with them to a dance. I longed to, but I was a cadet at Sandhurst receiving no pay, and my weekly parental allowance of a pound was not doing much more than pay my bus and tube fares. In four months' time, I told myself, I should be gazetted, with money of my own; then I could accept that kind of invitation.

We talked that evening, naturally, of *Mendel.* Mais wanted to meet Gertler and see his pictures, so Cannan wrote him a note of introduction. Gertler lived then in Hampstead. 'We'll go and see him tomorrow,' Mais said to me.

We breakfasted early, at Underhill, at eight o'clock. Mais ate, as he did everything, quickly. By quarter past he was on his feet. 'We'll go over to see Gertler now,' he said.

Walking across the heath at Mais's speed, we reached the studio before nine. It did not at the time seem to me an extraordinary hour to pay a social call, but it must have to Gertler who was not yet up and whose breakfast table was being laid. He concealed his surprise, however, and very courteously showed us round his studio. 'The Merry-Go-Round', with its strident orange and red canopy that later was the chief feature of the London Group Exhibition in the Mansard Galleries, was on an easel. I had never before realized how colours could sing.

Cannan at that period lived in a windmill at Cholesbury, a few miles from Berkhamsted, where W. W. Jacobs lived. I paid it a pious pilgrimage. Cannan was not there but we were shown inside. It had been painted in the fashion of the moment with bright primary colours. It was the only time that I have seen a windmill converted into a private residence. As far as I remember there was no miller's cottage. If there was, it must have been very small. The main rooms were inside the carcase of the mill. The tapering of the cone-shaped walls was most effective.

In the Gertler memorial exhibition in 1941 there was a picture of the windmill with Cannan walking in the garden; there was also 'The Merry-Go-Round', its colours as vivid as ever on that grey bomb-scarred day.

Cannan was disliked and disapproved of by many who did not know him, but he was well liked by those who did. I do not indeed see how he could have failed to be. There was nothing to dislike about him; he was well mannered and well-bred; he was never ill-tempered or impatient; he was temperate in drink; he never made scenes; he did not boast about his successes with women; he rarely discussed sex, as is often the case with men who lead full lives; he was single-minded in his devotion to the causes that he championed. As a writer he did nothing cheap.

He was a silent man. I have already described how on our way to a cricket match at Winchester, he and Sieg-fried Sassoon divided a third-class compartment into two groups of four. To some it may have seemed that he was haughty, arrogant and aloof. A small man can sit silent in a gathering and not be noticed but you are aware of a tall man's presence. He did not exert himself to be amusing. Myself, I was so stimulated mentally by his company that I talked a lot, but I can imagine that he may have made a self-conscious person more self-conscious. Some people may have found it hard to be themselves with him.

Perhaps he was not only silent but impersonal—a disability that I may not have noticed because I was myself, in my admiration for his work, so at ease with him. In the Gertler letters an interesting passage describes how Mary and St John Hutchinson, when they were staying at the mill, organized a trap so that they could get Cannan alone late at night and induce him to tell them his life story.

'As a life,' they said, 'it was very dull and he told it in a dull dreary voice, all even, but nevertheless it was very important to help us to understand him. You see, it is just as I thought, nothing ever *really* stirred him, nothing ever made a real impression. When for instance he came to the part of his life when a rich cousin comes as if from no-where and adopts him, puts him into a rich home suddenly after his own sordid environments and then to Cambridge, he did not seem at all impressed or excited. He did not seem to feel the change and was not surprised. He told it all in the same even bored voice, and so on and so on. . . .

'Many, many times we had to pull him up to prevent him from becoming vague and abstract. We would ask him, "What do you mean exactly?" or "Tell us the details".'

Yet they finally concluded, 'We really felt that we now understood Gilbert much more.'

His private life caused so much concern to so many strangers. Could it have been that he really was not very interested in it; that he was someone to whom things happened? Can it be that he was a temporarily embodied spirit, for whom eventually the frail fabric between two realities dissolved? His final novels were incomprehensible. He appeared to be travelling in a fog, yet with serene unawareness that bright day was not about him.

Was he overrated between 1910 and 1920? I question it. A novel has to be very good or to have very special qualities of interest to remain alive thirty years after its author's retirement or death. A novelist who is still around, publishing a book every so often, appearing in public, writing articles, being interviewed, replying to the Toast of Literature, sponsoring the work of the younger generation, retains the public's interest in his personality and a curiosity towards his early work. If W. L. George and Gilbert Cannan were still alive, I am confident that one or two of their earlier books would be on the bookstalls in a Pan, Penguin, or Pocket Library reprint.

My friendship with Cannan was a cause of considerable concern to my future father-in-law, W. W. Jacobs, who was very perturbed about the kind of people that his daughter would meet when she left his vigilance. Megan Rhys was a source of considerable concern to him. He refused to invite Cannan to our wedding on the grounds, so he wrote to me, of his conscientious-objector attitude during the war; but it was on moral grounds that he explained his fiat to my father. 'There is Cannan,' he said, 'able to go everywhere, and this wretched girl able to go nowhere, cut off for the rest of her life from decent people.' How that prophecy had been turned topsy-turvy within five years.

I have included a sketch of W. W. in my autobiography and my brother wrote of him at greater length in *A Little Learning*. The characters in Jacobs's stories were all rebels against authority. His most famous, Bob Pretty, was a village poacher, his sailors Sam Small and Peter Russet dodged policemen, the night-watchman lived on the windy side of the law, but on the two main issues of politics and sex Jacobs was extremely bigoted.

His reputation as a writer still stands high, deservedly. Few Englishmen have understood the technique of the short story so perfectly and he had a wonderful power of compression. No authors enjoy criticism, and he was indignant with the critic who complained that the night watchman was getting garrulous. 'If there is one thing he isn't, it is that.' Jacobs was right. The night watchman's ironic commentaries on life remained to the end caustic and concise. Arnold Bennett wrote an essay on him in the *New Age* called 'W. W. Jacobs and Aristophanes' in which he gave the following example of Jacobs's lean, bleak wit. A man offers a mistrustful wife as an explanation of his late return, the fact that he had seen a boy run over in the street. 'How long did that take you?' the wife said. 'Do you think that funny?' Bennett asked. 'I think it very funny.'

There was another criticism that Jacobs did not relish, but of which he admitted the truth. 'The Biter Bit.' All his stories fit into that formula. But then that is the classic formula. A situation is set out, a character attempts to solve it, but the solution is achieved in a manner completely opposite to the plan. Most of the best stories fit that formula—those that is to say that depend on plot—and when one has written that kind of story one is wise to ask oneself whether it does or does not conform. If it does not, there may be something wrong with it.

The publisher to whom Jacobs offered his first collection of short stories, *Many Cargoes*, suggested an outright purchase for £60, an arrangement that was not uncommon in those days. Jacobs insisted on a small royalty and a lease to publish for three years. 'Beatrice Harraden,' he would say, 'was offered the same terms for *Ships that Pass in Night*, and she accepted them.'

There was another story that Jacobs would recount with a chuckle in connection with *Many Cargoes*. A reviewer wrote: 'Jacobs is a neat craftsman, but he works in a narrow field of which he has already exhausted the yield.' 'That narrow field', Jacobs would say, 'has already yielded fifteen books.'

It was not till late in life that he reached his tether, he then stopped writing. He was a scrupulous and conscientious writer. Editors could trust him not to drop below his own high standard. J. B. Pinker arranged for him an exclusive contract with the *Strand* at £350 a story for the world serial rights. He believed this to be the highest *guaranteed* price offered to any English writer at that time, except Rudyard Kipling.

Once, but only once did the editor, H. Greenough Smith, return a story with many apologies, explaining that it fell so much below the Jacobs standard that publication of it would harm Jacobs's reputation. Jacobs did not want to create a precedent but decided eventually not to object and put aside the story. Three years later Greenough Smith was anxious to have Jacobs in the Christmas number. Jacobs was a slow worker and had not a plot in mind. He took out the discarded story and re-read it. It seemed to him all right. He altered three sentences, had it retyped and sent it to the *Strand*, saying that he had entirely recast it and believed that in its revised form it was improved. Greenough Smith was delighted, hailing it as vintage Jacobs.

'The Biter Bit' was the formula of *The Monkey's Paw*, that untypical Jacobs story that has, I suppose, appeared more often in anthologies than anything that he has written. He had a strong vein of the macabre that he rarely exploited. Perhaps he was afraid of it. I once saw a surprising sign of it, when he was staying with us in our Sussex bungalow. The dog—a friendly mongrel—slept in the same room as Barbara and myself. W. W. woke us in the middle of the night fearful lest the dog should turn on the tap of the gas-fire with his teeth. The tap in question was not one that turned but screwed. I doubt if the dog could have turned it with his teeth, even if he had wanted to. The dog had been sleeping with us for a year. Nothing could have been more unlikely than that he should now make the attempt. Jacobs was diffident and hated to appear ridiculous. He must have suffered acute agonies of apprehension before he woke us up. We appeased him in the end by putting a tumbler over the tap.

I may have suggested that because of the narrowness of his opinions in terms of politics and sex, Jacobs was uncongenial company. That was far from being so. He was affectionate, under his reserve; he appreciated the pleasures of the table and his mordant wit gave a sharp keen flavour to the talk. In early days I often found myself arguing with him, and he got impatient when he argued, but I soon learnt not to challenge his provocative statements and to steer the talk into calm waters. Had he married a worldly woman who 'took life easy', he would, I believe, have been a contented and benign family man, but perhaps if he had done so his wit would have lost its edge; 'The wife' in his stories was always an adversary. Perhaps it was constant domestic friction that kept his wit so sharp. If another kind of woman had made him happy, the night watchman might have become garrulous.

10

The Nail in the Coffin

HUGH WALPOLE

The 1914–18 war caused a reappraisal and sometimes a reversal of literary reputations. When the
race began again, the various contestants were
entered under different handicaps. No one's prospects at
that point seemed brighter than Hugh Walpole's. The war
had consolidated his position. Bad eyesight unfitted him
for the army, but he went to Russia in a Red Cross Unit,
acquiring an O.B.E. and a Russian decoration. In his
spare time he wrote two novels about Russia in the Russian manner. He also in January 1918 published *The
Green Mirror*—a very English novel on which he had
been at work before the war. With *The Green Mirror* he
changed publishers, leaving Secker for Macmillan.
Macmillan did not and do not take up a writer unless
they are satisfied that he has a long and honourable
career ahead of him. Their imprint was the imprimatur
on Walpole's reputation. He was then thirty-five and the
ball lay at his feet.

I never knew Walpole well, but I met him fairly often
over twenty years, particularly during the 1920s. He was
at that time an effective personality with his forces
impressively disposed. He had a large house near Regent's
Park where he housed his library and pictures and entertained his friends. He was a familiar figure at first nights,
at publishers' parties and at ladies' clubs where dinner
was followed by short speeches by seven or eight writers.
He had a cottage in Cornwall to which he retired for quiet
and concentration. He went to America most years.

Everything was going well, everything promised to go

well. Each book sold better than the last. His lectures were a great success; to American audiences he seemed the embodiment of all that was best in Britain. He was tall, broad with a bulldog chin. Incipient baldness accentuated his high-domed forehead. He was fresh complexioned; one interviewer nicknamed him 'Apple-cheeked Hugh'. He had a boyish eagerness; he looked thoroughly wholesome; no 'flim-flam' about him; he had an easy forthcoming manner. His father was an Anglican bishop and he had an inherited aptitude for oratory. He took trouble over his lectures. He phrased his sentences well. I heard him lecture once in Brighton, and I can well remember the spontaneous outburst of applause that greeted an eloquent tribute to Walter Scott. He enjoyed lecturing. He appeared to be sorry when his time was up.

He was active in literary politics. As a critic he was generous in his appreciations: always ready to introduce with a preface an American writer to the British public; on such occasions he would often contrive a compliment to one or other of his friends. His preface to Cabell's *Jurgen* is an example of this, with its dragged-in reference to J. D. Beresford's *Signs and Wonders*. He was anxious to have his friends share in his own good fortune. He was worried at the difficulties young writers were experiencing in getting their work published, and in the autumn of 1919 he wrote a letter to the *Times Literary Supplement* that started a long correspondence on first novels. Feeling that there should be closer contact between authorship and the trade, he founded the Society of Bookmen, where authors, publishers and booksellers discussed their separate and joint problems at monthly dinners. The Society, I believe, still flourishes. Its first secretary was Maurice Marston, then one of the partners of the now defunct publishing house of Leonard Parsons. Later when the National Book League was formed Marston was its organizing secretary. It is very possible that, but for Walpole, the League would never have been formed.

He had a full and happy life. I recall a lunch party of St John Ervine's at the Garrick Club in 1926. It was a mixed party, eight of us at a round table. Walpole was in high spirits. He did not monopolize the conversation, but the talk centred round him. I cannot remember anything he said. He was not a witty talker; he was good company not because he said clever things but because he was interested and enthusiastic. It was a small room and we took our coffee where we sat. We were still at table when a club servant announced that 'Mr Walpole's car was waiting'. As soon as he left the room we started to discuss him. We agreed that he was the happiest man we knew. St John Ervine wondered if he had ever had an unhappy hour. We were still discussing him when the door opened and he reappeared. There had been a mistake; it had not been his car after all. Conversation ceased.

Walpole looked round the table. 'Well, what were you saying about me behind my back?'

The pause continued. It was a little awkward. Then Mrs Theodore McKenna spoke. She was the senior person present, and one of his best friends. 'As a matter of fact Hugh, we were saying how happy you were, and how glad we were about it. We were wondering whether you have ever been unhappy.'

It was said on a note of genuine affection, but for a moment Walpole seemed disconcerted. I fancied that I knew what he was thinking. Dostoevsky's stock stood high. The man who had not suffered, had not lived. Art sprang from suffering. Walpole did not relish the suggestion that he had not suffered. At the same time he did not want to disparage his own good fortune. He had had bad times, he said, times he would not care to live again, but during these last ten years, well he had to admit that those years had been very, very good. He had been happy pretty well all the time.

That was in 1926. And he was not able to say that much longer. When he died fifteen years later, he was an unhappy man.

That for a writer is a fate by no means unusual. Fashions change; writers lose their talent and appeal; they are lucky if they saved money in their good years. Walpole's fate was different. Charles Morgan has told in *The House of Macmillan* that Walpole worked on a ten-year schedule and right to the end he kept to his programme. The last half of the 'twenties and 'thirties was a period of solid industry. *The Herries Chronicle*, a series of four long novels, sold very well. Between each volume he published shorter but creditable books. He made a great deal of money. He was knighted. To a foreigner, to anyone outside London and New York literary society, he must have seemed to occupy a highly enviable positon. In a sense he did. But he had lost the respect of the only people whose respect he valued. He had become a joke to the intelligentsia.

It has been said that no man has ever been written down by anyone except himself. That was not Walpole's case. A far better writer with a casual, almost a left-hand gesture collapsed his reputation and self-confidence with the portrait in one book of a minor character. As Alroy Kear in Somerset Maugham's *Cakes and Ale*, Walpole was presented and made ridiculous as a literary careerist busily grooming himself to be the G.O.M. of the English novel. His technique and tactics were explained, his motives were exposed. He was made ridiculous.

From Walpole's point of view, the timing of the book could not have been more unlucky. The Athenians wearied of hearing Aristides called the Just, and writers who were suffering the occupational hazards of a profession peculiarly subject to ups and downs, had begun to be irritated by Walpole's perpetual geniality. Need he always look as though he were the guest of honour at a party at which Life and Literature were the host and hostess? In 1926 Beverley Nichols in his *Twenty-Five* was amusingly malicious at his expense. After referring to his 'appearance of complacency' Nichols concluded 'he was born middle-aged, but he is rapidly achieving his first childhood'. Walpole was able to parry that attack. He asked Nichols to lunch and a recantation duly appeared in the *Sketch*. But the number of people who chuckled over that particular chapter was an indication of the way the wind was blowing.

Walpole again looked too well. Actually he suffered from diabetes and had to give himself daily injections of insulin. He drank little alcohol but he had a 'sweet tooth', and to correct his indulgences in candy he frequently increased his dose, a practice that ultimately undermined his health. Morbid streaks were detected in his work, in *Portrait of a Man with Red Hair* particularly. He remained unmarried; gossip did not link his name with any woman's; people began to wonder. 'That kind of thing' was all very well for willowy young men at Broadcasting House but it was scarcely appropriate to 'Apple-cheeked Hugh' and 'the roast beef of Old England'.

It was only an affair of whispers and if nothing more had transpired, such a temporary recession would have provided an effective background for an adulatory welcoming of *The Herries Chronicle*. 'In the later 'twenties,' so might the encomia have read, 'there were not lacking those who questioned Sir Hugh's qualities, but now incontestably the proof is here. . . .' That is how it might have been. But instead these whispers became a pedestal for the 'Aunt Sally' absurdities of Alroy Kear.

It is honourable to strive for fame, the pursuit of money is venial not venal, but to write in order to become 'a person of importance' is not a creditable objective. That is a goal for politicians. A professional writer could not be exposed to a more damaging attack, and the power of *Cakes and Ale* was accentuated by a complete absence of 'hatred, malice, and uncharitableness' on its author's part. Maugham has admitted that *Cakes and Ale* is the book he enjoyed writing most. It is told in the first person, and 'Ashenden' throughout is in the best of tempers. The atmosphere is sunny and good-natured. There is no suggestion that Maugham is trying to get his own back. He is just 'having fun'.

It must be admitted that Maugham drew several red herrings across the trail. He made Walpole a good golfer, which he was not, he attributed his celibacy to unrequited love, and there were a number of minor points of dissimilarity. J. B. Priestley, who collaborated once with Walpole, was dining with me shortly after its publication. One of my guests, my school-friend H. S. Mackintosh, whose ballades and light verse have recently received a more than cordial reception, but who was then no more than 'somebody in trade', referred to the caricature of Walpole. Priestley asked him why he assumed that it was Walpole. 'Walpole would never order a lunch like that,' he said. 'But who else could it be?' Mackintosh replied.

That was the point. The character was too lifelike not to have been drawn from life; too much in it rang true; too much could be confirmed; too many ageing novelists recalled the flattering tributes to their work from a young writer, which were followed a few months after by the advance copy of a novel graciously inscribed 'from a pupil to a master'; too many reviewers who had written in a lukewarm way about Walpole's work, had received if not invitations to lunch, at least long letters expressing

gratitude for the review, interest in the criticisms made
and a resolve to profit at a next endeavour; too many
literary 'punters' had noted how his apparently dis-
interested concern for his fellow writers—his letter to the
Times Literary Supplement about first novels for example
—had in fact provided Walpole with wide publicity without particularly benefiting the objects of his concern.

The red herrings, by and large, made the situation
worse. Where so many traits could be recognized, every
touch of the palette knife was accepted as direct portrai-
ture. Anthony West, reviewing Rupert Hart-Davis's
biography was to write (twenty-two years later) in the
New Yorker: 'Everything was there; the appealing charm
that Walpole could lavish on those who were successful
and might be useful, and the bland indifference with
which he could treat old friends who had betrayed him
by being neither, and most unkind of all his almost
complete lack of talent.'

That is unfair. Alroy Kear was based on Walpole but
it was not completely Walpole. It is not true that Walpole
dropped old friends who had ceased to be successful. He
was on the contrary generous with his loans of money,
and many writers now established stand in his debt for
kindness and encouragement. Nor was he by any means
without talent. He was industrious and ambitious. His
novels had both theme and plot. He was not afraid of
melodrama: he could evoke curiosity and maintain
suspense. He could build up a background. He rarely
created a vivid character, but he so enjoyed telling a
story, he was so excited by what he had to tell that the
reader became anxious about the outcome and was
sufficiently 'held' not to be worried by the flatness of the
actual writing.

Alroy Kear is a composite creation, and a cruel but
genuine portrait with 'warts and all' would have done

less damage. *Cakes and Ale* ruined the last ten years of Walpole's life.

The story has been told that he began to read it while he was changing for dinner, as a guest in a country house. He had propped the book on the mantelpiece. The story opens with Kear and before he had read ten pages he had identified himself. In fascinated horror he read on; he forgot his dressing, he forgot dinner, he went on reading. When his host finally came up to see if anything was wrong he found Walpole standing before the mantelpiece, his shirt-tails flapping about his knees and his unbraced trousers in a coil round his ankles. His own account of the incident in his diary is less dramatic, but it was the embroidered story that went the rounds.*

'How was Hugh taking it?' Everyone was asking that, and Edward Knoblock was reported to have earned a diploma for tact by having asserted at a lunch party in Walpole's company that it was 'a little caddish of Willie to have written quite so cruelly about poor John Drinkwater'.

How was he taking it? How should he take it? The worst human misfortune had befallen him. He had been made to look an ass; and what was there that he could do about it? The days of duelling were past. He could not have assaulted in public a man fifteen years his senior and six inches shorter. He could not have addressed a letter to *The Times*. Ninety-nine times in a hundred it is wise to ignore attack; Walpole in that respect was wise. Unfortunately he overdid it. He not only behaved as though nothing had happened, but went out of his way to insist that nothing had happened.

A year later Elinor Mordaunt published anonymously

---

* Robin Maugham's account in *Somerset and all the Maughams* is slightly different.

a novel of which Maugham was undisguisedly the central character. It was called *Gin and Bitters* in America, and *Full Circle* in England. Maugham brought an action against the book in the English courts and obtained its suppression.

On the book's appearance in America, Walpole attacked it violently. The book was published there by Farrar and Rinehart, and for many years there hung in the firm's office a cartoon by Will Dyson entitled 'The noble art of Self-defence'. It showed a small frail woman, holding a book before her face to protect herself from the assault of a man twice her size. Her assailant is umistakeably Hugh Walpole. The book in her hand is *Gin and Bitters* and the caption reads, 'Now no one can say that *Cakes and Ale* was meant for me.'

The caricature of Walpole is lethally vindictive. The name of Dyson may not convey much today. The reputation of a political cartoonist is fugitive. But his gift was great and individual. He worked for the extreme left wing, and no one could have rendered more bestially the profiteers of the First War and the moneyed worldlings of the 'twenties. He drew them half-animal, half-human, sometimes as pigs in overtight morning coats and overtall top hats, their fingers dripping blood that became gold sovereigns as they reached their moneybags.

It was with that technique that he drew Walpole. He posed him in a Rupert Brooke style open shirt posturing as the incarnation of careless youth; but you saw at once that he was middle-aged; there was a glandular obscenity about his retarded adolescence; his fingers were heavily ringed; they were long, pointed, pudgy; the fingers of a decadent. It exposed a basic unwholesomeness underlying a spurious healthiness. 'The Man with the Red Hair' showing beneath 'Fortitude'. It was hard to look at Walpole afterwards without remembering that cartoon.

I have been told that it was only by degrees that Walpole realized how much damage the book had done him. *Cakes and Ale* would not blow over. It was too good a book; as long as it was being read, and there seemed no likelihood of its not being read during his lifetime, he would look an ass. And it became in time apparent that he had made a mistake in letting himself still be numbered among Maugham's acquaintances.

Late in the 'thirties Maugham gave a large supper party at Claridge's in honour of his grandchild's birth. There must have been a hundred and fifty people there. There was no fixed seating, there were a number of small tables and you sat where you chose. Most of the guests were connected in some way with the arts, and the grandchild's health was proposed by Osbert Sitwell. Walpole was in any gathering, because of his height and chin, a conspicuous figure, and there was a whispered 'Fancy him being here', as he moved from one table to another. It was felt that he would have shown dignity had he stayed away.

His knighthood did his reputation little good. For no good reason, a knighthood has less prestige value for a novelist than it has for an actor or a painter, a critic or an historian. The best novelists have not been knighted and Galsworthy declined a knighthood. It was perhaps this reluctance of the novelist and poet to be addressed as Sir Francis or Sir George that encouraged Edward VII to institute the Order of Merit. When Walpole's name appeared in the Honours List, people said, 'Ah, it's a consolation prize for *Cakes and Ale*.' Walpole, to judge from the published extract in his diary, was aware of this. But he felt he would 'like to be a knight'.

During the last months before the war he contributed a critical causerie to the *Daily Graphic*, a paper now amalgamated with the *Sketch*, that had at the time no literary standing. One wondered why he accepted the assignment. He could not have needed the money, and it must have been boring to wade through mediocre books. Did he want to feel somebody of consequence? At the end of the 'twenties Arnold Bennett had written a weekly article on books for the *Evening Standard*. But that had been a different matter. The *Evening Standard* was an important and influential paper. It gave Bennett a pulpit. And he had enjoyed a sense of day-to-day eventfulness. He had felt in the swim. He 'made' several books, *Jew Süss* in particular, and every writer was anxious to be reviewed by Bennett. But the *Graphic* could not do that for Walpole.

As the 1930s moved to their shadowed close, a feeling of irritation towards Walpole became apparent among other writers, the result possibly of a sense of guilt on their part, the realization that they had been unjust to him. It would be idle to pretend that most of us had not taken a malicious pleasure in his discomfiture. The Malvolio motif is an unfailing formula, it is human to be jealous of success, and *Cakes and Ale* had been very funny. But all the same we recognized that he had been unfairly treated. We resented his having given us the sense of guilt.

In the spring of 1939 he was sent to Rome by the *Herald Tribune* to report the coronation of the Pope. In *Roman Fountain*, he used this trip as the framework for a variety of digressions. It is one of his better books, but it was published after the war had started and it contained much with which at such a time it was hard not to feel impatient. He wrote gratefully of the kindnesses he had received from Somerset Maugham when he was a young man in London. Why, one asked, must he maintain this pretence of friendship? He explained that he had given a false impression of complacence when he was young by holding up his prominent chin to keep his pince-nez-position. It seemed childish that he should be worrying about that at this late day. He described his loneliness in a hotel bedroom on his first night in Rome. It was a self-pitying passage. 'Really,' one thought, 'what is the old quean fussing about now, living in a comfortable hotel as the *Tribune*'s guest with a large cheque waiting him at the end!' He went on to wonder whether in such a hotel he might not one night feel the first symptoms of a mortal malady. A morbid passage. But, as I said, one was unfair to Walpole. Perhaps he did have a premonition then. At any rate, two years later he was dead.

He died in June 1941, when nerves were strained. For a year England had been carrying on a war single-handed. Russia had not yet been invaded, America seemed stable in neutrality. There had been the winter's bombing. Defeat was following defeat, in the Balkans, Greece, and Crete; the brief gains in the desert had been mostly lost. It was easy at such a time to snap. But making allowance for the temper of the moment, his obituary notices were astonishingly malevolent; they gave the impression that their authors had been smouldering for years with irritation, that they had not wanted to say what they felt during his lifetime because 'after all the old boy was likeable and they were sorry for him', but that now they could not wait to get it off their chests. Nothing could have surprised me more at Christmas 1918 than to have been told that in 1941 I should be reading such obituaries.

Maugham has said more than once that a man who has done you a bad turn never forgives you for it, and it would seem that he has not forgiven Walpole the injury he did him.

In *A Writer's Notebook* he unfairly compares in terms of popularity Charles Garvice and Walpole—unfairly because Walpole must surely have made very much more money than Garvice did. And in his preface to the American edition of *Cakes and Ale* which was printed on the front page of the Sunday Book Section of the *New York Times*, he identified Hugh Walpole as the original of Alroy Kear, describing him as a man whom you could like but could not respect, dismissing his work as negligible. The nail in the coffin.

Rupert Hart-Davis quoted in his biography, in particular reference to *The Times* obituary notice, the concluding sentence of Charles Morgan's section on Walpole in *The House of Macmillan*; 'So good a story-teller is likely at any rate to live longer than many a *petit maître* who sneered at him as soon as he was dead.' But with the driving of that nail home, it is probable that more and more readers will join Anthony West in a mistaken identification of Alroy Kear with Walpole, so that Walpole will be recalled not as the author of *The Herries Chronicle* but as a minor character in one of the world's best light novels. Literary history contains few episodes as ironic.

II

Two Poet Cricketers

CLIFFORD BAX, J. C. SQUIRE

Somerset Maugham in *Cakes and Ale* referred to the period when authors to show their manliness played cricket and drank beer, and between the wars, the name 'Authors XI' often appeared in the fixture lists of a number of minor public schools and southern villages. These sides were captained either by J. C. Squire or Clifford Bax. Squire called his side 'the Invalids' and Bax 'the Old Broughtonians', the former because the idea of launching such a side had come to Squire when he was visiting a friend in hospital, the latter name because between 1911 and 1914 Bax had owned the Manor House at Broughton-Gifford and made it the centre for an annual cricket tour. The qualification for membership was the same, a personal friendship with the captain.

No two men could have been less alike than Bax and Squire. Bax was tall and well built; as a young man he was handsome, in later life distinguished. At the age of forty he grew a short Shakespearean beard which made him look like an hidalgo. Squire was of medium height and stocky. He had no distinction of appearance, but he had a pleasant, friendly face. He was short-sighted and peered at you through heavy lenses. He was untidy and usually looked as though he had shaved with a blunt razor eighteen hours before. Arnold Bennett described him in a pre-war diary as 'Jaegerish'. At the end of his life he grew a long untidy beard. The last time I saw him was in 1956 at the luncheon Cassell's gave to celebrate the laying by Sir Winston Churchill of the corner-stone of their new offices in Red Lion Square. Squire sat at the same table as myself on the opposite side. I wondered who he was.

In appearance Bax had every advantage over Squire, but it was Squire who had the more definite personality; he had an air of attack on life while Bax was diffident, gentle, self-effacing. Squire was a countryman, Bax a townsman. Squire came of sound, unmoneyed, West Country stock. Bax was a man of substance, but he rarely spoke of his father and I do not know in which generation the foundations of the family's wealth were laid. Squire had the conventional upbringing of a man born into his class, Blundell's and St John's College, Cambridge. Bax was educated first by a tutor, then at Heidelberg.

Both married young but whereas Squire was temperamentally a family man, Bax was not. Squire had four children, and till they were launched in the world, maintained a home for them. Bax had one daughter, Undine, but his marriage broke up early and his wife refused him a divorce. Within a few months of her death in 1925, he remarried, but was soon established in a bachelor set in Albany.

Writers, because they do not have to keep fixed hours, are exposed to two main occupational hazards—gallantry and alcohol. Bax during the years when I knew him best, was perpetually involved in an emotional disturbance. One of his early poems begins,

> Snare me anew dear net of woman's beauty,
> I am too early free.

and concludes with a reference to the time when

> My own eternal spirit shall rule me wholly
> And all your charm be vain.

That time never came.

Squire, on the other hand, led a domestic life of exemplary decorum. His problem was conviviality. The cricketer who arrived late for a match of Squire's was wise to preface his apology with an account of how he had attended an Old Boys' dinner on the previous night. Bax was more inclined to be indulgent to the delinquent who began, 'The trouble was, there was a girl . . .'

Both were ambitious but their careers followed divergent courses. Squire had to earn a living. Bax had not. The label 'careerist' is applied to writers in a derogatory sense, but every man who has to earn a living must be a careerist if he is to amount to anything, and it is no criticism of Squire to describe him in his early years as a man with a sense of self-direction.

I first heard of Squire in 1915 from Gerard Meynell, a neighbour of his in Chiswick, the director of the Westminster Press who had an office in No. 11 Henrietta Street and lunched with my father at Gatti's two or three times a week.

Meynell lent me Squire's satirical war verses, 'The Survival of the Fittest', that contained the quatrain,

> God heard the embattled nations shout,
> Gott straffe England and God save the king,
> God this, God that, and God the other thing,
> Good God, said God, I've got my work cut out.

Squire was then contributing to the *New Statesman* over the signature Solomon Eagle a weekly causerie on books which I now started to read each Saturday with keen appreciation of its lively readiness to expose pomposity. I then, as others, thought of him primarily as a wit and parodist. But by November 1918 he was cast for a very different part. His contributions to *Georgian Poetry* *1916–17* had established him as one of the foremost of the younger poets. He was now editor of the *New Statesman*.

He contributed an influential weekly causerie to *Land and Water*. And in his collection of parodies 'Tricks of the Trade', he had taken leave of his old role of jester by dedicating them to Robert Lynd as 'these last essays in a not wholly admirable art'.

In 1914 he had been little known outside a narrow literary circle but by Armistice Day he was more than a coming man, he had arrived. Chance had been upon his side. In his early 'thirties, a man of great energy who worked fast, he had been rejected for military service for bad sight. Since most of his contemporaries were in khaki, he had been consequently subjected to a minimum of competition at the very moment when his powers were coming to their peak.

When the war ended he was well placed to take advantage of the boom that followed. He had friends with capital which they were ready to invest in magazines. They already owned *Land and Water*; they now launched a literary monthly, the *London Mercury*. That summer the Hawthornden Prize was founded, the best book by an author of under forty earning a gold medal and a cheque for £100. Squire was one of the committee. In the autumn he became the chief literary critic on the *Observer*. He had some connection with the publishing house of George Bell & Sons.

Not only was he himself in a position of power, but so were several of his friends. Edward Shanks, who had also been unfit for military service, was sub-editor of the *London Mercury* and of the *New Statesman*. Shanks appeared in the 1918–1919 volume of *Georgian Poetry* and was the first winner of the Hawthornden Prize. He had a serial running in *Land and Water*; he reviewed novels for the *London Mercury* and the *Saturday Westminster Gazette*—a paper of quality and influence.

There was also W. J. Turner who had appeared in the

1916–1917 volume of *Georgian Poetry*. He was an Australian and when I met him first in 1919 he was in uniform, but I fancy he had been on sick leave for some while. He reviewed the theatre in *Land and Water*. Squire's brother-in-law, Clennel Wilkinson, became a little later if not the editor of the *Outlook* the man who accepted manuscripts.

A fantastic situation had in fact arisen. Squire and his friends had control of, or an influence over *Land and Water*, the *Observer*, the *London Mercury*, the *New Statesman*, the *Outlook*, and the *Saturday Westminster Gazette*. The Hawthornden Prize was one of their subsidiaries. During 1918 a warm friendship sprang up between Edmund Gosse and Squire; that gave Squire the ear of the *Sunday Times*. Robert Lynd was a close friend of Squire and that accounted for the *Daily News*.

This situation was not the outcome of a 'deep-laid plot', but of Squire's career reaching a peak at a time when his competitors were away and of two close friends of his, who were also good poets and good critics, appearing simultaneously upon the scene. There were jobs going and no one was available who could fill them better. But it is not surprising that there should have been envious talk about the 'Squirearchy'.

Writers returning from the war and war work and, in some cases such as D. H. Lawrence, from the obscurity to which unpopular war views had consigned them, men as yet unadjusted to new conditions, many of them in financial difficulties, found that they could not get a hearing. Wherever they looked they saw 'the gang' at work. A monopoly had been established for the placid pastoral poetry of John Freeman, Francis Brett-Young, Martin Armstrong, Edmund Blunden; excellent of its kind, but there were other kinds. A whole group of poets lacked a forum—D. H. Lawrence, F. S. Flint, Richard

Aldington, T. S. Eliot, Ford Madox Ford, John Gould Fletcher.

I often saw Harold Monro during those years. I had worked for him for a few weeks at the Poetry Bookshop. We played squash together at the R.A.C. and dined together afterwards. Monro was warm-hearted, affectionate, very companionable, but he was a disappointed man. Before the war he had edited and published *Poetry and Drama* in which Brooke's 'Grantchester' appeared; he had issued chapbooks and volumes of poetry—Robert Graves's first book among them: he had organized weekly poetry readings. He had also published *Georgian Poetry*. The Poetry Bookshop had been a centre for the new idea. Now the centre had moved. He felt he had been shouldered out.

If Squire himself was aware of the hostile atmosphere that his success engendered, he never showed it. He behaved as though he had not an enemy in the world. There are very few people whom I have never heard say an unkind or spiteful thing about another person, and of those very few, some, I suspect, have been charitable partly through caution and partly through a lack of definiteness in their own personalities; tolerance is often no more than the child of laziness and indifference. Squire was not like that. He was too busy to have enemies and too large-hearted. He had supreme self-confidence. If there is such a thing as a superiority complex, then he had one. He was never boastful, but he had no doubt of his own talents. Poetry was to him the alpha and omega of existence. He knew he was a good poet, and if, so he felt, you are a poet, everything falls into place.

He was always welcoming, exuberant, enthusiastic. He was generous and open-handed. The members of his Surrey cricket tour were all of them his guests. In his days of affluence he befriended many young poets who had financial problems and he paid the college fees of one of them. His material fortunes were to know many fluctuations, but circumstance was powerless against him. He never looked crestfallen.

The 'Squirearchy' fell apart during the 1920s. Spain which under Charles V had been swollen by the satellite principalities of the Holy Roman Empire remained a power under Philip II: and so did Squire when Shanks and Turner followed separate careers.

He described himself as a centipede with a foot in a hundred worlds. In addition to his critical and editorial work, he found time to stand for Parliament as a Liberal —in 1918 he had stood as a Labour candidate—and each time he forfeited his deposit. For ten harried years he wrote little poetry, but in the mid nineteen-'thirties he enjoyed a St Martin's summer and *A Face in Candlelight* contains some of his finest work. In 1932 a large dinner which he appeared to have organized himself was given in his honour, and shortly afterwards he was knighted.

In March 1953 his seventieth birthday was honoured by a small dinner at the Garrick Club, organized by J. B. Priestley and A. D. Peters, and attended by his oldest friends. It was a genuine disappointment to me that I should have had to be abroad. It was a great success.

Squire died in 1958. In his last years he lived in the country, at an inn. He rarely came to London, but his friends visited him and the villagers revered him. He was one of Macmillan's chief advisers and his book page each week in the *Illustrated London News* had its own special quality. His reputation was firmly based upon high achievement.

I wrote of Clifford Bax at some length in my auto-biography. But he was then still alive—he died in the autumn of 1962—and I was anxious not to say anything that would seem to him too personal. He disliked publicity and had a stubborn regard for privacy. As it was, one of his friends upbraided me for contending that Bax's father had made a mistake in not sending him to Eton. Would Clifford, she argued, have been any more charming or sympathetic if he had. That was not my point. I believed and believe that Bax's career exemplifies the disadvantages of an unconventional education.

If a man departs from the norm, he should do so under the compulsion of his own temperament and not because of external pressure. It is a mistake to encourage a boy to consider himself exceptional. It is for him to prove that he is exceptional. A boy should be brought up among his equals. If you send the son of an earl to a small grammar school, he will be looked on as an oddity; it is unwise for a boy to be brought up with those much poorer or much richer than himself. A boy should feel himself at one with the group into which he is born, and incited to excel his contemporaries on their own ground.

If it is clear in the nursery that a boy is a freak, physically or mentally, then he should be prescribed a special treatment. But Clifford Bax was not a freak. He was healthy, athletic, with a love of games, with a fine alert mind. Born into the upper-middle class in 1884, he should have gone to the kind of school to which members of that class go. As he would inherit a considerable income and as he had no family links with another school, Eton was the right one for him. He would have learnt there that the possession of money is a privilege and a responsibility, shared by others. He would also by competing with his contemporaries have acquired a standard with which to appraise his own abilities. This is very important for an Englishman. He tends otherwise to over or underestimate his powers. Bax in his early years did both. His view of himself was out of focus.

When I met him first in June 1920, he was living in a top-floor studio in Edwardes Square. It was a large sunny room, with some fine pieces of furniture; warmed with a stove it was relatively comfortable, though the rain dripped through the roof and he arranged a series of vases on the floor to catch the drops. He had no resident maid but a woman came in daily to provide breakfast and to tidy up. He took all his meals out, except tea which he prepared himself. He had no telephone. He often did not open the door to visitors, preferring not to be disturbed; his friends devised a code of knocks, so that he should know who was on the door-step.

He dressed in unpressed tweeds. He resented having to put on evening clothes, and when he did he wore heavy brogue shoes, sometimes with rubber soles. In winter he wore a heavy, threadbare coat, fifteen years old; it had belonged to a poacher and had voluminous inside pockets. He was considering, he told me, the purchase of a new one, and was deliberating the wisdom of having it made for him by a tailor. He was apprehensive lest in ten years' time he should have put on weight and a coat that now fitted well might then constrict him. He wore dark felt hats with narrow brims. Once he bought a new one, and its contrast with the threadbare coat was disconcerting. I am not easily embarrassed, but I could not help suspecting that we looked an incongruous couple as we walked down Kensington High Street, myself short and dapper with a military bearing, he tall and undulant, like a scarecrow swaying in a wind.

When I met him first, he was in a morose mood. He had been writing for several years with limited success. Under no compulsion to earn a living, he had not

Squire's sense of self-direction. He was ready to accept any publisher's suggestion. He was not the man who brought ideas to publishers. His bibliography, in consequence, contains several minor books. The man who stage-manages a career realizes that it is important for a book to look important. Instead of writing a short biography of Bianca Capello to fit into a publisher's series, Bax would have been wise to have put three or four contrasted biographies inside a single volume, as Lesley Blanch did in *The Wilder Shores of Love*.

Taught by a private tutor, he made friends by chance. We all do that, but he did not in his early years meet the kinds of man with whom he had most in common. The nearest approach was Godwin Baynes, the doctor and rowing blue. Only meeting those who were also being exposed to eccentric forms of education, he did not become a part of his generation, and his marriage accentuated this divergence. His wife was several years older than himself and she did not, as a young wife might have done, open the door for him into the world of his contemporaries. On the contrary she encouraged him to take a house in Wiltshire and write poetry, which was all wrong for a young man who was by birth and tastes a townsman.

Within three years he had left Wiltshire and established himself in London with a young and attractive female. This in England before World War I was a highly unconventional procedure. The English are infinitely tolerant of anything to which they can close their eyes but even now convention decrees that unmarried couples should reside under separate roofs. The adventure showed a poetic courage on Bax's part since he had good reasons for fearing that his father would disinherit him. The fears proved unfounded, but so dubious a *ménage* cast his lot still further among the

unconventional, a set to which he did not by taste belong.
'I am tired,' he said to me in 1925, 'of failures and of
misfits.' The *ménage* did not last very long, but by the
time it ended he was nearly thirty.

The war would have given him a chance of finding the
type of friend he needed, but he was medically unfit for
service. As young men who were not in uniform in 1914–
18 inevitably did, he gravitated still further among misfits.

It was while he was emerging from this fog that I
first met him. I will not say that he was a disappointed
man, he was too young, too vital, too ambitious to be that.
But he was aggrieved at the lack of recognition that his
work had received.

He published that autumn a book of poems, *A House
of Words*, which contained a number of fine poems, but
received a small and lukewarm press. The *Saturday
Westminster Gazette* suggested that Clifford Bax's role
in the arts was not that of a creator, but of an appraiser
and interpreter, and the notice was editorially headed
'Mistaken Vocations'. This hurt his feelings very much.
It was illogical that it should, since he had no respect for
the critical standards of the day. But no one is logical in
this respect. Many people were surprised to learn from
her notebooks how much store Virginia Woolf had set
by her reviews. She had such little respect for most of the
objects of popular veneration that one would have
imagined that she would have suspected her own work's
quality if it had been greeted with a chorus of praise.
Why should an artist expect a public which he considers
mistaken on every other point, to assess his own work
correctly? Some writers expect to be acclaimed the
winner of a race for which they have not entered themselves as starters.

I am myself surprised that Bax's poems so rarely appear
in anthologies. For me they are deep in feeling, human

and finely wrought. He suggested to me once that his being a Buddhist had militated against their appeal since the philosophy at the back of them was foreign to a reader raised in a different faith. This may be true. In *Inland Far* he paints a sympathetic picture of the Buddhist who converted him, but he gives no reason for having found Buddhism more satisfactory than the faith of his fathers. Keyserling in his *Travel Diary of a Philosopher* stresses the influence of climate on religion and in his chapter on 'Colombo' argues that Buddhism is in tune with the heavy heat and lush luxuriant foliage of Ceylon. Is it fanciful to suggest that Bax's adoption of a faith alien to the bleak cold north is a corollary to his eccentric education?

He did have a certain measure of success. *The Rose Without a Thorn* had a long run when it was first produced, has been frequently acted by amateurs, and has been used on the radio and on TV. He wrote several charming ballad operas. He adapted *Polly* for the stage; *Midsummer Madness* was exquisitely staged by Nigel Playfair at the Lyric, Hammersmith with Marie Tempest in the lead. *Mr Pepys* too was a success. But in his choice of subject he was frequently handicapped through not having the same educational background as his fellow-countrymen.

In *The Rose Without a Thorn* he had in Henry VIII a character in whom everyone was interested; so had he in Mr Pepys, but it was a different matter when he wrote of fifteenth-century Italians. He himself considered *The Venetian* his best play, but my own interest in it was immeasurably diminished by my ignorance of the period; others were in my plight. It is hard to interest an audience in a period other than its own, unless the conflict of that period can be related to its own, unless a parallel can be drawn, or unless it is already familiar with it. Shakespeare's plays have, for instance, made certain historical characters familiar, so that Gordon Daviot's *Richard of*

Bordeaux presented from a new angle a man about whom
the public already had its own idea.

It is important for the writer of historical plays and
novels to recognize which these characters and periods
are. It is also important for a playwright—for any writer
for that matter—to gauge how much knowledge he can
assume in the public which he is anxious to address.
Nothing annoys a reader more than having a story hinge
on a reference he cannot catch. For the writer of historical
plays this is particularly important. The historical dramatist is in one respect at a disadvantage with regard to the
writer of drawing-room comedies. He is robbed of the
effects of suspense and of surprise because the audience
knows how it will all turn out; watching *The First
Gentleman*, for example, it knows that George IV's
daughter will die in childbirth, otherwise how could
Queen Victoria have reached the throne. But in compensation he has a ready-made sense of dramatic irony. In
John Drinkwater's *Mary Stuart*, the tension was heightened by the audience's foreknowledge that Rizzio had
only a few minutes to live. In *The Venetian* Bax assumed
that this sense of dramatic irony existed. He made a
duke reflect on the eve of battle, that five hundred years
hence men would be discussing what he achieved or failed
to achieve in the next few hours. But the greater part of
the audience had never heard of the battle or the duke and
were wondering why they were being invited to be
concerned over what seemed to them a remote tribal
skirmish.

'Birds of a feather', I suppose, and the lives of nearly
all my men friends have been convulsed by a series of
romantic crises. As their friend, I have received a number
of confidences from the ladies of their concern. Bax
attracted a great many women; though he had a soft voice
and a gentle manner he was intensely virile. He was kind,

generous, attentive in small things; in love tenderly forceful, concerned with a woman's pleasure before his own. He had an intuitive and sympathetic grasp of a woman's problems; women felt that they were understood by him. This understanding is exemplified right through his work, particularly in his rhymed *Plays for Girls*, in *Midsummer Madness* and in the character of Catherine Howard in *The Rose Without a Thorn*. He was a good friend to women, capable of deep and unselfish friendship. It was, I fancy, women more often than he who refused to be satisfied with 'just friendship'.

Though he was anything but promiscuous, he was rarely uninvolved in a liaison. He said to me more than once, 'I have had now all the experience that I can absorb. When this thing is over, I'm going to quit all that and turn my experience into plays.' But 'this thing' was always followed by another 'thing'.

His liaisons followed, unconsciously, the principle of the rotation of crops, a 'lady of quality' succeeding a Bohemian, and someone frivolous following someone serious. During 1923 he was occupied with an austere lady, not unattractive, but tall and grim, forbidding at a first and indeed seventh meeting. She was possessive, jealous of his friends, limited and exclusive in her tastes, insisting that he should only know people whom she thought 'worth while'. But I may be prejudiced. I was one of the friends who was not 'worth while'.

When her reign ended, in mid-1924, he completely altered the pattern of his existence, moving out of his studio into a comfortable house north of the Park, with an establishment consisting of a married couple and a valet. This move coincided with and was perhaps occasioned by the entry into his life of an old friend, Vera Leslie. *A House of Words* contained a number of character poems. One of them called 'The Flirt' was inscribed to her.

> Myriad-lovered
> Vain provocative
> Heartless, honeyed
> Exquisite girl.
> Are you merely
> Something enchanted?
> Could we unspell you
> What should we find?

Vera was a socialite. She was smart. She had a gift for
drawing. She appreciated elegance. Though her background was 'army and county', she preferred the company of artists. Her first husband had been an artist and
printer, Stanley North; her second and at that time
current one was Filson Young. There was not a great
difference in age between herself and Clifford and they
had been friends in youth. When I had questioned him
about 'Flirt' he had told me that she was one of the most
fascinating women he had ever known.

Under Vera's guidance he changed his appearance to
suit his new address. He went to a good tailor, bought
patent leather evening shoes, adopted a wider-brimmed
style of hat and grew a beard. He had a good cook and he
gave charming dinner parties for which he expected his
guests to change. I have very happy memories of those
dinners. He always maintained that four is the best
number for a party;* sometimes he invited three other
men, sometimes two women and a man. Sometimes he
wrote verses on the place cards. I cherish one on which he
combined within a couplet the titles of three of my books:

> *Myself when young* spurned *Pleasure* and sought Truth;
> Weave wiselier thou upon *The Loom of Youth.*

Nineteen-twenty-five was a happy year for him. He
was working well. *Midsummer Madness* was produced. He

---

* Myself, I agree with Cyril Connolly in preferring six, since that gives
opportunities for duologues as well as general conversation.

enjoyed his change of circumstance. He was a man who in some respects grew up upside-down, and he now at the age of forty was showing an undergraduate's interest in clothes. A valet was a great adventure for him.

He was also very happy with Vera. He was in the mood for a gay companion, after the gaunt guardian of his diary, and the fact that he and Vera had known each other when they were young gave him a sense of having the threads of his life drawn together. So often one feels incomplete with a new friend because one cannot talk about one's past; in the same way for that matter one often feels incomplete with an old friend because one cannot discuss with him one's immediate concerns. Vera and Clifford could let their talk wander at will over twenty years.

During this period he wrote several of the stories that were published under the title *Many a Green Isle*. One of them was inspired by Vera. In it he wrote, 'on a sudden I realized that as great a wonder had happened to me as if I had stepped into an enchanted pool and had come forth ten years younger. And my new self laughed at the arrogance of the self whom I had shed. After all then—the world had been right; the simple souls had been right; they were not mere sentimentalists because they assumed that the love between men and women was the inmost treasure obtainable from life. "Proud poet," I said to myself. "Now you are with the humblest. Now you are back at the beginning of wisdom and perceive that those who belittle love are those who could never find it."'

It is not impossible that this friendship might have been a lasting one, might have been the anchor for him that a later friendship was to become, but Vera's husband, Filson Young, took exception to it. Divorce proceedings were initiated and Vera and Clifford married. Vera was a person of much charm, was a good hostess, who knew how to decorate and run a house, but Clifford never looked himself in it. He needed to be alone. Four years later he took a set in Albany.

He was now in his late forties and it was here that he appeared to catch up with himself, to complete the process of growing up the wrong way round and stand square upon his feet, to reach a point of development that was in keeping with his nature. Both as a Bohemian and as a socialite he had been cast for the wrong roles, and he had been out of character in marriage. He needed solitude and freedom, and a setting in which he could meet and entertain different kinds of friend. He did not need formality but he did need comfort. He did not need a valet but he did need a good housekeeper.

He was in tune with the whole atmosphere of Albany with its quiet, its privacy, the college atmosphere of the ropewalk, the red-uniformed porter with his cockaded hat, and the rounded windows with their view of Vigo Street. Seeing him with his books and pictures round him, I felt that he was himself at last. His book, *Evenings in Albany*, a graceful blending of reverie and reminiscence gave a happy picture of his life there. It was during this period that he made friends with men of his own type— men like E. V. Lucas and C. B. Fry.

No two men could have been more different than Bax and Squire. They were very different too, as captains of a cricket side.

It might have been expected that Bax, who had shown little sense of stage-management in his career as a writer, would have been a vague and casual captain of a cricket side and that Squire, who had such a marked sense of self-direction, would have been on the field a brisk, military martinet. Not at all; though Bax looked like an Elizabethan poet, he was a business-like manager. The staff work of his tours was smooth, and his teams arrived on time with an umpire, a scorer and a twelfth man in flannels.

The Invalids were very different. *England, Their England* is dedicated to Squire. He figures in its pages as Mr Hodge. The book is comic and the comedian's licence to exaggerate is freely used. Into the famous cricket match are crowded the high spots of a dozen matches, and no real game could have ended in that kind of a tie with half the fielders colliding in mid-wicket. It is full, rich caricature. But in the presentation of Mr Hodge's captaincy and management there was no caricature at all. It really was like that.

I first met the Invalids as an opponent in the summer of 1921. I was living in Ditchling and captained the village side. Squire had wanted to make it a whole-day match. But it was harvest time, the villagers could not get away, so we agreed on a one-thirty start with a buffet lunch first for the visitors in my bungalow. I expected my guests around midday, but the first opponent appeared at half past nine, in the belief that it was a whole-day match. I have forgotten his name. I have never seen him since, he was a very silent man. I soon began to hope that other members of the side would be under a similar misapprehension, but the slow passing hours of the morning were only broken by a couple of telegrams for Squire from players who had been delayed. Noon came, half past twelve, one o'clock; then the solitary arrival and myself ate a portion of the lunch, covered over the remains in the hope that they would be reasonably fresh at suppertime, and made our way to the ground where the villagers were patiently waiting for the 'toffs from London'. Eventually the game began at five to four, with the last two places filled by an eleven-year-old schoolboy and the taxi driver who had driven half the side from the remote station to which they had been misdirected.

I will not call that a typical experience—but it was an effective introduction to the Invalids. Squire was at that time the busiest man of letters in the country: more often than not he was forced to leave the writing of his Sunday article for the *Observer* till the Saturday morning, and most regular members of his side can recall fidgeting in his study, beside the messenger who was waiting to take down his manuscript to the printer, while the Invalids, one by one, were assembling forty miles away in a Sussex pub. Every regular Invalid has his own pet story of a side six short without its captain being put in to bat and desperately trying to hold out till lunch when a further instalment of players might be expected.

No side can have been managed more capriciously off the field and its management in the field was unexpected. Squire, unlike Bax, had not had, well, how shall I put it— the conventional grooming of a cricketer, and he captained his sides, as Hitler led his armies, not from a study of the textbooks but by the light of poetic intuition.

In a half-day game once against a good side on a good wicket, he opened his attack with his second and third change bowlers. At tea, with the score at 165 for two, he explained his plan. 'I thought I would get two or three quick wickets, then loose my good bowlers, when they were fresh, against the tail.'

He enjoyed bowling, and some maintained that his tactics in the field were dictated by the subconscious need to create a situation when he would be justified in putting himself on to bowl. He had, as a bowler, some curious idiosyncrasies. The average captain, when deciding from which end he will prefer to bowl, studies the slope of the ground and gauges the direction of the wind with a wetted finger. Squire looked at the sun. 'I'll go on this end,' he would say. 'At the other end the glint of the sun upon the stumps would put me off.' 'Mr Hodge,' A. G.

MacDonell wrote, 'was a poet, and therefore a theorist and an idealist. Every ball that he bowled had brain behind it, if not exactness of pitch.' He took a four-step trot, and tossed high into the air a ball guileless of spin and swerve. It was astonishing how often he broke a partnership.

But the most remarkable feature of a remarkable eleven was Squire's capacity to get the best play out of his side. Was it an innate gift of leadership or did the memory of an earlier Sir John who would not 'march through Coventry with that', inspire or rather goad a reasonable club cricketer, who recognized how hopelessly the odds were laid against him, into a desperate resolve to put a face on things? Something of both most likely. Certainly most regular Invalids will admit that they played ten per cent above their normal form for Squire and two high victories stand upon his records—against a strong R.A.O.C. side at Aldershot, when that fine musician Walton O'Donnell took seven wickets and made over 80, and at the Oval against the Lords and Commons largely owing to a three-figure partnership between Clifford Bax and that sound writer of detective stories, Milward Kennedy, who appeared on the score card disguised by his baptismal name, M. R. K. Burge.

It is one of the anomalies of leadership that Squire, untrained as a cricketer, with no skill at the game and little knowledge of it, should have been able to get the best out of his team, while as editor of the *London Mercury*, with his great knowledge of literature and feeling for the humanities of literature, he should not have been able to get the best work out of his friends. The rates of pay on the Mercury were low but most writers would sooner have £10 from a paper they respect and an encouraging editor who takes pleasure in their work than £30 from an impersonal, commercially-minded magazine. Over the years a number of excellent poems, essays and stories appeared within the yellow covers of the *Mercury*, but few of Squire's juniors felt when they had reached a final sentence, 'This really is rather good. I'll let Jack have first look at it.'

12
My Brother Evelyn

I wrote in my *Early Years* in explanation of the fact that it contained so little about my brother, 'I lack the key to Evelyn. I cannot enter imaginatively into the mind of a person for whom religion is the dominant force in his life, for whom religion is a crusade. . . . You cannot appraise a stained-glass window if you look at it from the outside and, not possessing that key to Evelyn's nature, I might give in a full-length essay . . . a misleading picture of him.' I was afraid 'that I might get the picture out of focus. I might lay the wrong emphasis on certain episodes, and mislead rather than guide his readers.'

But when I wrote that, I could not have foreseen that Evelyn would never finish his own autobiography; and though for those same reasons I do not feel myself competent to draw a full-length portrait of him, I do feel that I owe it to his memory to sketch for the benefit of his readers a picture of his early days, up till his conversion.

During the last fifteen years of his life, I saw him so seldom that I can remember each separate occasion on which we met—there were fewer than a dozen— weddings and funerals, his libel action against Nancy Spain; once we lunched in London; once a trip of his to Monte Carlo coincided with one of mine to Villefranche. I twice visited him in his house in Somerset. But though we met so little, we were in constant touch. We frequently corresponded; I have a large folder of his letters which I shall one day annotate and edit for presentation to a university library. I was very conscious of him down there in Combe Florey, at work among his books or pottering round his garden. I was questioned about him constantly. Mutual friends would recount this or the other piece of gossip. When something happened I would think, 'That will make Evelyn chuckle. I must write to him.' I still involuntarily go on thinking that. I cannot believe he is no longer here.

The only period when we were really close was the decade between his going up to Oxford and my second marriage—January 1922 to October 1932. I saw little of him during his childhood. He was by five and a quarter years my junior. Two-thirds of the year I was away at a boarding school. He took no interest in athletics. When my father announced his birth, I said, 'Good, now we'll have a wicket keeper.' But my attempts to teach him cricket inculcated in him a permanent repugnance for the game.

He was, inevitably, something of a nuisance to me. Presumably I was to him. In our first home, in West Hampstead, my nursery cricket—a game I played by myself—was restricted by the danger of hitting a ball into his cot. When we moved to Underhill, a larger house, I at first left the nursery to him, and spent the winter day-time reading in my father's book-room. But after a while I became interested in billiards, and a small table was installed in the nursery. Evelyn must have regarded this as an invasion of his territorial rights.

It is probable that he realized that I considered him a nuisance and that he resented it. He made friends, soon after we moved to Underhill, with a family that lived a quarter of a mile away in a house called Wyldesmead. He has described how he and this family organized 'the Pistol troop', to resist the German invasion which at that early day was to them obviously imminent. A clay heap in a builder's plot was fortified, and provisions for a siege were buried. The parents of the family, who had not yet met my parents, were for a time under the impression that Evelyn was an only child. 'Oh no,' said one of them, 'he has a brother whom he hates.'

It is possible that I was not very kind to Evelyn. I can still visualize the occasion when my mother lectured me on this point. We were spending an August with my father's family, where I had to see rather more than usual of my brother. My mother said, 'I don't like hearing your aunts complain that you aren't kind to Evelyn.'

I fancy that I, an indulged child, very much my father's favourite, grew up with a superiority complex. I was confident that I was going to make a considerable mark in the world. Evelyn may well have felt himself relegated to a second place. He once said to his mother, 'Daddy loves Alec more than me. But you love me more than you love Alec.' This was indeed true, but my mother felt that she should not show favouritism. 'No,' she said, 'I love you both the same.' 'Then I am lacking in love,' he said.

When I returned for the school holidays, my father used to paste over the face of the grandfather clock in the hall, 'Welcome home to the heir of Underhill'. Evelyn's comment on this was—he was then only six—'When Alec has Underhill, and all that's in it, what will be left for me?' My father never put the notice up again. The incident had an amusing sequel; forty years later my mother, who had inherited my father's estate, apart from his library which had been left to Evelyn and myself, consulted me about her will. She had not a great deal to leave, apart from the furniture, most of her capital having been invested in an annuity. I was by then a resident alien of the United States. I had no need for furniture. Evelyn had six children; reasonable provision had been made by my father-in-law for my three children; Evelyn had contributed generously to his mother's support during her last years, so that it seemed to me both equitable and trouble-saving for me to disinherit myself. With some reluctance she agreed and made Evelyn her sole heir, so that in the end it was Evelyn who got 'Underhill and all that's in it.'

Cyril Connolly reviewing a life of Ian Fleming wrote in connection with the rivalry, fostered by their mother, between Ian and his elder brother, Peter, 'One can detect a similarity of predicament as between Alec and Evelyn Waugh and Peter and Ian Fleming, but one can strain Adlerian principles too far. Without Peter (or Alec) the second brothers might have done just as well.' But it is indeed possible that Evelyn as a second son was challenged to assert himself. He seemed to detect a conspiracy against him between his father and his brother, though he treated it jokingly; when he was sixteen or so he appeared in a tail-coat at an evening party. The neighbours to whom I have referred, commented on his smartness. 'It was my father's coat,' he said, 'then it was Alec's; now it is mine. In fact it has come down from generation to generation of them that hate me.'

Evelyn has described his childhood as being blissfully happy. He adored his mother and his nurse. He resented his father's intrusion on their life together. His day ended with the click of his father's latch-key in the lock, and the shout from the hall, 'Where is K, where is my wife.' My life, on the other hand, started with my father's return from work. I do not really know how I spent my Christmas and Easter holidays. I did not have a single friend in the neighbourhood, until during my second year at Sherborne, another boy from Hampstead came to the School House, H. S. Mackintosh, to whom I have already made reference in these pages. I was never lonely, but I certainly led a solitary life.

Evelyn had a sunny nature; he was emotional and apt to dissolve in tears. Our mother had in the dining-room a large high-backed chair which my father had given her, on condition that she did the carving. If my father or myself threatened him with discipline, he would throw himself into the back of this chair, shouting 'Sanctuary, sanctuary.' He could not be touched when he was there. He invented his own language of love between his mother and himself. The word 'goggles' stood for love. He would finish his letters, 'Evoggles goggles moggles'. His love was so special that it needed a special vocabulary, like Swann's Cattleyas.

In later life Evelyn may have given the impression of being heartless; he was often snubbing, he could be cruel. But basically he was gentle, warm and tender. He was very like his father, and his father's own emotionalism put him on his guard. He must have often thought, 'I could become like this. I mustn't let myself become like this.' *Brideshead Revisited* is the only one of his novels in which his poetic side was given a loose rein. He wrote it between February and June 1944. His father had died in the preceding summer. Is it too fanciful to suggest that that death gave him a feeling of release? The warning example was now removed.

In many of Evelyn's novels there is the portrait of the gentle loving man being exploited by self-seeking worldlings—Paul in *Decline and Fall*, Adam in *Vile Bodies*, Tony in *A Handful of Dust*. That was one side of Evelyn, the larger side, but he was also Basil Seal. Some people only saw that side of him. When he first read *The Diary of a Nobody*, he exclaimed delightedly, 'But Lupin's me.'

Only in Charles Ryder are the two sides of him fused. Ryder talks to his wife very much as Evelyn did talk to someone by whom he was irritated: but though *Brideshead* may be autobiography spiritually and emotionally, it is not factually. Charles Ryder was an agnostic. But Evelyn was devout from the beginning. As a child he

went to matins, in a small village-type church-room, where
the service was conducted by a man not in holy orders,
but from the age of, I should say seven, he attended with
the rest of us, choral celebration at St Jude's, in the
Garden Suburb, which was near Anglo-Catholic; its
priest being Basil Bouchier, a cousin of the actor, who
was satirized as the Rev. Boom Bagshaw in A. S. M.
Hutchinson's 1921 best-seller *If Winter Comes*. Evelyn
was confirmed there in 1916. He had a shrine in his
bedroom, at which he lit incense. In *A Little Learning* he
tells that in his later years at Lancing he had a period of
agnosticism, but I do not believe that it lasted long. In
The Ordeal of Gilbert Pinfold, he speaks of his conversion
as the inevitable crossing of a line, a step that could have
been foreseen from the beginning.

When he was quite young—I do not know the exact
date—his mother said to him before the beginning of
Lent, 'We are now starting Lent. We should always give
up something during Lent. We should also be on our
guard against our besetting sin. You know, don't you,
what is your besetting sin?'

He shook his head; no, he had no knowledge of it.
His mother explained: it was his quick and unkind
tongue. He accepted her criticism: pondered it for a
moment, and then said, 'You know, Mother, what is
your besetting sin?'

This was a shock to her. Conscious though she was of
her shortcomings in the world at large, she thought that
in the nursery, and in the eyes of her second son, she was
the image of perfection. But she supposed that she must
face the mirror. 'No, Evelyn,' she said, 'what is it?' The
answer came back straight: 'A lack of faith in Catholic
doctrine.'

'And of course,' she would say afterwards, in recount-
ing the incident, 'he was completely right. I do lack faith.'

As a child, I repeat, Evelyn had a sunny nature. He was always happily, busily occupied. He indulged in 'different arrangements' which meant moving round all the nursery furniture to see if it looked better with the wicker chair beside the door and the Peter Pan picture over the fire-place. He was the centre of his own group of children, the spokesman, the organizer. The Pistol Troop was followed by the W.U.D.S. (Wyldesmead Underhill Dramatic Society). I came across some of their programmes the other day. They were very professional: illustrated with photographs of the chief performers. He was very like his father in all of that.

Evelyn has described his preparatory school—Heathmount, a day school in Hampstead—where Cecil Beaton was a junior contemporary of his. He was sent there instead of to Fernden because his mother thought he had too gentle a nature for the Spartan discipline that I described in my autobiography. Fernden was extremely tough; so tough that everything that has happened to me since has in comparison seemed tame. It may seem surprising in view of the reputation for toughness which Evelyn acquired in after years, that anything could have seemed too tough for him at the age of nine; but it must never be forgotten that he had a very tender heart. The toughness was superimposed, in self-defence. Beneath it he was highly vulnerable.

A Little Learning contains an amusing description of Heathmount, but it does not mention a schoolmaster, Aubrey Ensor, who can be seen in retrospect as a formative influence in his development. Ensor, who became a good friend of mine and very much a family friend of my parents, was that not uncommon type, a young preparatory schoolmaster with literary ambitions, who regarded his hours in the classroom as a prelude to a substantial career as a dramatist. He did not realize his ambitions but he had a real gift for writing stage dialogue; with a little luck he might have 'brought it off'; and even so, he has had a not unsuccessful life, spent in congenial occupations. He was at one time connected with the Everyman Theatre and at another supervised the Iveagh Bequest in Ken Wood. For nearly every artist there is someone outside the family, a schoolmaster, a parson, who at a very early age lengthens his horizon, opening windows on new landscapes. Aubrey Ensor did that for Evelyn. He introduced him to Saki. In the letter that he wrote to me after Evelyn's death, he told me how surprised and amused he had been when Evelyn, as an eleven-year-old schoolboy, had remarked, 'Terrible man my father. He likes Kipling.'

Had Evelyn cared for cricket, he and I would have had many companionable times together at Lord's and at the Oval. But as it was there was nothing except the cinema that we could share until he was old enough to go to adult parties. That did not happen till he went up to Oxford, in January 1922, when he was eighteen. In that month my first marriage broke up; I did not take a flat of my own until January 1924. For most of Evelyn's time at Oxford, we were, during his vacs, living under the same roof. I did not start travelling until June 1926. So that for four and a half years we were constantly in each other's company.

During Evelyn's first two years at Oxford, we had a number of good times together. I introduced him to my friends, I took him to parties and invited him to my own. I felt very proud of him. He was excellent company; witty, lively, hopeful. He was good-looking in a faunish way. Everybody liked him. It is pleasant to be the initiator, to show to the inexperienced, places with which one is

169

familiar, and it was pleasant to have someone with whom I could talk over the parties afterwards. My father's sisters always gave him a Stilton cheese for Christmas and I can remember many occasions when Evelyn and I, returning late, would raid the larder and pick away at the dwindling cheese, discussing various aspects of the party.

A few weeks before his death, Evelyn told an interviewer that after an idle year, he was again at work upon his autobiography, the second volume of which was to be called 'A Little Hope'. He only left seven or eight pages. I was very touched that one of them should have paid a tribute to those times. He wrote of me as 'a host who introduced me to the best restaurants of London, on whom I sponged, bringing my friends to his flat and when short of money, sleeping on his floor, until the tubes opened when I would at dawn sway home to Hampstead, in crumpled evening dress among the navvies setting out for their day's work.' In return he immensely enlarged my life by introducing me to men like Harold Acton, Hugh Molson, Christopher Hollis, Robert Byron, Peter Quennell, Brian Howard and Terence Greenidge.

Evelyn wrote at length about his three years at Oxford, both in *Brideshead Revisited* and in *A Little Learning*. Like Charles Ryder, he was studiously industrious for his first two terms; he then had a year of abounding happiness, but suddenly the magic faded. Ryder decided that he had got the best out of Oxford and that he would be better employed studying art in Paris. Evelyn also thought he had got the best out of Oxford and asked his father if he could come down. But unlike Ryder, Evelyn had nothing to come down to. His father, as most fathers would, told him that it would be foolish for him to leave before he had taken a degree. It was only a matter of another year, then they could review the situation. Evelyn stayed on and took a third. Because he had gone up a term late, he would have had to stay on another term before he could take his degree: as he had had his scholarship taken away, because of his third, there seemed no point in delaying his start on life for six months in order to be able to put B.A. after his name.

Charles Ryder's ecstatic days at Oxford coincided with the peak of his friendship with Sebastian; it ended with Sebastian's decline into alcoholism, and the authorities' refusal to let him share rooms with Ryder. But there was no Sebastian in Evelyn's life. No one will believe that novelists create their characters by taking one trait from this person, and this from that, giving one character a situation that has perplexed another; and because the head of a titled family was forced at that time because of a scandal to live abroad, and because a younger son of that family drank himself to an early death, the world said, 'Of course the Flytes are the . . .' and no doubt Evelyn had that family in mind when he created Sebastian, Julia and Lord Marchmain. But they are not portraits; any more than Margot Metroland is the Mayfair hostess who in 1927 had a love affair with a prominent coloured singer and whom Evelyn must have had in mind.

Charles Ryder said, 'I sometimes wonder whether had it not been for Sebastian, I might have trodden the same path as Collins round the cultural water wheel. My father in his youth sat for All Souls and, in a year of hot competition, failed. Other successes and honours came his way later, but that early failure impressed itself on him, and through him on to me, so I came up with an ill-considered sense that there lay the proper and natural goal of a life of reason. I, too, should doubtless have failed, but, having failed, I might perhaps have slipped into a less august academic life elsewhere. It is conceivable, but not, I believe, likely for the hot spring of anarchy rose from

deep furnaces where was no solid earth, and burst into the
sunlight—a rainbow in its cooling vapours—with a power
that rocks could not repress.'

Presumably Evelyn was drawing a parallel between Mr
Ryder's failure at All Souls and his own father's third in
Greats.

But though there was no Sebastian in Evelyn's life,
there was, I think, an equivalent for Sebastian in the
number of brilliant and elegant young men from a larger
way of life who showed him in how narrow a world he had
moved at Heathmount, Lancing and at Underhill. For a
year he was enchanted at moving in this brighter wider
world, then he realized that he did not belong to it, that
he was only a sojourner, that if he wanted to stay in this
world after he went down, he would have to win his place
there. At least that is my diagnosis of the situation.

There was also the deep antagonism between himself
and the Dean of his college—Cruttwell. Evelyn wrote at
length about Cruttwell in *A Little Learning* and his
attack provoked in the public press a burst of epistolary
shrapnel from pupils who had different experiences of the
Dean. No man could reach and hold such a position as
Cruttwell did without having considerable merits. The
dislike between Evelyn and himself was mutual, instinc-
tive and as irrational as love. They hated one another.
How Cruttwell must have enjoyed writing the letter
announcing Evelyn's third and the loss of his scholarship.

Evelyn, subsequently, was implacable in his pursuit
of Cruttwell. If in a novel there is a dreary character who
can always be asked to dinner at the last moment, it is a
Captain Cruttwell. The bogus ex-Indian army officer who
sells tropical equipment in a department store was
Brigadier Cruttwell. *Mr Loveday's Little Outing*, the story
of the lunatic who is allowed out of his asylum for a single
afternoon and promptly strangles a schoolgirl on a bicycle,

was originally entitled 'Mr Cruttwell's Little Outing'. Evelyn was anxious that Chapman & Hall should write to the Dean, saying that they were proposing to use this title for a collection of short stories. The Mr Cruttwell in the story was a homicidal lunatic; if the Dean of Hertford thought he would be mistaken for this character, they were prepared to alter the title. But the letter was never written. It was felt that the joke had gone far enough, and by then the victim had suffered an adequate humiliation.

At that time certain universities were allowed the right to an independent representative in Parliament, and Cruttwell had in 1935 been chosen as the official Conservative candidate for Oxford University. Up till that day the actual voting was regarded as a mere formality and Cruttwell had arranged for a party in his rooms on election night to celebrate his appointment. This year, however, A. P. Herbert decided at the last moment and in a spirit of jest to have himself proposed as a rival candidate; he swept the polls and Cruttwell's party was never held.

The good news reached my brother when he was a war correspondent in Abyssinia. The jubilant letter that he wrote my wife is one of her most prized possessions. 'Cruttwell's ignominy' had made his week he said. He had needed cheering up as he had just returned from an unsuccessful attempt to reach the front. He had been arrested by a one-eyed sheik and kept under guard for a whole day and night. On his return to Addis in dejection, he had found 'Cruttwell's failure supremely comforting. It must be the first time in history that the official Conservative has bitched things so thoroughly.'

Evelyn gave the coming-out dance for his daughter Teresa in a marquee in a London square. It had been a singularly cold and rain-swept summer. But this particular night was warm and starlit. I congratulated Evelyn on his good luck. 'Not luck at all,' he said. 'The Sisters of —— have been saying masses for it for a week.' 'Do you really believe that?' I asked. 'Do you question the efficacy of prayer?' he answered. I thought of Cruttwell and all the pins that had been stuck into his wax image.

From the summer of 1924 to the summer of 1928, when *Decline and Fall* was in the Press, Evelyn was, though casually employed for the most part of the time, definitely not engaged on a career. He entitled the chapter describing this period as 'In which our hero finds himself in very low water'. The book ends in July 1925; and the low-water period had another three years to run. Four years may not seem a long time in the retrospect of fifty years and as a prelude to an unbroken series of successes, but at the time those four years were interminable in their passing, a constant source of anxiety; after all there was no means of knowing that they were a prelude.

In the autumn of 1925, I arrived one morning at Chapman & Hall's to find my father in a state of considerable perturbation. Evelyn had come up to London for the night, had taken a number of his friends to the Gargoyle Club, settling the bill with a cheque; the cheque had bounced.

The secretary had rung up my father: what did he propose to do about it? My father answered that it was none of his business; his son must settle his own problems. The secretary had her reply ready. The matter would have to come up before the committee. The committee included some very prominent literary figures, Arnold Bennett among them. Did Mr Arthur Waugh want the matter of his son's cheque to be brought before Mr Arnold Bennett? Clearly Mr Arthur Waugh did not.

My father was at his most histrionic. I listened with sympathy. 'You know father,' I said at length, 'if Evelyn turns out to be a genius, you and I might be made to look very foolish by making a fuss over ten pounds, seventeen and ninepence.' My father raised his hand to heaven. 'Would I, would we, that's not much consolation now.' It was not an easy period for my father, and as Evelyn admitted in *A Little Learning*, 'the intermittent but frequent presence of a dissipated and not always respectful son disturbed the tranquillity of the home to which he always looked for refuge.'

At the time, those years seemed marked with a steady retrogression. Evelyn has told how after a few weeks at Heatherley's Art School, he went to Oxford for a hectic week of parties. On his return he felt in no mood to continue as an art student and became a schoolmaster first at the preparatory school in North Wales which he described in *A Little Learning*, then at the school near Aston Clinton for backward young men, which was the model for Dr Fagan's academy in *Decline and Fall*. The two schools were merged into one for the purposes of fiction, Grimes being transferred from North Wales to Buckinghamshire.

At Lancing, Evelyn had kept a diary which he had abandoned at Oxford. He now resumed it. 'It reveals,' he wrote, 'a warmer and altogether more likeable character than its predecessor; even though it is a record of continuous failure.' If that is what it reveals, then I would suggest that here the embryo novelist was at work; subconsciously recognizing that the hero, the 'I' of a narrative must be '*sympatico*', and it should be noted that one of the most marked characteristics of Evelyn's novels is the likeability of all his characters. Even the grisly Mrs Beaver has her own repulsive fascination. One would be glad to meet her; if not to linger in her company; while with every one of his other characters, one would be happy to spend quite a little time. Of how few novelists can that be said.

It is for that reason, I am very sure, that the E. W. of the 1924–8 diaries is 'a warmer and altogether more likeable' character than the E. W. of 1920–22. For in point of fact the Evelyn of those four years was very far from being that.

It would have been surprising, if he had not been. At Oxford he had been one of the most prominent of a brilliant group. The highest achievement had been predicted for him, yet he alone of all that group seemed now to be headed nowhere. He must have been conscious of his own latent powers. He must have known that potentially he was more gifted than those who had passed him in the race. Yet at the same time he must have had torturing moments of self-doubt, when he asked himself whether he was so brilliant after all. He explained publicly his failure in schools with the excuse that he had not really tried, but actually he had worked much harder than he had let his friends suspect. It was not surprising that he should have in self-defence disparaged the successes of his contemporaries. What did what they were doing amount to after all? Were they not trivial time-servers, accepting the standards of the market-place? He looked for their weak points and then attacked them. His quick tongue was like a snake's.

Nor should it be forgotten that as a master of dialogue, he was as sensitive to clumsy speech as is a man with an acute sense of smell to odours that the majority of us do not find offensive. The opening of the third chapter of *Black Mischief* is the supreme example of his gift in this direction. The revolution in Azania is being discussed in England by anonymous characters. There are ten or so short sections of dialogue, the longest of six lines, but you know exactly from what social milieu each group came. You even know the sex. 'But of course you remember; that madly attractive blackamoor at Balliol,' could only have been said by a young lady of quality.

A man with such an acute ear for language could not help being irritated by phrases like 'kind of', 'sort of'. I remember very many years later, using the word 'you' when I should have said 'one'. I was referring to the way in which two people are so close that they do not need to explain themselves to one another. 'You'd say,' I remarked, 'that they could talk in shorthand.' 'I wouldn't say anything of the kind,' he snapped. His irritation was due to his being more sensitive than the rest of us; had he not been, he could not have written such superb dialogue. His sudden explosions of irritability were the penalty his friends had to pay for the immense pleasure that he gave them as a novelist.

In 1924, however, he was not giving them that compensating pleasure, and it was unlucky that he should have fallen in love with the last person equipped to restore his self-confidence and self-esteem. Evelyn has written in *A Little Learning* about Olivia Plunket Greene. I only met her a few times. She was pretty, gracious and well-mannered. She was not negative, since on several points she held strong opinions; but she was profoundly indifferent to the forces that activate most creative lives. She was without personal ambition, and could not understand the hold ambition takes on others. She was supremely un-Balzacian. The need 'to be famous and to be loved' was incomprehensible to her. Many men seek fame in the hope that it will secure them the favours of a woman. But Evelyn must have known that no public success of his would enhance her opinion of him. She was a profound depressant. One values the women who make one feel better about oneself. Olivia invariably diminished Evelyn's self-esteem, not willingly, not consciously: she was basically good natured, but through her indifference to his problems. He would come up to London from his exile as a schoolmaster especially to lunch with her and would return in heavy gloom. He was loyal to her and chivalrous. 'Down there at my school I see her as the symbol of everything from which I am cut off,' he said to me. 'I expect too much; it isn't fair to her.'

Her apathy towards ambition increased his contempt for his friends' complacence over their small successes. They might think themselves terrific figures, but their posturing cut no ice with Olivia Greene. Perhaps in this respect, her indifference was a bond between them. I never saw her after 1927. I have no idea how she reacted to Evelyn's subsequent success. I question if she was much impressed by it. She was consistent.

Evelyn's second school which was the model for Dr Fagan's academy was very much more congenial than the preparatory school in North Wales; it was within reach of London; the pupils were older, it was a training ground for misfits who ordinarily would have been at their public schools; they came, the majority of them, from good families; many of them had charm and intelligence. Evelyn did not feel that he was wasting his time with them. They were capable of appreciating what he had to give. I paid him a couple of visits during the spring and early summer of 1926, staying at the local inn. Once I lectured on the modern novel and found them a responsive audience. He seemed happy enough. He acquired a motor bicycle which made it possible for him to visit friends. But he was headed nowhere. Such a school could only be a dead-end road.

It may surprise many that it was not apparent to himself

and to his friends that a career as a novelist awaited
him. But he did not seem at this time to have any inclina-
tion to write, and what little he did write, did not seem
exceptional. He had not revealed his capacity for satiric
comedy. On the other hand his drawings had a very
definite individuality. At Oxford he designed book
jackets, letter headings and book plates. The illustrations
to the first edition of *Decline and Fall* surely show a very
special talent. It seemed to all of us that it was in this
direction that his true bent lay. It was also what he most
liked doing.

Evelyn was, in fact—at any rate until 1945—almost
the only writer I know who did not like writing. In those
early days he resisted his fate. He was, perhaps, subconsciously aware of the demands that it would make on
him. He was reluctant to yield himself. 'My ambition,'
he wrote, 'was to decorate, design and illustrate. I worked
with the brush and was entirely happy in my employment
of it, as I was not when reading or writing. Later in this
chronicle, I shall note various attempts to escape from
my literary destiny into pleasanter but less appropriate
work with my hands.'

Yet he was doing some writing. Early in 1926 he wrote
a long *avant-garde* short story, *The Balance* which I
included in *Georgian Stories 1926*, of which I was the
editor. Several writers—G. B. Stern in particular—
recognized its originality, and Michael Sadleir asked him
to contribute to his symposium the *New Decameron*. I
have not read *The Balance* for forty years. Evelyn did not
think it worth including in *Mr Loveday's Little Outing*.
But I hope that it will appear in the eventual canon of his
writings. It gives me pleasure to be able to boast that I
was his first editor.

In June 1926, I started on a tour round the world. I

was away nine months; there was no air mail in those days. I made one or two changes of plan. The last letters that I received from England were waiting me in Sydney in December. They had been posted in October. I cannot remember now when I learnt that Evelyn was no longer employed at Dr Fagan's. I never learnt the exact conditions under which he had left. I am not sure that he knew them himself. He had returned late at night on his motor bicycle; the matron had complained and next morning Dr Fagan had reluctantly informed him that he did not consider that a man of his particular qualities was really fitted for an establishment such as his. Dr Fagan did not bear Evelyn the least ill-will. The letter of sympathy that he wrote him four years later, after his divorce, could not have been bettered, even by its recipient.

He reluctantly took Evelyn's side against the matron; an unmarried lady in her middle thirties should have been flattered by nocturnal attentions. But the matron was an essential bulwark in his establishment. To keep her in a good humour, the temporary inconvenience of a young man must be sacrificed. Evelyn had to go.

No doubt my father wrote me a gloomy letter announcing Evelyn's enforced return to Underhill, but I never received it and when I returned to England in mid-March it was to find Evelyn in high spirits. Tom Balston, one of the partners in Duckworth's publishing house, had decided to invest a certain amount of capital in *Young Oxford*. He published Harold Acton's poetry and he gave Evelyn an advance of £50 on an unwritten book about Rossetti. My father, who as a publisher never made an advance without a manuscript, shook his head gloomily. 'Balston will never see that book. I suppose I'll have to make it good.' But rarely has £50 been invested more profitably. Duckworth not only got the book on Rossetti, but all of Evelyn's subsequent travel books. They would have got his novels too, had not Duckworth in Balston's absence been scared of the audacities of *Decline and Fall*. Evelyn was very loyal. As Father Caraman pointed out in his Requiem address, he had the same publishers and the same agent all his life.

In addition to this commission to write a book Evelyn had been taken on the staff of the *Daily Express* as a probationary reporter, and he was in funds. 'I am so glad that you came back now,' he said, 'when I don't need you: I can welcome you without any thought of self advantage.' London in that early summer of 1927 was very gay. A year earlier the general strike had been defeated. The political climate was encouraging and though there was no equivalent in London for the stock market boom in New York, a lot of money was being made and spent. Florence Mills and her 'Blackbirds' were being courted by Mayfair and Belgravia hostesses. 'The Bright Young Things' were news and Evelyn joined the rout. He seemed to be seeing less of Olivia, and more of Evelyn Gardner, a daughter of the late Lord Burghclere.

For him the rout did not last very long. Towards the end of May he invited me to dinner at the Gargoyle Club. He said, when I joined him there, 'We had better make this a good dinner. It is probably the last one I shall be able to give you for quite a while. I was fired from the *Express* this morning.'

It was at that time the practice of the large dailies to hire university graduates as probationers, at less than union rates. If they retained them after six months, they had to pay them the minimum union salary. It was a satisfactory system for everyone. The newspapers got good work cheap; they might make 'a discovery'; the young men got valuable experience. Evelyn's period was up. Not one line that he wrote during it was printed. Fifteen months later the same editor who had fired him, was offering the author of *Decline and Fall* twenty-five guineas a thousand words to write on anything he liked. But at the moment our hero was once again in exceedingly low water.

I was due to catch in mid-June, at Marseilles, a slow French steamer for Tahiti. I was to spend a few days on the way with my parents, who were taking a holiday in Nîmes. I suggested to Evelyn that he should come along with me. On my last evening in London, I gave a goodbye cocktail party. It was composed, as my larger parties tended to be at that time, partly of Bohemians, partly of athletes and their attendant nymphs. Evelyn and I were seen off at Waterloo Station by a group of 'football hearties'. One of them was to serve later as a partial model for Rex Mottram. In the train afterwards, Evelyn said of him, 'I feel awkward with men like that; but I wonder whether he wouldn't be right for Olivia. Vulgar but not common.'

It was a very happy few days that we spent together. We travelled south by daylight; between Dijon and Beaune we rose and bowed reverently to the sacred vineyards, Chambertin, Clos de Vougeot, Corton. We changed trains at Tarascon, and with an hour to wait, drank Tavel, I for the first time, with our sandwiches. In Nîmes we watched in the arena, the film of Conan Doyle's *The Lost World*. Evelyn found it 'appropriately inappropriate'. The photograph of Evelyn and his father sitting at a café table, which illustrated his article 'My Father and I' that appeared in the *Sunday Telegraph* in November 1962, was taken then. As my ship sailed at 11.30 in the morning, Evelyn and I spent my last night in Marseilles. Our evening in the *Vieux Port* provided him with material for *Decline and Fall*. Later he went on with his parents to Les Baux, with which he was delighted. Both my parents agreed that their five days there were among the very happiest that they had spent with him.

It was to a very different atmosphere that I returned early in November. I was myself involved in a love affair with an American married woman, which I have described in my *Early Years*. I knew inside myself that it could have no future; but I had to act as though it had. I had to make quickly enough money to be able to finance the start of a joint life if she elected to elope with me. I did not want to spend money on a flat in London, so I decided to go down into the country, to a small inn, during the week and work upon a novel, spending the week-ends at Underhill. I was no doubt in an edgy mood.

My father had lost during the autumn a dearly loved sister: he was becoming increasingly worried about the future of Chapman & Hall. Evelyn, also, was living at Underhill with his fortunes at their lowest. During the autumn, he had been knocking on innumerable doors. At one point, he had been interviewed by the headmaster of an excellent preparatory school. He had liked the head-master; the headmaster had said, 'You seem to be exactly the man I'm looking for.' Evelyn had returned home jubilant. 'Mr Toad on top,' he told his mother. But the headmaster knew Cruttwell, and that was that.

He had letters of introduction to a few London editors. They all said the same thing. 'The market's crowded; not a glimmer of an opening, old boy; fix up something with the provincial press, then worm your way in from there.' I have not known a single prospective journalist who has not been given that advice. I have not known one who has taken it. Either they have 'crashed Fleet Street' on their own, as buccaneers; or they have failed and sought some other source of livelihood.

Evelyn was receiving from his father a dole of four pounds a week—which he preferred to call an annual allowance of two hundred pounds—and he was a part-time instructor at a third-rate day school in Golders Green. I learnt of this from his mother; he was himself too ashamed to mention it. It is not surprising that he was fractious. I would not care to re-live the November and early December of 1927. Eventually it was agreed that Evelyn should be apprenticed to a carpenter. A premium was paid, and he was to enter into residence with a master of the craft in January. But before that could happen he announced his engagement to Evelyn Gardner.

I was very curious to know what he would say in 'A Little Hope' (which was to have followed *A Little Learning*), of his first marriage. It may well have been that doubt of how to deal with it, contributed to 'the writing block' that held him inoperative during his last year. He must inevitably have held harsh feelings for Evelyn Gardner, but he must have known that nearly everyone found her a delightful person; certainly I did. She was pretty and neat and gracious; she had winning ways; she had *race* but unobtrusively. She was friendly, welcoming, and cosy. She spent Christmas at Underhill. It was a modest house, compared with the many grand ones with which she was familiar. But she was appreciative of everything that was done for her. She made herself very pleasant to my parents. Recognizing that Evelyn and I were 'at outs' she put herself at once 'to set that straight'. And she succeeded.

She and Evelyn were a delightful team; they were so at ease, so affectionate together, their having the same Christian name was an amusing bond. They were called 'He-Evelyn' and 'She-Evelyn'. But of course from every worldly point of view, it was a ridiculous engagement.

Lord Burghclere, a man of great distinction, was from one point of view a self-made man. His widow, who had adored him and was bitterly disappointed at not having had a son who could carry on the title, was one of the Carnarvon Herberts, so that when at a later date Evelyn became engaged to Laura Herbert, the same great-aunt Lady Victoria Herbert who had protested against his marriage to her neice was able to exclaim, 'What, this young man again, I thought we'd seen the last of him.'

She was far from being the only relative who objected. Lady Burghclere was not rich. She had two other daughters; no doubt the family could have rallied to a deserving cause, a hundred from this uncle, three hundred from that aunt. But my brother did not seem a deserving cause. The Baroness made enquiries at Oxford. And Cruttwell for the last time had the satisfaction of performing 'his unwelcome duty'. My father and Lady Burghclere met; there was, as politicians say 'a frank exchange of views'. Evelyn remarked on how useful it was at such a time to have a father with an unblemished reputation. But there was no public announcement of the betrothal in *The Times*. One thing was certain, if He-Evelyn was to marry She-Evelyn, the union could not be supported by cabinets and chairs from Sussex. Evelyn could evade his literary destiny no longer. As P. G. Wodehouse would have said, 'he bit the bullet' and went to a small country-inn to write *Decline and Fall*.

At the end of January I went to California. I was not back until early May. This time I found Evelyn in high good humour. *Decline and Fall* was finished and his book on Rossetti had either just been or was shortly to be published. A critical study of Rossetti cannot expect a large sale, but it was well reviewed; the *Times Literary Supplement* noticing it at length, referred to its author as Miss Waugh, which gave Evelyn the opportunity of making an amusing ripost, and he was delighted to receive a letter of congratulation from Rebecca West in which she praised in particular his flashes of wit, recognizing in advance of anyone the eventual direction of his writing. The two Evelyns were as charming a team as ever and though there was still no definite engagement, there was a general understanding that if *Decline and Fall* was a success, family opposition would be relaxed.

I read *Decline and Fall* while it was under consideration at Duckworth's. I had no doubt of its quality. I found it hilariously funny, and was astonished at the ridiculous corrections that Duckworth's wanted him to make in it. They were shocked for instance at a 'debagged' undergraduate running round the quad without his trousers. Tom Balston was, as I have said, away on a holiday; and Gerald Duckworth who was a considerable friend of Lady Burghclere was nervous about her reaction to the book. Evelyn could not accept their emendations. He knew that the book was good, though he wondered whether he should not publish it under a different name, on the principle that a poet publishes his detective stories under a pseudonym. Could a serious literary critic sponsor Captain Grimes?

I do not keep a diary and cannot recall the exact sequence of events. My parents went for a holiday in early June, and it is my belief that my father left his fellow directors to decide whether or not Chapman & Hall should publish *Decline and Fall*. He admired the book immensely but he was hypersensitive on the use of the firm's money to finance his family. Ironically enough the decisive vote in Evelyn's favour was cast by a scientist who three years earlier had been voted onto the board after a stormy shareholder's meeting, to ensure that the firm's money was not wasted on *avant-garde* belles-lettres when such sound profits could be made on 'mathematics for engineers'. When the final acceptance letter was sent I do not know, but it was certainly while my parents were still away on a holiday that Harold Acton and Evelyn came round to my flat to announce that the Evelyns were being married clandestinely in two days' time, to invite me to the ceremony at St Paul's Church, Baker Street, and to luncheon afterwards at Boulestin's.

In *Memoirs of an Aesthete* Harold Acton has given a charming account of the occasion. There were only six of us there in all, Lady Pansy Pakenham (later Lamb) and Robert Byron being the other two. It was all very sweet and touching. She-Evelyn appeared to giggle when He-Evelyn promised to endow her with all his worldly goods. They looked so young, so innocent, and so defence-less, to be launched upon such rough seas. One prayed for charitable tides.

Five months later it seemed that our prayers had been amply granted. London mantelpieces were adorned with cards of invitation to his housewarming cocktail party at 17a Canonbury Square. This was in Islington, a section of London that had been occupied by city merchants in the middle of the nineteenth century. The houses were solid, well built, in the Georgian style. You would imagine yourself in Bloomsbury. For fifty years it had been occupied by humble families and Evelyn got a spacious first-floor flat, unfurnished, for a pound a week.

The invitation cards were decorated with maps showing guests how to get there. Buckingham Palace was marked on its left hand side and the caption read 'Routes from Buckingham Palace to 17a Canonbury Square'. Actually his home was far from inaccessible. It was a minute's walk from the Angel tube station and a 19 bus could get you there from Piccadilly Circus in twenty minutes.

The party was also in celebration of *Decline and Fall*. It had been published a few weeks earlier. It was not a best-seller, but it was a seller and it was being 'talked about'. It was recognized that a new and exciting figure had appeared upon the stage. The road to success ran broad and clear.

The large flat was crowded, with new friends and old. It was there that I saw for the first time Diana Mitford, whose friendship was later to mean so much to Evelyn. She was then, on the brink of her marriage to Bryan Guinness, in the full, rich spring of her flowering beauty. I have seldom been to such a genial party. Everyone was so happy for the Evelyns' sake. They had gambled on one another—a hundred-to-one chance—and they had 'brought it off'.

On the first Monday in December, I sailed for the West Indies. On the Sunday evening I had a very small good-bye party at the Gargoyle to which the Evelyns came. They were in high spirits. The company that owned the luxury cruising liner the *Meteor* had offered them a free holiday in the Mediterranean, in return for publicity in a travel book. They were to sail directly after Christmas. It was to be their real honeymoon. In June they had only been able to afford a fortnight in a country inn. I looked back a year, to that grim December when Evelyn unemployed and seemingly unemployable, had been so cantankerous. What a miracle She-Evelyn had achieved! But for her he would never have written *Decline and Fall*: he would still be fiddling with fretsaws; and was there any reason to believe that he would have been any more resolute as a carpenter than he had been as an art student at Heatherley's? How much could happen in a year!

I was away for five and a half months. Once again I frequently changed my plans; inter-island travel was not easy then; mail accumulated in ports I failed to reach when I was expected, so that I did not learn of the drama of the Evelyns' trip until afterwards. Nineteen-twenty-nine provided one of the most tempestuous Januaries within record. It snowed in Monte Carlo, and She-Evelyn caught pneumonia. She was dangerously ill, and her brother-in-law, Geoffrey Fry, who was then Stanley Baldwin's secretary, was active on the diplomatic telephones. Evelyn had to spend several weeks in a hotel in Port Said, visiting his wife in hospital; a stay that gave him unique copy for one of his most amusing travel chapters. It was an anxious time, but by the time I learnt of it, she had recovered.

We returned to England almost simultaneously. They dined with me their first week in London. It was delightful to see how affectionate they were together. Evelyn was getting well-paid commissions from the newspapers. He had acquired the right material for his travel book. He asked if he might dedicate it to me, sharing the dedication with Alistair Graham, the 'Lennox' of *A Little Learning*, inscribing it 'to two other travellers'. I fancy that the idea of the dedication was She-Evelyn's. On that same evening she said to Evelyn, 'Have you told Alec about the dedication?' She was consistently resolved to keep Evelyn and myself on good terms with one another. And I believe that it was because the dedication was her idea that when the book was eventually published, it was dedicated not to Alistair and myself, but to Bryan and Diana Guinness. He wanted to expunge every trace of She-Evelyn's influence. In England the book was entitled *Labels*, but in the U.S.A., *A Bachelor Abroad*—an ironic title for a description of one's honeymoon.

Climatically the summer of 1929 offered a full rich recompense for the appalling winter. On the vineyards of the Médoc grapes ripened to a lovely vintage. Socially there was a general heightening of tempo. There was, as I have said, no equivalent in Europe for the boom on the New York stock market, but a great many Americans in

Paris and London were living in terms of Wall Street. They helped to set the pace. Parties became more eccentric. By the Charing Cross Pier, a river boat, the *Friendship*, was hired for private parties. I remember a tropical party there—of which Vyvyan Holland was one of the hosts. It was a hot, still night; there was a curious kick out of misbehaving in a sarong in the dusk of the bows when along the embankment and over Westminster bridge dutiful citizens were hurrying to catch a last train home to Surbiton.

The pace was so keen that Evelyn, who had to get the back of his new novel broken, decided to go into the country for three weeks, to the cœnobitic refuge of a small hotel bedroom; She-Evelyn had two sisters in London and innumerable friends. She would be all right. On the third day of his retreat, he telegraphed 'Novel moving fast all characters seasick'. The novel was *Vile Bodies*. A novelist is at his most serene when he is working in a small hotel bedroom, for the sake of somebody he loves, thinking at the end of each day's work, 'I'm five pages nearer to her'. I imagine that those three weeks must have been very happy ones for Evelyn. He must have been well aware of how supremely excellent those first chapters were.

To myself, not working at the time and caught up by the movement of a crowded season, it seemed only half a week later, when dining at Underhill my mother said, 'Did you know that Evelyn was back?' 'Already, I must ring up.' I called directly after dinner. She-Evelyn answered. Her voice sounded strange. A sentence or two and I realized that she was crying. 'It's terrible, it's terrible. I can't talk on the telephone. Can I meet you somewhere?' We arranged to have supper at the Gargoyle. My parents were next door in the book-room while I was telephoning; they had not heard the conversation. My

mother was expecting me to stay the night, but I explained
that I had writing to do next day and that I wanted to
wake early beside my papers.

In the Gargoyle, my sister-in-law told me that she had
fallen in love with John Heygate, a young man on the
fringe of authorship, who later inherited a baronetcy from
his uncle, and who was currently employed on the B.B.C.
I had met him once or twice. He was a perfectly pleasant
fellow. There was nothing against him; most people liked
him, mildly. He was not particularly good looking. He
was not particularly anything. 'How long has this been
going on?' I asked.

'It's only just begun.'

We were together for close upon two hours. It was one
of those long, wandering discussions that keep returning
on its tracks.

'How is Evelyn taking it?' I asked.

'It's terrible. He's drinking much too much. It makes
him feel ill. And he thinks I'm trying to poison him.'

Poor, poor Evelyn, racked by a 'Belladonna' hallucina-
tion.

'You always seemed so happy together,' I said.

'Yes, I suppose I was,' then after a pause, 'but never
as happy as I've been with my sisters.'

That seemed an extraordinary thing for a wife to say
about a husband.

'What are you going to do?' I asked.

'That's what we've not decided yet.'

They did not take long deciding. Within a week
Evelyn telephoned to ask if he could come round to see
me. He told me that he was going to divorce his wife, and
asked me to tell our parents. 'It's going to be a great blow
to them,' I said. He laughed wryly. 'What about me?' At
the end of our talk, he said, 'The trouble about the world
today is that there's not enough religion in it. There's

nothing to stop young people doing whatever they feel like doing at the moment.'

I have no doubt that the break-up of his marriage hastened his conversion to the Roman Catholic faith. Recently I wrote and asked Christopher Hollis whether Evelyn had ever discussed the matter with him previously. Hollis replied that he had not; and that when *Vile Bodies* was published in January 1930, he made, in a letter of congratulation, a light-hearted reference to Father Rothschild. To his surprise Evelyn told him that he was taking a course of instruction. Evelyn was received into the Church that summer.

The news was a great shock to my parents, particularly to my mother. My father was distressed primarily on her account. 'Your poor mother,' he said, 'your poor, poor mother.' Everyone who discussed it at the time talked of it in terms of her. Only she thought of it in terms of Evelyn.

It was a blow that left a permanent scar on Evelyn. He had given himself to She-Evelyn and to his marriage, without reservations. He had trusted her completely; he was vulnerable from every angle. He had no armour against her betrayal of his trust. He was too much an artist to indulge a personal resentment in his novels, yet the characters of Tony Last and Charles Ryder show how incessantly the old wound throbbed. His tongue would not have been so sharp, his riposts so acid, had not that throbbing needed to be assuaged.

The whole thing was tragic, yet even so, it is impossible to doubt that 'the divinity that shapes our ends' was serving its own purposes in bringing Evelyn Gardner into Evelyn's life. But for her he might never have begun to write. My mother indeed who was distrustful of the written word, said more than once, 'If it hadn't been for

that She-Evelyn, he might have designed lovely furniture.' 'But Mother dear,' I would protest, 'think of the
books he's written.' 'I know, Alec dear, I know; but
furniture is so useful; besides he would have been happier
designing furniture.'

There she was no doubt right; but the implacable
destiny, whose slave he had become, is unconcerned with
the individual's happiness. 'Half a beast is the great god
Pan.' Maugham would not have been the writer he
became had his marriage been a success. Nor would
Evelyn. He made his first trip to Abyssinia in the
autumn of 1930; for six years he was on the move. Until
his marriage had been annulled he could not remarry.
Those six years of travel gave him the material he needed.
He could not have taken a wife upon those travels,
certainly not She-Evelyn, who was delicate in health. A
novelist to get the material he needs must travel alone
or with another man. Had the Evelyns' marriage been a
success, he would with his absorption in the world of
fashion, have concentrated as Maugham would have
done, on social satires that might well have become brittle
and superficial.

Did She-Evelyn subconsciously realize that? Her
marriage to John Heygate was short-lived, but she was
genuinely in love with him at the beginning. Would she
though have been prepared to let herself fall in love with
him—there is always a point at which one can draw back
—had she not felt that since the success of *Decline and
Fall* she was cast in the wrong role? The 'He-Evelyn, She-
Evelyn, "Orphans of the Storm" Idyll' had been one
thing; it was quite another to be the wife, companion,
confidant, counseller and bastion of a great man of letters
—the role that Laura Herbert was to fill later, so gladly,
so proudly, so lovingly, and with so triumphant a success.
I do not suggest for a moment that She-Evelyn argued

it out to herself that way, but I believe that her instinct warned her that the marriage would not work.

Evelyn did not remarry till the spring of 1937. It was an extremely successful marriage. The war intervened and he was not able to settle down to domestic life until the autumn of 1945. By then he had assembled his material. The conditions of a happy home life which he described in *The Ordeal of Gilbert Pinfold* provided him with the calm he needed for his writing. But all the time he was drawing on his past—on his years of travel and the war years.

Our mother was afraid that the break-up of his marriage would cause a collapse similar to that which followed his failure in schools. She was afraid that he would start drinking. She thought of him still as her little boy, who needed protection, for whom she provided sanctuary, but now that he had at last accepted his destiny, there was no looking back. He was armoured, professionally. He started the legal machinery for his divorce, disposed of his interests in Canonbury Square, moved his clothes back to Underhill; then went into the country to complete *Vile Bodies*. There is no sign in that brilliantly comic book of the unhappiness through which he was passing; there is no change of tempo or of temper between the later grief-shadowed chapters and those earlier ones which he had written in the excited expectation of a return to Canonbury Square as soon as he had earned his right to be there. There is no undercurrent of gloom.

He worked fast; and the novel was finished by December. I read it in proof at Christmas, which we both spent at Underhill; the last Christmas, as it proved, that we were both to spend there. It was very far from being an unhappy time. My father had just retired from the manag-

ing directorship of Chapman & Hall. We were happy
for his sake that he was spared those bleak, chill hours on
the windswept platform at Golders Green tube station.
Evelyn was constantly in the company of the Bryan
Guinnesses, who had a share in a large family house on
the edge of the Whitestone pond. Diana's first child was
shortly to be born. Evelyn must have had these weeks in
mind when he wrote *Work Suspended*. Their friendship
was a great consolation to him then. They gave him for
Christmas a gold pocket watch that he dearly prized. A
year before at my good-bye dinner at the Gargoyle, I had
thought of how much had happened during the last year.
How much more had happened during this.

Vile Bodies was published in early January. My father
had little doubt that it would, in terms of sales, largely
surpass *Decline and Fall*. 'The Bright Young People' and
the eccentricities of the Cavendish hotel had far more
popular appeal than the staff of an unusual school.
His prophecy was abundantly fulfilled. Best-sellerdom
depends on timing, and the timing of *Vile Bodies* was
exactly right. When I read the MS., I asked if the slang
of 'drunk-making' and 'shy-making' was his own inven-
tion. No, he said, the young Guinness set was using it. A
month later, a few days before the publication of the book,
I noticed that its use had spread beyond the narrow radius
of that set. In another two months it would have reached
the far fringes of the fashionable world. Within six months
it would have been 'old hat'. Evelyn caught the tide at its
flood. Ten days after publication, every conversation was
peppered with 'poor-makings', 'drunk-makings', 'rich-
makings'; Evelyn had set a vogue.

In early February I caught a French liner for East
Africa. I had planned to go to Zanzibar, but I learnt on

my arrival at Mombasa, that my travel book *Hot Countries*
was the Literary Guild choice for May. I ought certainly
to be in America for its publication. I shortened my visit
and made back for France, where I would be within easy
reach of letters and of cables. I decided to spend two weeks
in Villefranche, before sailing for New York. Evelyn
wrote to me that he was planning a trip to Monte Carlo
and that he would leave a little earlier, so as to join me on
the way.

We had five days together. Though we did not know
it, they marked the close of that succession of shared
experiences that had begun in boyhood. We had each
reached a watershed. When I had received that cable at
Mombasa, I had visualized its consequence in terms of an
Elizabethan, piratical plundering of the Spanish Main. I
did not realize that my projected visit to the U.S.A.
would begin that absorption in and ultimate identification
with the American scene that was eventually to make New
York my operative base instead of London.

Evelyn, too, was at the start of a new life. He was
without responsibilities; he had money in the bank; there
was every reason for believing that the flow of money
would be maintained, as indeed it proved to be. He had,
he told me, a romantic rendezvous in Monte Carlo. He
was able for the first time in his life to say to an attractive
female: 'What ghastly weather we are having. Don't
you think three weeks in Monte Carlo would be a good
idea?'

He was undergoing instruction as a Roman Catholic
and expected to be received into the Church during the
summer. This would involve a complete reorientation
of his inner life. Mentally and spiritually he would be at
peace. Socially too, his life would have a different focus.
He was to find himself increasingly at ease with fellow
Catholics, and less at ease with members of other faiths.

The fact that he could not, until his marriage to Evelyn Gardner was annulled, remarry with the Church's sanction, was to place him in an anomalous position. He was neither bound nor free.

C. M. Bowra in a warm and interpretative passage about him in his *Memories*, speaks of his falling in love but not with the right girl, and from this he suffered acutely. The incident is placed between the annulment and his second marriage. I do not know to whom Sir Maurice refers, and I wonder whether he has not chronologically misplaced Olivia Greene. I suggest this because he gives the date of Evelyn's marriage as 1936 when it was 1937, and writes on the previous page, 'In the later twenties Evelyn led a very varied social life, if only to console himself for the collapse of his marriage.' Evelyn's social period was 1930–6.

It is my belief that such *passades* as Evelyn may have had in this period were brief and shallow, and I do know that he drew back from what might well have been a profound emotional experience with a young and prominent actress, who was in a mood to welcome enterprise from him, because he did not want to involve a women whom he respected in the kind of confusion in which the Catholic hero of Graham Greene's *The Heart of the Matter* involved the heroine. 'I am sorry,' says the priest, 'for anyone happy and ignorant who gets mixed up, in that way, with one of us.' Evelyn was resolved to avoid that. In compensation his emotional nature was consoled and released by one or two deep Platonic friendships—*tendresses* is, I think, the word for them—in particular that with Lady Diana Cooper.

But all that lay in the future. At the moment he was on the brink of things, as I was. We were both at anchor, waiting to embark on the high seas, in a state of suspended animation.

That is the reason, probably, why I can remember so little of what we talked about during those five days. I can remember the things we did; he gave me an excellent champagne luncheon at the Ruhl. Josef Bard—Dorothy Thompson's first husband—was living at Cap d'Ail with his second wife, the painter Eileen Agar, and we lunched there, cosily and amply. Evelyn had brought a sword stick, I cannot think why, which he flashed very impressively in the sailors' bar in the Rue de Poilu that I frequented. There was a shop in Nice that advertised as '*fou rire*' practical jokes of which we used to take back samples to the waitresses who served that bar. It was a happy, harmonious time. Most days there would be in my hotel box the grey-green envelope of a cable and I would walk up the hill to the post office to send an answer. Where so much has been pulled down there and rebuilt, the post office is unaltered behind its flowering garden plot. I never pass it now without remembering those almost daily visits. My thoughts were in America; I was really living somewhere else, as Evelyn was.

The five days went by quickly. I planned to catch in Nice the train for Paris that is now called 'Le Mistral'. Evelyn wanted to lunch in Monte Carlo. Our trains went within ten minutes of each other; so we took the same taxi up the hill. There was no station bar where we could pour a final libation to our fortunes. I crossed to the southern platform; and we sat by our suitcases in the sun, facing each other, with the tracks between us, waiting for our different trains to take us on our different roads.

Theodore Dreiser, Grant
Richards, Sir Hugh Lane

Grant Richards, 1920

The Noble Art of Self-defence, cartoon by Will Dyson. Caption:
Now no one can say that *Cakes and Ale* was meant for me.

Opposite:
J. B. Priestley's Cricket Eleven. Top row: left to right—
Gerald Gould, Miles Malleson, James Laver, R. C. Sher-
riff, Alec Waugh, Ivor Brown. Seated: A. J. Cronin,
Arthur Bliss, J.B.P., J. C. Squire, Ralph Straus

L.N.A.

Evelyn, outside his home at
Combe Florey

The two Evelyns (E.W. and his first wife)

Evelyn's family, containing everyone except Jerisa's husband (she is third from the left). Auberon Herbert is on the extreme left. The fierce female in the center is E.W.'s mother-in-law, the Hon. Mrs. Aubrey Herbert.

Mme Yevonde

Alec and Evelyn Waugh, 1953

E. S. P. Haynes—"The Lawyer" in his garden

Caricature by Will Dyson of
Vyvyan Holland, on the occasion
of his reading a paper on Bores
to "Ye Sette of Odd Volumes"

STUDYING HIS SUBJECT

Michael Arlen

Alec Waugh with W.S.M., Villefranche, 1963

Alec Waugh, at the MacDowell Colony, March 1965

PART TWO

13
Arthur Waugh's Last Years

When I was young, we were taught history in terms of battles and betrayals; of treaties and capitulations, of crowns and dynasties. Henry V was addressed as 'England' and Louis XIV as 'France'. It was assumed that a country prospered or declined as its monarch's stock rose and fell. No one wondered how the people fared under these capricious changes. Spain was England's enemy through the second half of the sixteenth and most of the seventeenth century. We were taught to assess the power of Spain by the defeat of the Armada. We were never taught that for a century and a half the stupendous wealth of the New World was poured into the coffers of Seville, while the people of Spain starved.

It is fashionable today to regard the 1930s as a period of ignominy for England and the start of the next decade as Britain's Finest Hour. Yet actually for many Britons the world continued to be navigated on an even keel. My father who was born in August 1866 died in June 1943 and I suspect that the last ten years of his life were the happiest.

My father has been described at length in my brother's autobiography *A Little Learning* and in my *Early Years*. Both pictures are drawn with love, devotion and in admiration. They are supplementary to each other. I was closer, far closer to him than my brother was. I was in far greater sympathy with him. Evelyn and he were constantly in conflict. They were irritated by each other. In my mother's opinion they were too like each other. For that very reason, my brother understood him better. *A Little Learning* gave me a fresh insight into a number of facets of my father of which I was aware only subconsciously. In a novel there is nothing more difficult to depict than the 'good character', the 'good influence', the man or woman of integrity. There are not enough contrasting shades. For that reason the reader will get a more vivid picture of my father from *A Little Learning* than from my *Early Years*. And it is a very sympathetic picture. Any father would be proud to have had such a tribute paid to him.

A Little Learning stops in the year 1925. My *Early Years* stops in 1930. Nineteen-thirty was, as I have said, a watershed for me. So was it for my father. At the end of 1929 he resigned his managing directorship of Chapman & Hall, retaining his chairmanship of the board, and acting as reader and adviser, working at his home in Hampstead. His salary was less, but it was adequate now that he had only himself and my mother to support.

It was a great relief for him. The years between 1925 and 1930 had been hard. He was over sixty and he was tiring. His chest was troubling him. In camp as a volunteer when a quite young man he had, through sleeping on a wet pillow, set up trouble in his left ear and he was very deaf. During the war he had as an economy taken to coming home for lunch and he put a heavy strain upon himself by continuing this habit. He spent three hours a day travelling between Henrietta Street and Underhill; he was exhausted by the pull up the hill before lunch and the hurried departure afterwards. He had reached the age when he needed the restorative of a nap after lunch.

In winter, Underhill was a cold house. The wind blew straight under the front door into the hall. There was no central heating. The book-room was uncarpeted, and the French windows opened onto a veranda. There was a direct draught through the house. My father had grown

corpulent. He should have dieted, but he had a Latin
love of bread. Often after dinner he would be forced to
stand up beside the mantelpiece struggling for breath.
When he left the warmth of the book-room, the change
of air struck chill upon his chest, and he would be convulsed with asthma.

The office had become a worry. Hypersensitive to
criticism, he had not felt since the *coup d'état* which I
described in my *Early Years* that he was master there.
Evelyn's Oxford friends had referred to him as Chapman
& Hall, which later they abbreviated into the nickname
Chapman; he had liked it at the start but now, so my
mother told me, he discouraged it; he no longer felt that
he was 'Chapman'.

He had no cause for doubting his staff's loyalty. On
the twenty-fifth anniversary of his appointment to the
managing directorship they staged a surprise for him: a
lunch in a private room at the Florence attended by every
member of the staff where he was presented with a book
signed by all of them. He was very touched. But in small
ways and all the time he was conscious of his changed
position.

He was also worried by the yearly balance sheet. The
basic financial situation was unsound. The firm was not
doing badly. It was publishing good books, and at a profit,
but not at a sufficient profit to recompense both cumulative
preference and ordinary shareholders. I was very glad that
I was no longer a member of its board. As an outsider I
could give my father sympathy in a way that I could
never have done had I been still employed there, teased
by the knowledge that something must be done, and soon.

As to the ultimate outcome I had little doubt. Two can
live as cheaply as one, and amalgamation with another
firm would reduce overheads. With double the capital
four times as many books could be issued without adding

to the salary list. I foresaw this, in the same way that early in a long novel you foresee the eventual end—whose fortunes will rise and whose will fall and who will marry whom—but how it is all to be brought about you have no idea; if you had, you would not bother to go on reading. I knew how it must end but I did not see how the inevitable amalgamation was to be achieved without my father losing his appointment.

His retirement from the managing directorship offered him a respite. It also gave him leisure for his own writing. Nineteen-thirty was the firm's centenary year and he wrote its history under the title *A Hundred Years of Publishing*. The book was written as publicity, and certain of the later chapters were phrased so as to give pleasure to authors, members of the staff and personalities in the book trade: but its early chapters with their anecdotes of Dickens, Trollope and Meredith are part of literary history and give it a real value as a work of reference. John Farrar has told me he invariably ends his lectures on publishing by reading its last paragraph with its picture of the publisher sitting at the end of the day among the books that bear his imprint.

As soon as this book was finished my father set to work upon his autobiography. He was happy writing it, yet even so he was fretted about Chapman & Hall's future. He still dreaded the annual shareholders' meeting. Though the meetings were attended by a mere handful, there were innumerable other shareholders scattered over the country whom he had never seen, to whom one day it might occur to wonder whether some use might not be made of these apparently valueless scraps of paper. He felt he was sitting on a volcano, with no right to hope as the father of the founder of the firm's fortunes had, that 'something would turn up'.

But in fact it did.

Carl Brandt once said to me, 'If ever you have a fluke or a coincidence in a short story it must be an unlucky one for the chief characters.' And it was by one of those interventions of providence that occur in real life, but in a novel would appear contrived, that the fortunes of Chapman & Hall were salvaged.

The *deus ex machina* was Philip (now Lord) Inman. Inman is a mystery figure, much of his mystery lying in the fact that he does not look in the least mysterious. He is tall, handsome, affable, hospitable; he enjoys good company; he is determined but not aggressive. He is one of those busy men who never look as though they were in a hurry. He first made his mark in public life as the secretary of the Charing Cross Hospital, which like all hospitals at that time was supported by voluntary contributions. Inman had a genius for raising funds. He had an eye for politics and in Attlee's second government he was Lord Privy Seal: yet he was never part of a party machine. He is an independent man, the cat that walks by itself. That is in large part his strength. He knows what he wants and what he does not want.

His intervention in the affairs of Chapman & Hall made the last decade of my father's life a happy one. In his autobiography Philip Inman has told how he came to be associated with the firm. I, as my father's son and an ex-director, saw the situation from a slightly different angle. For me it had an element of comedy.

Chapman & Hall had published a kind of autobiography by Inman called *Oil and Wine* describing how he had raised funds for the Charing Cross Hospital. The book had been suggested by the secretary to the company, A. W. Gatfield, who was by now on the board. During the negotiations a certain measure of friendship grew up between Gatfield and Inman and it seemed to Gatfield that Inman was the kind of man who was needed on the board. Today Inman is a well-known public figure, but in 1934 no one knew very much about him, apart from his connection with the hospital, and the board could not see in what way he was likely to be of help to them. They turned down Gatfield's suggestion.

'I am not used,' Inman said to my father at a later date, 'to having the offer of my services declined.'

An affluent but humbly born citizen of New Orleans, who had been blackballed by the Jockey Club, bought up the race track and turned it into a cemetery which acquired so much chic that the patrician families who had refused his application for membership now requested the privilege of taking up their ever-lasting rest on the ground they had denied him. Inman decided to buy up Chapman & Hall, and Gatfield gave him his assistance.

It was a palace revolution. For the moment my father's position looked uncertain. But Inman, on realizing the kind of people with whom he had to deal, decided to work with and not against the existing régime.

Inman achieved a miracle at Henrietta Street. He acquired the ordinary shares, pacified the preference shareholders, wrote down the capital and within a few months Chapman & Hall was flourishing. For him the enterprise was a kind of hobby. He got fun out of it. It was something new, another iron in his well-banked fire. For my father it was a relief and a release. He had no longer to worry about the firm's future or his own. He ceded the chairmanship of the board to Inman and concentrated as vice-chairman on his duties as consultant. At about the same time his domestic routine was simplified. In the summer of 1933 he sold Underhill and took a first and second storey maisonette in Highgate, a few yards above the school cricket ground, in a short row of houses that stood back from Hampstead Lane behind a row of elms. The two main rooms faced north, but the room that my father used as a combined bedroom and study, faced south and was warm and sunny; there was a certain amount of traffic along the road, but he was too deaf to be disturbed by it.

He could scarcely have made a luckier choice. Highgate village has maintained many of the characteristics of a small county town. It has a life of its own. There is The Grove with its long trail of literary associations, from Coleridge to John Drinkwater and J. B. Priestley: there is the Highgate Institute; the tradespeople have the manners of those who have been used to dealing with the same families for generations. There is the school cricket ground where my father went every Saturday in summer. Not so far away is Ken Wood, acquired by the nation, where he took his walks.

When he first moved to Underhill, North End itself had had certain village attributes which Evelyn described in *A Little Learning*, but they have not survived the coming of the Tube and the creation of Golders Green. Being a householder in North End Road did not make my father a member of a community whereas being the sub-tenant of a flat in Highgate did. He began to make friends among his neighbours, which was what he needed now that he went into London only once a week. He soon became a familiar sight in Highgate, with his grey Homburg hat, his white hair curling above his collar, his short thick-set figure, his slow walk and the black poodle by his side.

His health was better now that he did not have to make those early starts for Henrietta Street; and the board meetings that had been such a penance to him when he was managing director, when he had felt that every

Friday his week's work was being subjected to criticism, were pleasantly dramatic interludes now that he arrived as the adviser, the elder statesman, patient, wise, encouraging. He looked forward to Fridays.

Nor did he lose the close touch with authors which had been one of the recompenses of his routine. He read every manuscript and corresponded with the authors, who very often would come out to take tea with him at Highgate.

The following letter that he wrote to Douglas Goldring is a typical example of his tactfully encouraging approach to authors.

I have just read 'Pot Luck in England' with very great enjoyment. It seems to me, if I may say so, full to the brim of personality and appeal. The descriptions of scenery and character are intimately interpretative. I know many of the places well and you have pinned their very souls to the paper. The book ought to inspire the wandering spirits of road and meadow and comfort those who now have to linger in the loggia. It is a rare good book indeed.

BUT—(there is always a but—) I wondered if you could be induced to reconsider a few of the phrases and references here and there, which in a world where no two people think alike, might conceivably affect the book's popularity. I know you like to speak your mind; and that the acid of your *ripost* is to you like the woodcock's trail to the *gourmet*, but if you could deny yourself the satisfaction, here and there, I honestly believe you would be glad later on. I was asked to read the MS. for libel. I found no libel but I did trip over a few comments . . . The Author's Society, Lord Londonderry, Sir Thomas Inskip, Howard Spring? I sent a list to Gatfield. If it finds its way back to you, may I commend it to your sympathetic consideration? At any rate it was made in the friendliest possible spirit by Yours sincerely,

Arthur Waugh.

As I said at the beginning of this chapter, the historian of the future will present the English of the late 1930s as anxious and apprehensive: shaken by crisis after crisis; the Spanish War, the Abdication, the trade recession, the Anschluss, Munich; a gradual drifting to disaster, but actually, as regards the individual, life went on for many very much the same. Arnold Bennett has told in his preface to *The Old Wives' Tale* that he realized as he was approaching the middle of his book that Sophie would have been in Paris during the siege of 1870. To acquire local colour he made enquiries of his concierge as to what he remembered of the siege. Bennett was surprised to find that he remembered very little: that the landmarks of his life were the death of a parent, marriage, the loss in accident of a child, this christening and that funeral. The details of the siege were as fugitive as the headlines of last week's paper.

It was that way with my father. From the year 1934 onwards, he was able to enjoy his leisure. He woke early and on fine mornings took a short stroll before breakfast. He could read his letters quietly and think out his answers to them. He had not to sandwich his replies between telephone calls and office interruptions. He would read a manuscript, then he would take another walk; if it was a cold day he might go to the Institute to read the weeklies. He had fallen into the modern habit of taking before lunch a glass of sherry and a biscuit; very often he had company. After lunch there was the crossword puzzle, till he dozed off in his chair. There was then a manuscript to finish, or perhaps a report to draft. He was in daily touch with Henrietta Street. As often as not someone came to tea: or else there would be a visitor between tea and dinner. His friends knew that they would always find him in. By staying in one place you can see more people than by rushing round in circles. He let life come to him. When I read his diaries I was surprised to find how much he had found to do, how many people he had met during his years of retirement. At no time in his life did he go in for organized entertaining. He did not give lunch or dinner parties, but there was a constant coming and going: a continuous informal hospitality. The spare room was in use most weeks.

In 1932 I married, in 1937 Evelyn married. My father was delighted with his daughters-in-law: he was proud of being a grandfather.

Not many Englishmen of his age were happier than he was on the first of January in that year of unlucky omen 1939. Nor would I say that he was in a very different mood, two years later, when the worst had happened, when for so many the future was completely black. Evelyn was under orders for the Middle East, my wife, who had been brought up in Australia, had taken our children there. But I had been posted to London as a staff captain in the Ministry of Mines.

I had a flat in Buckingham Street, Adelphi, but I spent every week-end at Highgate. My mother would lunch with me in London and we would go to a film afterwards, returning to Hampstead Lane by six o'clock. They were happy times. We did not talk much about the actual war, we gossiped of what our different friends were doing, of the difficulties of war-time publishing, of how one writer's stock was going up while another's was going down, talking as we had ten years before, assuming that we should be talking in just that way in 1950; never letting the thought intrude that in ten years' time England would be a very different place, that there might indeed no longer exist an England that we would recognize as England.

At a War Intelligence course at Swanage that I had attended early in the year we had been set problems beginning, 'It is the year 1943, we have invaded the continent of Europe. . . .' As my syndicate sat down to work out its solution, I would say to myself, 'What with?' Many must have been thinking the same thing, but they said nothing, nor did I. There were certain possibilities we declined to look at. That is one of the advantages of not being a logical race. The French were too logical. They added up the score and then packed up.

Did my father ever wonder what would happen to himself, his home and his wife if England were invaded? He never did out loud. In peace-time he had been apprehensive, worrying in September about what would happen in April at the shareholders' meeting. But in war-time he went on quietly with his routine, writing to his friends, having friends in for tea or sherry, reading manu-scripts and preparing reports on them, discussing the manuscripts with authors, taking out the poodle on the Heath, telephoning the office daily, reading the weekly papers at the Hampstead Institute, in the summer watch-ing the school cricket matches at the Highgate Ground and talking with the groundsman, the old England cricketer A. E. Knight.

From the business point of view he had little to worry over. Books invariably do well in war-time, they did particularly well in this last war when the quota of paper was strictly rationed and every book sold out, irrespective of its quality. Publishers were able to dispose of old stock that had not moved for years and had been written off as valueless. A large part of Chapman & Hall's stock was burnt and they received in compensation £18,000. Normally they would have been delighted at such a deal, but in 1941 they would have got even more for it from the public. It was a puzzling time for authors. They had no idea how many copies would have been sold if the demand could have been met. They could not tell how they stood. It was cruel luck on those authors who published their best books during the war.

Publishers had their problems but they were very different from those which had harassed them in peace-time. They had not to worry about selling books but about producing them. They were fretted by government controls, by delays in printing and in binding, by the crippling demands of income-tax. But my father was spared such worries. His post as reader and adviser had never been so simple. He had no longer the two-pronged problem, was a book good, was it the kind of book to sell; now he had only to decide if it was good. It could not fail to sell.

One major change took place at this time in Henrietta Street. In 1938 Inman had taken over the chairmanship of Methuen. The firm was in difficulties and on E. V. Lucas's death, Lloyds Bank had invited him to take Lucas's place. He soon found that he had created an awkward situation for himself. In his autobiography *No Going Back* he said, 'When manuscripts of new books were sent to me personally, as they often were, it fell to me to decide to which of the two firms they should be given. I found myself in a clash of loyalties. . . .' It was finally agreed that a solution of the problem would be for Methuen's to purchase the share capital of Chapman & Hall. The arrangement worked satisfactorily for all sides until September 1939.

Inman then found that his official war-time commitments were too heavy for him to remain in publishing and asked Lloyds Bank to release him from his contract. During the distractions of 1940 the interior economy of a publishing firm did not seem as involved as it would have done at another time. Directors were ready to accept compromises. The amalgamation of Methuen and Chapman & Hall took place without dissension and my father resumed his chairmanship of Chapman & Hall. My prophecy for the firm's future had been fulfilled, in the happiest possible way, without any member of the staff being forced into unemployment.

The flourishing condition of the two firms today is ample testimony to the debt that they owe to Inman.

I was posted overseas to Spears Mission (Syria) in September 1941. One does not look ahead in war-time and I did not ask myself whether I was seeing my father for the last time, nor did he make any of the remarks that had come so easily to his grandfather: he did not dramatize the occasion. I had been away so many times on so many voyages. A few months earlier Evelyn had sailed with his Commando for the Middle East and he was already back, to join a new formation. I, too, might be home within a year. Nine months was the longest I had ever been away.

Evelyn had landed at Plymouth a few days before I sailed, and his first week-end in London was my last. I was leaving on the Saturday night and Evelyn came out to lunch that day at Highgate. It was a cosy lunch, the four of us together. I gave a small good-bye cocktail party in my flat and Evelyn came for the first hour before leaving to write for *Life* the article on Commandos which caused so much confusion with the censorship authorities when it appeared later in the *Evening Standard*. From the restaurant where I dined after the party, I rang up my parents to say good-bye and tell them how the party had gone; just as I had done so often in the past on the eve of a sailing for New York or the West Indies.

It was not till four days later when the convoy left that I realized how different this sailing was. The first night on board, the O.C. ship addressed us. The journey round the Cape, he told us, would take eight weeks.

I remembered his talk when I saw the great massing of ships at Gourock. Eight weeks and all these men and ships and all these preparations. The War Office would not send us on an eight weeks' journey unless it was going to keep us there for a long time. This was not like those other sailings.

My father died on 26 June 1943, three and a half months before the golden wedding day to which he had so looked forward. He died suddenly and very peacefully, on a Saturday morning. He had been in bed only two days, and the previous Saturday he had spent the whole afternoon on the school ground watching a cricket match.

During those twenty months he and I were closer than we had been since the winters of 1915–17. We wrote every four or five days to one another, first by airgraph, later when they became generally available, by letter card. He was a wonderful letter writer. I knew exactly what he was doing, thinking, feeling. He had wanted to die in harness and his wish was granted him.

He had two special protégés on Chapman & Hall's list, Alex Comfort and Elizabeth Myers. He had met Comfort as a schoolboy. Comfort had caught his hand in a machine, mangling it badly. His father, to help him recover from the shock, took him on a long sea voyage to Central and South America. Comfort's account of his trip seemed so remarkable that the school authorities showed it to my father. He published it under the title *The Silver River*.

I only saw Comfort a few times, when he was still at school: he was shy and awkward then, very conscious of his injured hand which he wrapped round in his school cap. But I felt that I knew him well. I heard so much about him in my father's letters, about his career at Cambridge, his marriage and the various discussions of his first novel. I was happy that my father in his last years should have sponsored so vital a talent.

My father's last letters were very occupied with Elizabeth Myers whose *A Well Full of Leaves* was then in the press; he unfortunately did not live long enough to see it published. I only met her once, several years later, a few months before her death, but I could well understand how magnetic and instantaneous a fascination she exerted on her friends. She was tubercular, with a frail look, but she had immense energy. She was lit with a bright inner flame: one was conscious in her of a spiritual quality, the same poetic quality that shone through *A Well Full of Leaves*.

She was a frequent visitor to Hampstead Lane during 1942. My father's encouragement and belief in her work and future sustained her when she was worried by ill health and lack of money. Indirectly he was responsible for the happy and comfortable conditions in which the last years of her life were spent. She had never been to Sherborne: she was anxious to visit it and he gave her a letter of introduction to Littleton Powys, the one conformist of the Powys brotherhood, who had been in charge of the prep. for many years. Powys was a widower, and within a short time he and Elizabeth married. The one time I saw her was in their house at Sherborne. Powys's care and love made her last years her happiest.

My father kept a diary from the day he gave up the managing directorship of Chapman & Hall. He wrote it in a large Boots's diary, sixteen inches long, with ten lines to every day. He was most punctilious about its upkeep. In one sense it is of no public interest since it is a day-to-day, hour-by-hour record of everything that he did and everyone he saw. He made no attempt to spotlight events that might become important twenty years later. Yet it has so many references to books and writers that I have given it to the Boston University Library in the hope that it may be of value to the research student. In a case like this for instance: an entry that is typical of the way in which he intermingled events of permanent and trivial interest, putting things down in the order in which they occurred.

Alexander Woollcott shortly before his death wrote to Mrs Belloc Lowndes that, 'one of the good things I got out of my last trip to London was a talk with Arthur Waugh about Wolcott Balestier.' The entry in my father's diary reads:

1941 Nov. 4. Woke at 6.50. Another dark, cold day, raining as well. Once more could not go out all day and felt very bronchial. Heard from Haynes about an entry in his notebooks which he wished me to read, from Beazley a very interesting letter about Oxford in wartime, and from Mrs Wingate sister of Eustace Heriz-Smith, who wanted advice for her boy now serving in the Navy, with regard to the chance of getting into a publishing house. Wrote a report on the American novel by Fannie Cook and K [*my mother*] did it up for post with proofs of 'Botany Bay'. Wrote a card to Haynes and a long letter to Joan [*my wife*]. At 10.30 Alexander Woollcott of N.Y. called in a super saloon car to talk to me about Wolcott Balestier. I found that he knew 'The Road' [*his autobiography* 'One Man's Road'] quite well, so the best I could do was to lend him Edmund Gosse's little brochure from The Century and answer any questions. He proved a genial fellow and the hour went all too soon. In the p.m. Nannie [*my children's former nurse*] came to tea and stayed 2½ hrs talking much about Florence Desmond and a row they had had. When she had gone I tackled the crossword and did it all, K making two successful shots. Listened in to Alexander Woollcott on Benedict Arnold, so it was certainly Woollcott's day. Again very bronchial at bedtime, but again had a good night with only a short interval for tea at 2.45.

To me as his son, the fourteen volumes of his diaries are of absorbing interest. They give me a picture of his life that I could never have acquired otherwise. It is very hard for children to visualize their parents' lives in the round. Parents alter their own plans to suit their children's; tea parties and expeditions are promptly cancelled and friends put off when a daughter rings up at the last moment to announce that she will be bringing down two friends for the week-end or when a son returns unexpectedly on leave. Children forget that their parents have real lives of their own and do not go into hibernation in their absences. My father's diary showed me how much he was doing all the time; particularly during his last twenty months.

There are many references to my brother in his final entries. Evelyn had a dramatic war. He was a regimental officer the entire time, first in the Royal Marines, later in the Blues, attached to a Commando. He went on three separate campaigns, in the summer of 1940 to Dakar, in 1941 to the Middle East where he was in the raid on Bardia and in the Crete evacuation. Later he went to Yugoslavia, with Randolph Churchill, as part of a military mission and was lucky not to lose his life in an aeroplane crash. But from the close of 1941 through mid-1944 he was stationed in England.

It made a great difference to our father; Evelyn was now a director of Chapman & Hall as well as a Chapman & Hall author and they worked together in easy harmony. During a part of 1942 Evelyn was stationed at Sherborne, in the Digby Hotel where my father had always stayed when he came down to see me, which was an added bond. That Christmas when food was scarce, Evelyn managed to acquire a goose which he sent up to Highgate by his batman; a no doubt highly irregular operation which touched my father as much as the goose delighted him. If only my father could have lived long enough to read *Brideshead Revisited*. How proud of it he would have been.

Three weeks before my father died, he presided over Chapman & Hall's annual shareholders' meeting. 'Of course there were no shareholders left,' he wrote to me, 'except the directors of C. H. and Methuen. Chamberlain spoke most generously, that they were all pleased to see me looking so well, long to reign over us, happy and glorious and so on. It really looks as though the old firm would live out its need of me. It will be very pleasant if we manage to keep light at eventide.'

The first two pages of the letter were written in his firm, clear Greek script. Earlier in the year I had been worried by a change in his handwriting. He seemed unable to control his pen and the sheet was scored by scratches. Occasionally it was impossible to read. But the warm spring had brought improvement. I remembered the old adage of the creaking door. He was only seventy-six. As I read his account of the shareholders' meeting, I saw no reason why he should not celebrate his golden wedding day in October, but on the third page of his letter the script was again criss-crossed with scratches. 'My hand seems wearing out, but I have been two hours over this,' he wrote.

It was with no real surprise that I received the telegram that announced his death.

The funeral service was in Hampstead Parish Church, on a day of sunlight, with the friends of a lifetime gathered round him. He had chosen for the inscription on his tombstone a line from Revelations: 'And another book was opened which is the book of life'.

Half a week later I received in Baghdad the last letter that he had written me. There are words in it which try as I could I have been unable to decipher.

I have been feeling villainously guilty in my relations *vis à vis à toi*, having had 3 really splendid letters from you and being prevented from replying by this exasperating failure of my writing hand. I was plugging away when your mother said 'My dear you can't possibly send that, it is illegible'. So I tore my letter to pieces and had not the endurance to begin again. But here is another attempt which I hope may be more successful.

I am pretty well in myself, except for bad sleeping which is bound to knock me up. I feel very like the dyspepsia I got in 1931. At any rate I feel very much as I did then, before we went to Villefranche, but I have never felt anything like as bad as I did then.

My one pleasure has been watching the school cricket which has had many good days and successful wins. . . . I never remember a boy not

much higher than the stumps getting 102 not out twice as young Laws did
while Maclure was getting 74 and 30.

Evelyn has been over to see us several Sundays. He has had Laura with
him. He has been most agreeable and has brought me some wine. . . .

Well, I have looked through what I have written, but I must confess
that it has made me sad. So often I have said to myself 'Well, when I am
growing old and ugly, at least I shall have the old gift of communication
and if I can still speak in the old language, I shall be able to bring the old
look back. . . .' But alas it will not. I can see the old secret vanished and
when a letter comes, my dear ones can no longer. . . . The old clouds lose
their colour in the sky. Never mind, God bless you, son of my soul, there
will never be shadows in the . . . With every tender remembrance. May
every base be broad in honour. . . .

Your loving and grateful
Father

14
My Second War

When I returned to New York in September 1945, an engaging female enquired if I had had 'a chic war'. No, I answered, but I had had a lucky one. My birthday, 8 July 1898, which had made me old enough for the First War, made me just young enough for the Second; as a Lieutenant in the R.A.R.O. (Regular Army Reserve of Officers) I was recalled to my regiment on the first Monday of the war, and was not demobilized till June 1945. Those six years away from my desk gave me a much needed 'breather' in midstream. I had been writing for twenty years and was beginning to be conscious of the strain. In the autumn of 1945 I returned to professional authorship refreshed. I also returned with sharpened susceptibilities, with broadened interests. I never rose higher in rank than major, so that my opposite numbers were always men considerably younger than myself. In the early 'twenties most of my friends had been older than myself. Now the balance was adjusted.

In September 1941 as I have already mentioned I was posted to the Middle East—six months in the Lebanon and Syria, two months in Cairo; then thirty-three months in Baghdad. But for the war, I might never have seen the Arab world. How much I should have missed if I had not. Moreover I gained an insight into the machinery not only of military intelligence but of police procedure; this insight has been invaluable to me as a novelist.

There are two kinds of military intelligence, offensive and defensive. Offensive intelligence tries to discover the enemy's intentions, defensive to conceal one's own.

Offensive intelligence operates in an enemy or neutral territory. It is invariably exciting and often dangerous. Defensive intelligence operates in one's own or in an allied country and, in spite of its importance, can be extremely dull, since it often has to concentrate on preventing one's own troops from acting in a manner that would give information to the enemy, if there were an enemy agent on the watch. It is a negative activity employed against an imaginary and often non-existent foe. Defensive intelligence can, however, be exciting when it is pitted directly against active offensive intelligence and it was on this kind of work that I was employed for two years in Baghdad.

My particular job was to watch the subversive elements of Iraq, in particular the agents and groups of agents who were sending information to German Intelligence in Turkey. Though the actual fighting was by now many miles away, it was important for the Germans to be mis-informed about the quantity and quality of the troops stationed in Iraq; it was important that saboteurs should not interfere with the transport of aid to Russia; nor with the oil installations in Kirkuk and Abadan; it was important that *agents provocateurs* should not cause civil trouble and thereby necessitate the maintenance of troops who could be better employed elsewhere. Thirty years before Baghdad and Mosul had been vilayets in the Ottoman Empire. Many of the elder Iraqis had been educated in Turkey. The Turks had been allies of the Germans. There was no lack of disaffected persons ready to assist their former friends. At times I felt that I was living in a novel by Phillips Oppenheim. Could this really be happening to *me*?

I was present at the arrest of several men who were working for the Germans. It was invaluable for a novelist to observe how men who have had no reason for suspecting that they are being watched behave when they are arrested. To my surprise not one of them showed surprise or fear. The only man who did show fear was completely innocent. He was a barber. In the old quarters of Baghdad, where the streets are narrow and congested, and it is difficult for a postman to find his way, barber's shops are used like an Englishman's club as a *poste restante* and when we arrested the members of a subversive group who had used a particular shop in this way, we had to take its owner into custody as well.

We arrested him on a Sunday morning when his shop was opening and I have never seen a man more harassed and distressed. We took him back to his house so that he could collect some clothes and inform his family. He was desperate with despair. He ransacked his trunk for paper money and scattered a quantity of it among the womenfolk who were squatting on cushions round a coffee-pot. He had no idea what it was all about, he told them. His ignorance, no doubt, accentuated his alarm. He had read stories of innocent people caught up in a plot. This was now happening to him. Anything might happen next. The other men who knew precisely what they had done, were stoical. The barber was back with his family within three days but those three days must have been a torture for him.

I also while I was in Baghdad saw the C.I.D. at work. When Iraq acquired its independence after World War I, a number of British experts were appointed as technical advisers to organize the various Ministries. They were all of them men of the highest quality and they worked no less loyally because their efforts were devoted to the making of their own posts unnecessary through rendering these organizations so efficient that there would be no need for technical advisers.

The technical adviser to the police was Colonel Wilkins, a Scot who had been trained by Scotland Yard. He was in his middle sixties when I met him, tall, white-haired, urbane, with a twinkle in his eye. I saw him on an average twice a week.

Within three minutes of my arrival, as in all Arab offices and houses, a cup of strong black coffee would be offered me. During Ramadhan, so that the drinking of coffee should not offend orthodox Moslems, the cups were brought in cardboard boxes. We would sip the coffee and gossip and then Wilkie would begin to talk.

Interviews with him tended to last two hours. He was never in a hurry. He did not go home for lunch. It was believed that he brought sandwiches down with him but I never saw him eat them. He would pull out the bottom drawer of his desk, place his foot in it and on this leverage rotate himself in a swivel chair. He would talk round and round a subject, thinking it out as he was talking, reading a report slowly, lifting it to his nose and shaking his head, 'No, no, I don't like the smell of it, I don't like the smell of it at all.'

In the heavy heat of a Baghdad summer when for days on end the temperature does not drop below 110° F. and often rises into the 120s, it was hard not to feel drowsy, sitting there while he talked. To cool the room brush-wood was stacked outside the window with an arrange-ment that let water trickle over it. As he swung in his swivel chair I would sit there half mesmerized watching the drops drip from twig to twig as his voice droned on.

I cannot say exactly what it was I learned during these long hours in Wilkie's office, but I believe I gradually absorbed an atmosphere. Friends have told me that in my West Indian novel *Island in the Sun* the character of the policeman Whittingham rang true. If it did, it was because of those long hot noon-day visits to that shaded room, with the water dropping twig by twig and the taste of strong sweet coffee on my palate and the sound of that voice going on and on. There he was, the spider at the centre of the web, benign, friendly, humorous, but inexorable in the pursuit of justice.

I also learnt how large a part chance plays in criminal research. Much depends on how busy the investigating officer may be. If he has three important cases on his hands, he is likely to dismiss cursorily a minor case. If, however, he has nothing particular to do, he is likely to raise a hornets' nest; and the enquiries that he initiates often reveal conspiracies of quite another nature.

The police know both more and less than is generally recognized, and in war-time when a man is suspect, they proceed to find out all they can about him—which are his clubs, who are his friends, what are his tastes and habits. Not only is his correspondence censored, but that of his friends. Several cases of tax evasion came to the notice of authority in this way. Once we were watching a man who had come to our attention because a friend of his was a pro-German suspect. The man was, we eventually found, a person of blameless political affiliations but his correspondence proved him to be a homosexual who in company with an acquaintance made a practice of picking up Air Force personnel in cinemas, taking them back to his house and doping them with arak into acquiescence.

It is the general practice to leave a suspect at liberty as long as he is not immediately dangerous, so as not to frighten his friends and to obtain information from his correspondence. But a time may come when his activities become so quiescent that more information can be obtained by taking him into custody for interrogation. Such a position was reached on one occasion in the case of a man who was, we were very certain, concerned with a pro-German conspiracy. We had not enough evidence to ask for his arrest by the Iraqi Police—Iraq being a sovereign state—but when he applied for permission to take a holiday in Beirut we had our chance. He could be arrested by the French and taken to Cairo for cross-examination. I was in charge of the case and it was for me to decide whether it was more advantageous to arrest him or leave him at liberty.

This is not, I must explain in advance, a story that confers any credit on myself.

In Baghdad there was an almost complete lack of eligible feminine society. Iraq is a strictly Moslem country and my three years there were celibate. My only relief from the consequent strain was an occasional 'mental orgy' with the kind of book that is catalogued as 'curious'. Such books were unobtainable in Iraq but they were in copious supply in Cairo. If the arrest was made, I should be sent there to assist in the interrogation, and I could replenish my library. I weighed the reasons for and against the making of the arrest. They seemed to balance out exactly. If I had had no personal preference either way, I should have flicked a coin. But I had a personal preference.

There are those who out of an exaggerated sense of duty would have chosen against their own wishes; in the same way there are those in authority who deliberately ignore the claims to promotion of a friend or relative. I am not like that. I tabled every pro and con, decided that the score was level, and ordered the arrest.

Perhaps more often than one would think, some frivolous equivalent of the need of a sex-starved officer for a dirty book leads to the click of handcuffs.

I did not, as it happened, go to Cairo. The suspect either in fright or in an attempt to commit suicide fell off the train in which he was being taken as a prisoner. He was in hospital for several weeks. By the time he had recovered, the situation in Baghdad had shifted. I was heavily occupied with another case, and a younger officer who had recently had a bad attack of sand-fly fever and who was felt to need a change of climate was sent instead. The cross-examination of the suspect did not produce any very conclusive evidence, but my brother officer returned glowing with recovered health after a rumbustious romance with a member of the Palestinian A.T.S.

In another respect too, my six years' breather was a great piece of good fortune. It gave me an opportunity to review my own writing from a detached critical standpoint and to reassess it.

In January 1945, when the Battle of the Bulge had been converted into victory, and it had become clear that the war in Europe would be over early in the summer, it was rumoured that the oldest soldiers and those with the longest service records would be demobilized at once. By the end of the year, therefore, I should be back at my desk, at work on novels and short stories. I looked forward confidently to their resumption, but I presumed that I should find the machine a little rusty when I set it into motion, that it would take me a short story or two and half a novel to get back into smooth production. I thought I would be wise to read some of my earlier books and see what standard I had set myself. I wrote to England to have three or four sent out.

The reading of them was a considerable shock. I was disconcerted by the slovenliness, not in their actual writing but in the development of the plots. I would construct a situation, for fifty or sixty pages the narrative would mount rapidly; then there would be a break; the story would start somewhere else. There would be fifty or sixty effective pages, then once again there would be a break; eventually at the close there would be an attempt to gather up the loose threads in a final situation that would give significance to the whole.

A novel is a parabola. The curve is gradual; about a third of the way up it steepens; four-fifths of the way along its length it turns into a sharp decline towards the climax. When you are going downhill, writing is easy and very pleasant; it is a gallop. The opening when the situation is set out and the characters set in motion can also be—though it is not invariably so—easy and pleasant writing. The difficult part comes when the rise of the curve steepens with every implication of the story pointed, in a gathering momentum, to the peak. Look at any major novel and you will see this principle at work. What I had done, I now realized, time and again, was to shirk that extra effort that was required to send the curve to its peak; instead I had taken a short cut and reached the climax along the level. By so doing I had not got the full dramatic value out of the situation, nor had I raised my characters to the summit of experience where they could reveal themselves and their potentials. I had never exploited to the full the situation that I had set out in the first fifth.

I had taken 'short cuts' and that is fatal, not only for the artist but in every walk of life. How had I come to do it? I exposed myself to a personal inquisition. I had known all along that the novelist's problem was three-pronged. He had to find the material for his books, he had to find the leisure and peace of mind in which to write them, and he had somehow to fit into that pattern the human beings with whom he was personally involved. Looking back at the five years before the war, I recognized that I had not given myself enough leisure in which to get my writing done.

Before my marriage, I had gone into seclusion when I had a book on hand. In the early 'twenties when I had a half-time employment with Chapman & Hall, I used, during the autumn and winter, to go every Monday night to a small inn in the country, work for three solid days and return to London on the Friday morning. During the later 'twenties, when I was no longer working for Chapman & Hall, I would leave London for long periods; I never found that I could work in London, any more than I was to find later that I could work in New York: too many things were happening, the air was too electric. I would go to the South of France, to Villefranche; or to an inn in Devonshire, the Easton Court Hotel at Chagford on whose stout tables many writers have inscribed many solid books. A small hotel bedroom has its link with the monk's cell. There is the discipline of contemplation. On my long trips abroad to the South Seas, the West Indies and the Far East, I had found that same discipline. There were no Pan-American Clippers in those days. I would sit for hour after hour, in my cabin or in the smoking-room, at a table; then at the end of the day I would walk round the deck, breathing in the clean sea air, planning out my next day's work. I would find that a transatlantic crossing gave me exactly the right amount of time for a ten-thousand-word magazine short story. My best work during the five years before the war was the short stories that I wrote on transatlantic crossings. But I had not, during those years, given my novels a chance.

I thought I was doing so, but in point of fact I had not. My wife had bought a comfortably sized Queen Anne house on the Hampshire-Berkshire borders in which I had a comfortable study. But we also had a small service flat in London. I spent on the average a couple of nights a week there. I was a Clubman. The Wine and Food Society started in 1932. There was a sudden specialized interest in wine. We all carried around little ivory cards tabulating the good vintage years. There was a good deal of entertaining.

During the summer I played cricket two or three times a week and went on a couple of tours. I also played golf regularly. We had week-end guests. We entertained and were entertained both in the country and in London. My magazine market in the United States was developing, and I went to New York most years. I was, in fact, leading a varied and entertaining life, but I was not giving myself those long, quiet, uneventful periods which a novel requires, which I had given myself during the 'twenties, but had not since my marriage. With only one of my novels written in the 1930s was I satisfied, a West Indian novel on which I was at work when the war broke out.

I had begun it in late June. I was short of money. I wanted to go to New York in September, so I decided to avoid London until then and stay in the country, writing continuously. I went to work on the book again in January 1940. I was then back in the Army, at Dorchester, organizing the training of recruits in the manipulation of track-lined vehicles. I have always found the atmosphere of regimental life conducive to writing. You are leading a healthy open-air life: you are in touch with human beings, you have congenial company; your mind is not greatly exercised. You have plenty of opportunity to brood. When I was in the Army in 1916, I wrote *The Loom of Youth* in two stretches of three and three and a half weeks, writing for two hours before parades and two hours after them. In 1940 I wrote the last fifty thousand words of *No Truce with Time* in seven weeks, getting up every morning at half past two and going to bed every night at eight.

During those seven weeks I lived with the book. It

came out at an unlucky time, in February 1941, when neither in England nor America was anyone likely to be enthusiastic about an unsociological story dealing with characters who, though contemporary, were not affected by the war. It was, however, serialized by *Redbook* and the film rights were bought by M.G.M. though the picture was never made. I think it one of my better books. Certainly, as I re-read it in Baghdad, on the eve of my return to authorship, I accepted the lesson that it had to give; that I must, in future, give myself the proper atmosphere in which to write long novels. I must build for myself a routine of day-to-day eventlessness, so that I could dig deep into my subconscious and discover how much the particular subject had to offer.

Nearly always the idea for a novel or short story comes in a flash, but that flash—flash is the wrong metaphor, but it is an accepted cliché—is the first showing above ground of a plant that may have deep roots. You cannot tell till you have tended it, watered it, protected it, given it time. It may be a tree, it may be a flower; but you must not dig it up and transplant it right away. That first showing of green is nothing in itself. You have to wait. And that was the vow I made myself in the spring of 1945, in far Baghdad. I would turn over a new leaf. I would give myself the time to write.

If I had not had that six years' break, if I had not had that opportunity of taking stock of myself, of seeing my books, from a distance, with new eyes, I do not believe that I should have been able to stay the course into the 'sixties. Between 1919 and 1939 I published fifteen novels. Since 1945 I have published only five. The last three certainly are better than any of their between-the-wars predecessors, and have been considerably more successful.

15

The Lawyer

E. S. P. HAYNES

I returned from the Middle East in mid-June 1945. Almost the first number that I rang was that of E. S. P. Haynes, one of my oldest friends, whom I had first met in January 1917.

I was home then from Sandhurst for the Christmas recess and S. P. B. Mais was staying at my parents' house; he had dined on a Saturday night with Haynes, returned late and noisily and disturbed the poodle. On the following morning he was not at breakfast. When I returned from church he was still in his room. He sent down a message that he was supposed to be going for a walk with his host of the previous evening but that he did not feel like walking; could Haynes be telephoned? At that time there was no telephone in my parents' house. Oh, well, Petre Mais replied; it did not matter. He did not suppose that his host would feel like walking either.

At a quarter past twelve, however, a large, hatless, comfortably-dressed man of middle age arrived. I told him that Mais had not expected him to appear that morning. Our visitor looked perplexed. 'Why not?' he said. Those two words made a rapid thumb-nail sketch of a personality. They defined three traits, a strong head, a refusal to let the new day be disturbed by the accidents of the previous night, and a rigid observance of routine.

During over thirty years of friendship, he retained those characteristics.

By birth a Pollock, by marriage a connection of the Huxleys, a scholar of Eton and of Balliol, a lawyer and a man of letters, thirty or so books stand against Haynes's

231

name in the British Museum's catalogue. Some of them are of the type that booksellers list under the generic title of 'belles-lettres'; the most successful were his *Lawyer's Notebooks*—a four-volume series of reflections, comments, recollections; others were controversial; *Divorce Law Reform* and *The Decline of Liberty in England*. He was a persistent propagandist for man's right to live in the way he chooses, but it is not as the champion of individual liberty but as an individual that his friends remember him. He was one of the last of the eccentrics.

Everything about him was unusual, his time-table, his habits, his appearance. He was the untidiest man that I have ever seen. He never discarded a pair of trousers while its seat held together, and at least one key button was invariably unadjusted. The spare bed in his own room was piled with books and pipes, though I never saw him smoke anything but a cigar. He had some twenty pairs of shoes all of them half-worn. His end of the dining table was arrayed with small jars, bottles, tins of chutney, garlic, sauces, charcoal biscuits. Evelyn Waugh must have had him in mind when he created in *Scoop* the character of Uncle Lionel, who regarded the dish that the servant handed him as the raw material for a meal, onto which he worked from the stock of small bottles spread before him.

He was Rabelaisian in his conversation and in his behaviour. The plumbing in his chambers at Lincoln's Inn was primitive and to save himself the trouble of walking down a passage and up a flight of stairs, he kept in his cupboard a chinaware utensil; at least one female client was astonished when in the middle of a conference he rose to his feet, turned his back and availed himself of its convenience. It never occurred to him that he was doing anything unusual. He never did anything for effect, that was his great charm. He was of a piece. He 'did what came naturally'. Having evolved a pattern that was congenial to himself, he observed it rigidly.

Shortly after his marriage he acquired the lease of a stucco-fronted four-storey house in St John's Wood Park. He lived in it until a few months before his death in 1950. In Lincoln's Inn he had the same chambers in which his father had worked and for forty-five years, for six days every week, his horizon was bounded by two long lines of Georgian windows. He did the bulk of his work between ten and two. He had a family practice. He was a rare and unwilling litigant. His appearances in the lower courts were exceptional and at half past two o'clock he went out to lunch.

He lunched in Chancery Lane in the back room of an oyster shop. It was unlicensed, so he provided his own wine, a light Moselle and a tawny port. His lunch consisted of shellfish and cheese. Talking more than eating he remained at the table till four o'clock. He had nearly always a guest with him at lunch; more often than not between a quarter and half past three a friend at the end of his own luncheon would arrive for a glass of port.

It never occurred to him that this time-table was unusual, that the general lunch hour was quarter past to half past one and that many of his guests found themselves by quarter to two driven by hunger to a sandwich bar. Half past two was an hour that suited him and he expected his friends to adjust themselves to his preferences. He would be in little mood for work when lunch was ended. There would not be a great deal of work to do; letters to sign and a conference with his managing clerk. He left his chambers at five. Occasionally he would take a Turkish bath; more often he returned straight home. More at his ease as a host than as a guest, he dined out seldom and reluctantly. He had a wide acquaintance and could be sure in his own house of surrounding himself with the people that he liked, and of eating the food and of drinking the wine that he preferred. He kept a good table; he also kept early hours. That, five days of the week, was his routine.

On Saturday, unlike the majority of Londoners in a senior position, he went down to his chambers to work as strenuously as on any other day. He left, however, at half past twelve, a walk to his club entitling him to a carnivorous lunch—butcher's meat was his description of it. After lunch he slept.

The routine of Sunday was equally time-tabled. Choosing a different companion each week, he started from his house at eleven o'clock for the same two hours' walk. Climbing Fitzjohn's Avenue, pausing to relieve himself at the Hampstead tube station, he would proceed past Romney's studio to the Whitestone Pond; turning left across the Heath to the Leg of Mutton Pond he would cross Golders Hill Park into North End Road. He returned past the Blake cottages and the Spaniard's Inn. From the middle 1920s on, he formed the practice of breaking his walk at my parents' house and taking a glass of port or beer there. He arrived home at twenty past one; while his guest was entertained by his family he would take the bath which would make him five minutes late for lunch—a typical English Sunday luncheon, a joint, a fruit tart and cream, Stilton or Cheddar cheese. There were no cocktails. The apostolic succession of drinks would be observed; sherry, claret, port, and brandy.

That was his routine when I knew him first in 1917. That was still his routine when war broke out. Haynes was then over sixty. His wife and second daughter were living in the country and he was in London alone during the blitz, looked after by a Belgian refugee who, embarking from Antwerp in the belief that he was to be taken to

Cherbourg to join the army, had found himself to his astonishment in Hastings.

The Belgian, a man of forty, an expert at sauces who wasted nothing, proved both ingenious and economical as a cook.

'I have never been better looked after in my life,' said Haynes.

He did not allow the blitz to interfere with his routine. He lunched every day at the oyster shop with only such variations of menu as the necessities of war forced on him. He paid his Sunday visit to my parents' house, with a companion and his poodle Wuff, named after my preparatory school nickname. The evenings he arranged methodically, drawing up a duty roster of those of his friends who did not mind travelling in the blackout, and could be relied upon to arrive punctually to dinner in an air raid; each man to his own night.

He continued to sleep in his own bed, on the first floor, even after a stick of bombs, pitching in his corner of the street, completely destroyed the house adjoining his, riddling his roof, shattering every window in the house and breaking great chunks of plaster off the ceiling. His family urged him to leave and take a flat, but he refused.

'I've lived here for thirty-five years. How many Londoners can say that about their homes? When I think of all it's seen, all the friends who've dined here—Rupert Brooke and Edward Thomas, Belloc and Max and H.G.—why should I want to leave?'

His resolve to lead his private life was as strong as ever. He would explode with wrath against municipal authorities, against the various lackeys of officialdom who bothered him with forms. Once, when he was sitting in the garden after dinner, a wireless in a neighbouring garden was turned on over-loudly. He jumped up from his chair. He stamped his feet.

'It is intolerable,' he shouted. 'Is one allowed no peace, even in one's own garden? Wireless. If it hadn't been for the wireless that wretched demagogue, that cheap German Cleon would never have got a nation even of subservient fools to follow him. Wireless, Munich.' His face went red with anger. 'They might, though,' he growled. 'Germans—they'll do anything.' Then as suddenly his anger left him. 'I'm sorry,' he said, 'but when I think of what Germany has done—ruined my life twice. Taken all my friends from me, the friends of my youth, and now the friends that I had found to take their places. Germans,' he'd say, 'I've always known them for what they were. I've never made a friend of one. I've never asked one to my house. When I've had for business reasons to entertain one, I've taken him to a restaurant.

'I've only once slept with a German woman, in Chicago, and anyhow,' he added in extenuation, 'she was a Jewess.'

I had kept in touch with Haynes while I was in Baghdad, yet it was with some misgiving that I went round to see him on my return. I wondered how he would have survived austerity. The oyster shop had been bombed out, his Belgian cook had returned to Belgium; and he with his violent attachment to personal liberty would have been irked more than most by the innumerable controls and regulations by which the existence of every Englishman was hampered.

To my surprise and my relief, however, I found him barely altered and if I had sought a figure symbolic of London's survival through the war I could not have found a better example.

American and Dominion post-war visitors to England were surprised at the small amount of apparent damage except by the docks and round St Paul's. London looked much the same to them with its squares and crescents, except that in practically every street a house was missing, with the general effect of a mouth from which a tooth had been extracted. Built over a series of small rivers, London is a city of low houses, of parks and gardens, and does not lend itself to concentrated saturation bombing and spectacular effects of ruin. The visitor needed to look closely, to peer behind gates and fences to recognize how much damage had been done. Then he had the sense of being in an equivalent of Cairo's city of the dead; whole areas had been gutted and abandoned; the walls stood but the windows were shattered, the roofs had gone, the exposed floors and stairways were rotted with damp and mildew, the gardens were a tangle of high-growing weeds.

St John's Wood Park was that kind of ruin. Haynes's house was the only one still inhabited, and I fancy that only he could have continued to live in such a shambles. The roof had fallen in and though a tarpaulin had been slung between the chimney pots, the top floor was derelict. Every window on the front of the house had been covered over with netted plastic that filled the rooms with twilight. In the drawing and dining-rooms the plaster had fallen from the ceilings and splintered woodwork was showing through. With Mrs Haynes living in the country, disorder had spread from the bedroom to the drawing-room. Undusted books covered the chairs and sofas and the disarray of pots and bottles that had characterized his end of the table now swamped the sideboard. Anyone who did not know Haynes well would have been appalled by the general atmosphere of disrepair, but I had the cosy sense of being back in a familiar place. I had no sense of an army in retreat, but of a siege conducted gallantly. Haynes had gone on leading his own life while the skies had thundered over him.

It was on a weekday that I lunched with him. 'I never go down to work on Tuesdays or on Thursdays,' he

explained. 'Three days at an office is quite enough. I can
see any urgent client here and my clerk comes out to
report to me at tea-time.'

I asked him how business was. When I had left in 1941,
he had been worried about declining revenues and rising
costs. But now apparently all was going well. One or two
profitable estates had needed winding up. He had
received one or two personal legacies from clients; everything would be satisfactory if the Government did not
worry him with forms. His managing clerk had been
killed in an air raid. He could not find anyone who understood the forms. It was intolerable, he said, the way these
jacks-in-office pestered him. 'I ignore their forms. I don't
even read them.'

He had invited me for half past eleven. By quarter past
twelve he was ready for the walk. It was a grey cool
morning. There was always the danger of catching a cold
when you went out with Haynes. In his forties and
early fifties he had stormed at a violent pace up Fitzjohn's
Avenue. At the Hampstead tube station he had entered
the lavatory and remained there for five minutes, leaving
a sweating guest at the mercy of five-way draughts. Now
on the brink of seventy he proceeded at so slow a pace
that one might just as well have been standing still. Wuff
had never been subjected to discipline. Haynes insisted
on putting him on a lead every time he crossed the road,
and there are several roads to be crossed between St
John's Wood Park and Primrose Hill which was now his
routine walk. Moreover every quarter of a mile or so, he
would stop, convulsed by a fit of coughing. His health
had clearly deteriorated during these last years. Sitting
in his bedroom while he dressed, I had noticed how thin
he had become. Before the war, because I had associated
him with the pleasures of the table, I had fancied him to
be heavier than he was, and since he still wore the same

shabby but voluminous clothing, he presented externally the same appearance.

I wondered with some misgiving what manner of lunch I should find waiting me after my chilling walk. I need not have. A dish of skate was followed by cold chicken, nor was there any lack of wine. The litter at his end of the table was indeed increased by the presence of several half-bottles quarter full, and curiously labelled. He was at the mercy of what his wine merchant chose to 'give' him and he had several wine merchants. In regard to debts he had always quoted to me Dr Johnson's remark that you can dodge the cannonballs, but the bullets get you—you should, that is to say, as a debtor, concentrate on your overdraft, your tailor, your hosier and your wine merchant. I had followed Haynes's advice with the result that having only one wine merchant I was limited to two bottles of Scotch a month. Haynes had not followed his own advice, had scattered his custom and from innumerable sources small packages of diverse wines refreshed his cellar. He regaled me with Big Tree Chablis, Algerian claret, South African hock, and something from Australia, thick, sweet and yellow, that was more like Madeira than Chartreuse. By the time we had finished lunch the sun had broken through the mist and it was really warm. He suggested that we should sit out in the garden.

As the house was, so the garden was—a wilderness of flowing grass with here and there a rose bush or a scarlet runner breaking through. The gardens on either side were in a similar condition. We took out deck chairs. Haynes hesitated for a moment. 'Let's go next door,' he said. The fence dividing the gardens had been broken down, and we pushed our way through waist-high grass to the adjacent terrace. 'I've always wished I had this garden too,' he said. 'Now at the end of my life I've got it.'

I asked him about the lease of his house which had expired in 1943. He chuckled. 'They're trying to evict me,' he said, 'and I'm refusing. They say they want to build but I know they can't, with all these war controls. No one but myself would ever think of living here. I've paid my rent, but they won't cash my cheques. If they did they'd admit my tenancy. I've lived rent free for the last three years. Will you have some brandy?'

Curious though the wines had been, the brandy was as good as ever. As I sat there out of the wind in the shelter of the ruins, I had a vivid sense of London's capacity to survive, of the deep ingrown nature of London's life. Whereas other cities have been sacked and pillaged, London's streets have remained through close now upon nine centuries untrodden by foreign feet. Kings have been dethroned, a King has been beheaded, a Commonwealth has been proclaimed, but the citizens of London, undisturbed by the passage of great events, have continued to lead their personal and private lives of clubs and sport, maintaining their own rights and privileges. Even through this last calamity, the rhythm of the city's life had beaten steadily. Cricket had been played at Lord's, football had been played at Highbury: Club committees had deliberated the claims of candidates, publishers had argued about terms with authors' agents; on Sunday afternoons lovers had strolled on Hampstead Heath. And here at the end of it all, a symbol of survival, was Haynes sipping brandy in his neighbour's garden, inveighing against the 'intolerable' interference of the bureaucrats with the inherited rights of the individual. There could have been no firmer reassurance that the essential London had survived, that however the totalitarian bureaucrats might try to clip their liberties there would be no lack of Londoners ready to assert their rights and flout authority.

Yet at the same time I could not help feeling some

misgiving on Haynes's own account. It seemed to me that he was taking on, at his age, too much; or rather that he was opposing the forces of bureaucracy with outmoded weapons; that just as the benevolent liberalism of Asquith's day had no place in a world of sharply defined issues, the individualist of the second half of the century would need to develop a new technique if he was to get his way, if he was to preserve his independence, a technique that it was too late for Haynes to learn. It was no use in 1945 to refuse to fill in forms.

I had had one of my happiest reunions. But when Haynes as was his wont fell asleep with his cigar half-smoked and I walked out into the Finchley Road, to pick up a bus at Swiss Cottage, I could not restrain misgivings on his account.

Three years later, in November 1948, I was returning to England from New York. My first act at London Airport was to buy a copy of the *Evening Standard* and as always I turned first to the 'Londoner's Diary'. In the centre of the third column I read this paragraph:

Struck off

Lawyers are startled to learn that E. S. P. Haynes, well-known solicitor with offices in Lincoln's Inn, has been struck off the Roll by the solicitors' Disciplinary Committee.

There was a technical description of the complaint. It was a question of improperly kept books. The paragraph then continued:

Haynes is 71, an old Etonian, author of some 30 books, and a prolific writer of letters to newspapers. He is an authority on laws affecting divorce and marriage. His 'Divorce and Its Problems', written in collaboration with Derek Walker-Smith (now MP) was published in 1935.
'The war has done this,' said Haynes. 'Up till the war I was well off and solvent. But I am a child in finance. Perhaps I gave too much time to

writing. When I no longer had people to look after my money affairs, this happened.'

Stooping, grey-haired Haynes recalled to-day a remark by his father (also a solicitor). 'He told me, no matter how idle I was I could expect about £1500 a year.'

Says Haynes: 'I have not been idle, and I have earned much more than that. But those days are ended now.'

Haynes plans to spend his time writing now, has a book due for publication soon.

I re-read it, trying to envisage all its complications. I had been away a month and on our last walk Haynes had told me that he would be appearing shortly before some board. 'It was intolerable,' he had grumbled. All these forms. With his old managing clerk alive he had known exactly where he was. The accounts had been prepared for him. A man like himself should not have to bother about trivial details. He was concerned with the strategy not the tactics of a campaign. As I read the paragraph again, I recalled the misgivings that I had felt on his account on that first walk with him. Those misgivings had been justified. He had taken on too much.

I was going straight from the airport into the country. I was not planning to spend much time in London before Christmas. I should have no chance of finding out the facts from mutual friends, of discovering from a neutral source 'how Ted was taking it'. I thought it was better to write than telephone. I dropped him a note, telling him that I was back, asking if he would suggest a day for lunch. Five days later having had no answer I rang up. He was always hard to hear over the telephone. He regarded the telephone as a commercial convenience, to be used by secretaries, not by principals. His voice gave me no indication of his state of mind.

We made a date for the following week. I went up to London with some trepidation. My last walk had been a painful one. It had been a chill, bleak day. Wuff had been more than usually fractious. Haynes had been more than usually asthmatic. Every few hundred yards he had stopped and choked and coughed. We proceeded at a glacier's pace. My fur coat was in cold storage in New York. I was very cold. Haynes himself had been in a gloomy mood. He would never, he said, get through this winter. He had nearly died last February. This February would finish him. His face was pallid like stale plaster. He was very thin. This might well be, I had thought, the last time that I should see him.

That had been in late September. Now in early December, by a caprice of climate, the sky was blue and the air vivid with a sense of spring. The stucco-fronted house took on a golden tone in the mild amber sunlight.

Haynes was no longer living in St John's Wood Park. The proprietors had at last succeeded in obtaining his eviction. But his youngest daughter had a house half a mile away in Hamilton Road. It was a smaller house, but it had been built in the same period; early nineteenth century. It had the dignity of solid unpretentious things that are built to last. He had moved his furniture across— the John Wells portrait of his wife in the wide-spreading gold skirt, the eighteenth-century ancestor, the dresser with its Wedgwood dinner service. On my first visit it had all looked uncomfortably tidy, but within a few weeks the old litter of books and pipes had been restored, and the curious smell, a mixture of leather, garlic, cigar smoke, undusted magazines, a smell that was by no means unpleasant but that was peculiar to Haynes, pervaded again the rooms and passages.

As always my reception from Wuff was boisterous. He ran past me into the front garden and barked for a full three minutes. 'Don't your neighbours object to that?' I asked. It had been one thing to bark in the wilderness of a bombed area; it was quite another to disturb a respectable residential district. 'Yes,' said Haynes. That laconic 'yes' was as typical, as symptomatic as his first 'Why not?' Nothing could have been more complete than his refusal to have his personal preferences disturbed.

As usual, though I had arrived a little late, it was to find him in his night-shirt. His dressing proceeded slowly. Although his litter of half-worn shoes matched his litter of half-smoked pipes, he had bought a new pair of shoes the week before. It was the first time I had seen him with any new article of attire. I fancy that he had only bought them because shoes were at that time rationed and he felt that by using his clothing coupons he was getting his own back on the Government. He had great difficulty in getting into these shoes, and could not find his shoe-horn. Finally with the leverage of a spoon I effected the introduction.

In September Haynes had looked pasty and exhausted. Now there was a buoyancy in his step that reminded me of the days when he had taken Fitzjohn's Avenue in his stride. He did not once stop for breath. Wuff was relatively docile. Instead of stopping at the foot of Primrose Hill we had time to mount its summit. We sat on a wooden seat looking over London.

'I suppose you've heard about my being unfrocked,' he said.

To the ordinary person, being struck off the Roll of Solicitors would be a disgrace, comparable to the cashiering of an officer. But Haynes was not an ordinary person. He ordered his life by a different set of rules, and by his own standards he had done nothing of which he needed to be ashamed. Several solicitors have assured me that he had done nothing except be casual and muddled, that since his managing clerk's death he had not bothered to keep his accounts in order; a negligence that is in a solicitor reprehensible but implied no reflection on the

E. S. P. Haynes whom his friends knew and loved. It was in character.

He could not have taken his reverse more calmly. When an Englishman goes bankrupt, or fails to meet his obligations, he is expected to resign from his clubs, because he might put a club servant in the awkward position of having to refuse a member's cheque. But Haynes could clearly not be bothered with unnecessary correspondence, and he had been amused by the devices adopted by the various club committees to remedy this omission. A personal friend of long standing at the Achilles had written to say that as the subscription was being raised in January he would probably prefer not to continue his membership. A city company on the other hand gilded the pill by returning him not only his entrance fee but his subscription over thirty years. He could not have been more delighted with his cheque for three hundred pounds.

He was as full of plans now as ten weeks earlier he had been despondent. At last he would have the leisure to write the kinds of book he wanted.

I had never known him so self-confident. His confidence was not bravado; a need 'to show people' that he still 'had it in him'; to justify, to vindicate himself. He was genuinely relieved to be rid of the necessity for paying daily visits to his chambers; to have the whole day free for writing.

Confident though he was, however, I had never seen him feebler. He looked well, but he looked very old. As Christmas was near, I had brought him as a present a bottle of champagne. He insisted on our drinking it together there and then. It was pleasant to drink it with him; it was pleasant to watch his enjoyment of it; but he kept falling asleep at table, a thing I had never seen him do before, even when he was bending his head over the broad-brimmed goblet inhaling the aroma of the wine. His talk grew vague and indeterminate. I did not believe that he would have the vitality to complete his reminiscences. At the same time he would be happy working on them intermittently. The next two years might be among his happiest; an Indian summer.

On several earlier occasions on grey cold days when I had taken those freezing walks with him, when he had stopped and choked and Wuff had disobeyed him, I had stifled my irritation with the thought, 'This may be the last time you'll ever see him. You must make a happy occasion of it.' This time I had no such feeling. Many more lunches were awaiting me in these next few years. We went upstairs for coffee. He lit a cigar. I have no recollection of what we talked about. Before the cigar was a quarter finished, he fell asleep. As was my wont, I let myself out quietly. It was the last time I saw him.

A few days after Christmas as he was standing in his bedroom in front of the gas fire, the tails of his shirt caught fire. The burns were serious: pneumonia followed: he died in his sleep.

The funeral was at the crematorium at Golders Green. It was the first time that I had been to the funeral of anyone for whom I closely cared; in thirty years our contact with each other had been unbroken. There are those who say that the crematorium service is cold and clinical. I did not feel it was. On the contrary I felt my heartstrings pulled as they never had been at the scattering of earth, by the symbol of the coffin passing out of sight, towards the furnace, followed by the words 'Go Christian soul'.

They were discussing Haynes at the Savile that day at lunch. 'What a pity,' someone said, 'that he didn't die four months earlier, before the trouble broke.'

I could see what that someone meant: and for his

family the trouble inevitably must have been a cause of grief. And he himself may have been saddened by the suspicion that no obituary might appear of him in *The Times*. At the same time that trouble gave a sense of classic completeness to his life; it rounded the thing off. His full stature became apparent in those last weeks when he displayed in adversity his full stoic calm, his capacity to carry on, to remain an individualist to the end. I would not have had Ted Haynes in himself one iota different: he was of a piece. I would not change the end.

16

Son of Oscar Wilde

VYVYAN HOLLAND

A traveller such as myself relies on clubs to give a cohesion to his scattered life. I belong to four clubs in London, and two in New York; in addition I have several dining clubs. In London none has mattered to me more than Ye Sette of Odde Volumes. Founded in the 1870s by the bookseller, Bernard Quaritch, who grew tired of paying for his friends' meals and decided that by forming them into a club he could ensure that his intimates became self-supporting, the Sette is, I believe, the oldest dining club in London. Bookish in its inception somewhat in the trade sense of the word, the rules and ritual suggest a Mason's handiwork. There are elaborate initiation and inauguration ceremonies. The members wear badges, and the officers assume chains of office. The master of ceremonies carries a seven-foot silver and ebony wand. Until very recently full evening dress was worn. In fact, almost the only times since the war when I have worn white tie and tails have been at the Odde Volumes. Each member has a special cognomen and is known and addressed as Brother Idler, Brother Spectator, or Corinthian. The president is called 'His Oddship'.

The constitution was drawn up in terms of what the 1870s considered humorous; facetiousness is the prevailing note. Rule XVI provides a typical example:'There shall be no Rule XVI'. It is the habit for the brethren to introduce their guests, one by one, in a speech. It is traditional to insult one's guests. The more distinguished the guest, the less veiled the insult, Vyvyan Holland once remarking of a well-known publicist, 'I joined the

Sette because I needed somewhere to entertain the kind of man I could not invite to my own house. Mr ——— is the kind of guest I had in mind.' The wittiest introduction was that of Eustace Hoare by Maurice Healy. 'My guest is a member of the second oldest profession in the world. Mr Hoare is a banker.' Evelyn Waugh in *Brideshead Revisited* made an amusing and irreverent reference to the Sette—Bridey was a member—as 'a curious association of men, distinguished in their professions, who met once a month for an evening of ceremonious buffoonery'.

The first half of the evening is conducted on that note. Then the Sette proceeds to justify its claim to be regarded if not as a learned society, at least as a gathering of specialists in different fields. A paper is read, and a relatively serious discussion follows. These papers are twenty to forty minutes long and very often they are printed in a standardized format at the expense of their author and presented to the members. They are listed as *opuscula*, and over a hundred have been issued. The early ones are considerably the longer, and as I have turned their pages I have wondered how the Odde Volumes of the 1890s, after consuming the many-coursed banquets that were then the fashion, managed to stay awake while they were being read. But most of the more recent *opuscula* have intrinsic merit; are something more than collectors' items.

I joined the Sette in 1920, am now its senior member, though as an Emeritus Odde Volume I take no longer an active part in its affairs, and have seen several changes in its atmosphere over fifty years. The members are now a much livelier lot, and the ritual is treated, as the plays of Wilde are acted, as a period piece. The papers are a good deal shorter. Probably the Sette was at its best in the 1930s, when its membership included doctors like

Moynihan and Arbuthnot-Lane, jurists like Norman Birkett, Roland Oliver, and Walter Monckton, wine experts such as André Simon, A. J. A. Symons, Maurice Healy, and Vyvyan Holland, while David Low designed its menus. Surprisingly enough, it did not number many authors, Ralph Straus and J. G. Lockhart being the only professional writers besides myself, but it was during this period that the best *opuscula* were issued. Perhaps some of the best writing is produced when a man of taste and scholarship writes on his own subject, out of direct personal experience.

I have an idea that our guests were sometimes bored by the 'ceremonious buffoonery' of initiation evenings and by the heavy-handed facetiousness with which some of the brethren introduced their wives on Ladies' Night; I know I was. But an Odde Volumes evening always led to something else and I enjoyed the back-stage politics, the small lunch and dinner parties that members of the Sette gave each other when they were plotting a palace revolution, smoothing out a difficulty or electing the next year's officers. These parties because they were convened for a purpose created a genuine link between the four or six men who were grouped round a table. We shared a fraternal bond. During the 1930s I became friendly with several men of eminence in the law and medicine whom otherwise I could scarcely have hoped to know as other than chance acquaintances. In particular I am grateful to the Odde Volumes for having converted a pleasant acquaintanceship with Vyvyan Holland into a friendship that has become one of my most dear possessions.

In 1954 Vyvyan Holland described in *The Son of Oscar Wilde* how his father's tragedy affected him. It is a moving story told with restraint, dignity and warmth. It had a large sale on both sides of the Atlantic and I can assume that anyone who reads these pages will have read or have read about it. In it Vyvyan limited himself to his subject, writing about himself only as 'the son of Oscar Wilde'. He told us nothing about himself apart from that. This restraint gave his book a special unity.

His book closes in 1914, and it was not till nine years later that I met him in January 1923 on the evening of my election to the Savile Club. It was a friendship of pleasant but slow growth, possibly because he is not a cricketer and I had not yet started to play golf, and it was in the 'thirties that with the Odde Volumes as a link, we found how much we have in common. We like the same kinds of person, we played the same kind of golf—though he would not confirm this—we each have a collector's taste in first editions, we enjoy the pleasures of the table. I have had many of my best times with him.

He is a man of many interests. After leaving Cambridge he was called to the bar and though he never practised, when Roland Oliver became a judge, he travelled with him on circuit, as a Judge's Marshal. He has worked off and on in publicity with Richard Temple. He has translated a number of books, but except during the Second War when he was employed in the foreign section of the B.B.C. he has never been a man who went to an office after breakfast. He has worked hard, but intermittently, a man of apparent leisure.

Between the wars when his father's books and plays were in copyright, he was comfortably off financially. He had married young, but his wife died tragically in a fire while he was in France with the R.F.A. He returned to peace-time with an O.B.E. and the resolve to enjoy himself.

He did it as thoroughly as anyone that I have known. There was no reason why he should not have. He was in his early thirties, he was popular, witty, unattached, he had money, he had good health, and tastes that it was not difficult to indulge in post-war London, particularly in post-war Chelsea.

H. G. Wells said that the two essentials for gallantry were leisure and convenient premises. Vyvyan Holland had both. He was a generous and skilful host and he gave every kind of party in his house in Carlyle Square. I remember a dance there. I remember many luncheon parties. I remember men's dinners and ladies' dinners. I remember dinners for those who were especially interested in wines, when you would sit down at a table faced with three or four glasses, each one numbered, and four decanters of red wine that had taken the room's temperature, so that you could drink one wine against another. And how many evenings elsewhere did not conclude with Vyvyan's invitation to 'finish it in Carlyle Square'. On such occasions he would produce from his cellar a sparkling wine which he called 'Cutie Champagne': to the discerning he would whisper out of the corner of his mouth 'I recommend the whisky'; every kind of party except a cocktail party.

He did everything with grace and elegance. He was always involved in some romance and, as his friend, I have received many confidences from the ladies who were involved with him. I have never heard one say a spiteful or revengeful thing against him, though I heard one say wistfully, 'It's too bad really, I think I'd have been right for him, but I've known all along that marriage was not his game.'

He enjoyed the pleasures of the table, but he was temperate in their indulgence. The early 'twenties was a wild time in Chelsea but he had his own technique. Going to an evening party that began at nine o'clock, he would 'case the joint'. If the party appeared likely to continue until 4 a.m. and if he saw a girl there who attracted him, but had an escort, he would return unobtrusively to

Carlyle Square, go to bed, sleep for five hours, wake up fresh, take a shower and shave and return to the party. More often than not the escort of the girl who had attracted him would be on the verge of passing out, with she herself ready to welcome anyone capable of a practical appreciation of her charms.

When I left for the Middle East in September 1941 I felt I knew Vyvyan Holland as well as I have ever known any human being. I knew him in terms not only of what he had told me about himself, but of what a number of his friends had told me; nothing would have surprised me more then than to have been told that fourteen years later one of the best-selling books of the 1954 autumn season would be *Son of Oscar Wilde*.

I had scarcely heard him mention his father's name, and was surprised when going over an old guestbook of the Odde Volumes, to have him pause as he turned a page and point without comment to his father's signature. He had a passion for anonymity, which anyone who has read his autobiography will readily understand. He detested notoriety as much as his father had delighted in it. On the title-page of his translations he sometimes reversed his own initials—appearing as H.B.V. He hated having to be explained. He declined the presidency of the Odde Volumes because he did not want to have guests saying, 'Who on earth is that fellow sitting up in that big chair?' He was erudite and witty. The paper that he read to the Odde Volumes on *The Mediaeval Courts of Love* is one of the very best in its archives, but when his friends urged him to attempt a larger task he would shrug, and mumble something inaudible out of the corner of his mouth. It is natural for the son of a highly successful writer to be diffident about following in the same profession and inviting comparisons. But he carried his love of anonymity to an extreme point. His friends carefully avoided a mention of his father.

Part of his reluctance was a form of self-defence. No one could be more completely normal and he resented being pestered by homosexuals, foreigners for the most part, who wanted to pay their respects to the sacred memory of 'Oscar, the martyr'. There was another point too. He had adored his mother, he had seen the misery which the case had brought on her. He resented his father's having inflicted this misery upon her. Yet loyalty would not allow him to speak a word against his father. Better remain silent. Perhaps, we would think, he would have liked to talk about him. He seemed the least inhibited person in the world, but this refusal to discuss a subject that must have been constantly on his mind may have created barriers inside himself. But it was not for us, we felt, to bring up the subject.

When I returned to London in the summer of 1945 after very nearly four years in the Middle East, I found changes in many of my friends, but nothing surprised me more than to find Vyvyan talking freely about his father, without embarrassment, with affection, with wit, treating the sudden vogue in Wilde as a piece of comedy that would have made his father chuckle.

During the war he had married Thelma Besant, a very attractive Australian woman who is one of the chief figures in Cyclax. Thelma, who is several years younger, had grown up when the scandal of the 'nineties was half forgotten; to her the name of Oscar Wilde was one to be acknowledged proudly. Gradually and with great tact she broke down the barrier.

If that barrier had not been broken down, *Son of Oscar Wilde* would not have been written and the world would have been the poorer. The Wilde saga would have lacked its coping stone.

17

Michael Arlen in Retirement*

The King Cole Room in the St Regis Hotel, New York, is open at lunchtime to men only. On most days of the week during the early 1950s the table on the left of the desk was occupied by a small thin man in his later fifties, with a short clipped moustache and closely cut hair that was turning grey. He wore a dark suit that had been cut for him in Savile Row, a stiff white collar with a plain silk or satin tie and a pearl pin. He had a Continental air.

He arrived at a quarter to one, alone. He would order a dry martini and light a cigarette which he smoked through a long holder; four places were laid at his table, and by the time he was half-way through his martini, one or two of those places would have been filled. His table was a club where each man paid for his own drinks and food, and his friends rang up a day or so before to ask if their presence would be convenient. If no one had rung up by ten o'clock he would take steps to assure that he would not lunch alone. He did not need to often; he had a large acquaintance and was excellent company. There was constant laughter at his table. He was a good listener, who could appreciate good talk, but the loudest laughter came when he himself was talking.

A few years earlier as a result of a motor accident he had been forced to carry a walking stick and as he told a story, he would lean forward on it. When he was a very

---

* Michael Arlen died in the summer of 1956.

young man, the first Lord Birkenhead gave him this advice on public speaking: 'If your hands are right, everything will be all right. Get a chair or table in front of you and hold on to it.' He now used his walking stick as a lectern and gesticulated with his cigarette holder. You were reminded of those oriental tale-tellers of the market-place, whose hands were as eloquent as their voices.

He ordinarily took three martinis before he ordered lunch. Half past one became half past two. The room was now almost empty. Quite often at about quarter to three, a waiter would whisper, 'Your wife's outside, sir.' She was small, neat, and dark, with a short, pointed aristocratic nose. She too had a foreign air. She had looked in on her way to her hairdresser to ask if anything had happened during lunch to change the plans that they had made that morning. He would talk to her for a couple of minutes then return to his table. A newcomer to the King Cole Room would think, 'That must be somebody.'

The newcomer would be right. It was Michael Arlen. And the story of the long journey that had brought him to that corner table in the King Cole Room is as romantic as any of those which brought him fame and fortune in the 1920s.

I met him for the first time in 1920. Heinemann was then advertising a book by an unknown writer with a quote from the *Daily Express*: 'All reading London is guessing at the authorship of a slim book entitled *The London Venture*. Some clever people think that Mr George Moore has recovered his dead youth in this extraordinary little volume, half essay, half novel, wholly delightful.' Reviewing it in *John O'London's Weekly* I gave my reasons for not believing that it was by George Moore. A few days later W. L. George, at an afternoon party, brought up to me a quietly but exceptionally well-dressed young man. 'It's as well,' George said, 'that you didn't try to pretend there was no such person as Michael Arlen because here he is.' George amplified his introduction. Arlen, he said, was an Armenian born in Bulgaria and christened Dikran Kouyoumdjian who had prudently rid himself of a name no bookseller could pronounce.

Of that first meeting I can recall one thing only, but it was symptomatic. George showed me a copy of *The London Venture* that Arlen had inscribed on the title-page '*Per ardua ad astrakhan*'. From the start Arlen knew whither he was bound.

Four years later *The Green Hat* was a top best-seller on both sides of the Atlantic. Subtitled 'A Romance for a Few People,' written in a highly mannered, almost precious style, peppered with allusions that the general reader could scarcely catch, it was presented to the public as belles-lettres rather than a novel in the genre of Max Beerbohm and George Moore; yet it caught the public fancy like a dance tune.

Today, forty years later, it is easy to see why it did. It was set in the post-war London of fast cars and expensive night clubs, and its heroine, Iris Storm—a woman with 'a pagan body with a Chislehurst mind' (perhaps 'Boston' is the nearest American equivalent for that), star-crossed in her first love by a parent's intervention—stayed faithful to that love 'in her fashion'.

'What I said at eighteen is true now at thirty. I have never said I loved him to any man but Napier for it hasn't been true. I have given myself in disdain, in desire, with disgust, with delight, but I have kept to that silly childish boast of mine.'

In *The Green Hat* Michael Arlen was the spokesman of a new type of woman who was demanding a man's right to live her life in the way she chose. Several recent books—*The Far Side of Paradise*, for example—have accepted Iris Storm as a symbol of the 1920s. And in telling her story Arlen was also the spokesman of a disenchanted generation that after four years of the trenches was eager to welcome extravagance, frivolity, and display.

The story is told in the first person, with the narrator constantly in the centre of the stage, so that the personality of the author was an essential ingredient in the book's success. Every discussion of *The Green Hat* became a discussion of Michael Arlen.

His Armenian birth gave him an air of mystery. He rarely lifted the curtain on that foreign background, even to interviewers. Only once, in *Confessions of a Naturalized Englishman*, which appeared in his collection of short stories *Babes in the Wood*, was he autobiographical. In that story he told how he was brought to England at the age of five, and spent his boyhood in Southport, where there is a large Armenian colony. For three years he was 'instructed in team work and pulling together at Malvern College in Worcestershire', a school that is famous for its cricketers. At the age of seventeen he came to London on a weekly allowance of £2.

That was in 1913. A year later the outbreak of war made his position difficult. He had no legal status. Bulgaria had disowned him because he would not serve as a conscript in her army. Bulgaria was an ally of Germany, so he could not become a naturalized British subject during the war, nor could he change his name. As he was not eligible for military service, his lot was cast among those who for reasons of health, age, or political opinions were non-combatants. He was befriended by Orage, the editor of the *New Age*, a paper which rewarded its contributors parsimoniously. He made friends with Aldous Huxley, who was debarred from service by his eyesight; with D. H. Lawrence, whose German wife was under police surveillance and whose *The Rainbow* had recently been suppressed by the public prosecutor; and with Nancy Cunard, who was then, as she has been so often since, in conflict with her day. He was one of the patrons of the White Tower restaurant in Percy Street, whose proprietor Stulic, a Viennese by birth, was also under police surveillance.

As far as I know none of his friends of this period have written of him in their autobiographies, but there is an illuminating passage in a letter that D. H. Lawrence wrote to Lady Ottoline Morrell in December 1915:

Kouyoumdjian seems a bit blatant and pushing: you may be put off by him. But this is because he is very foreign, even though he doesn't know it himself. In English life he is in a strange alien medium and he can't adjust himself. But I find the core of him very good. One must be patient with his jarring manner and listen to the sound decency that is in him.

Arlen once remarked to me that self-pity was a useful formula for a best-seller but he never exploited it. Until 1916 he lived in a third-floor flat in 46 Redcliffe Road, a dreary little thoroughfare. Margaret Irwin, later famous as the author of *Young Bess*, was living on the first floor. They never met, but after he left for the flat in Shepherd Market which he described in the first chapter of *The Green Hat* a curious thing happened. The second-floor flat was taken by a Scot with second sight who was disturbed night after night by ghostly but emphatic pacings of the floor above, which were interrupted by rushings to the window whenever a taxicab stopped below. Margaret Irwin was to learn later from G. B. Stern that Arlen had spent many hours pacing that floor, waiting for a capricious lady. Margaret Irwin made those pacings the theme of a novel *Knock Four Times*; but Arlen never used his own material, except in that one short story. He did not want to write about poor young poets waiting in their garrets but of the big and brilliant world in which they aspired to shine.

He saw that world, as a foreigner, with dazzled eyes. D. H. Lawrence shrugged when Arlen asked him his advice. 'I am a realist,' he said, 'you are a romanticist. You have your own way to make. I cannot guide you.' Orage told him the same thing. Arlen began *The London Venture* as a parody of George Moore. Orage said, 'This is no parody, this is your best stuff. You've digested what I told you years ago. Don't be realistic. Your strong point is artifice.' Osbert Sitwell wrote of him in a poem-portrait, 'Alone of all popular writers, he dares to use the art of imagery.'

Arlen wrote vividly but colloquially, with unusual inversions and inflections, with a heightened exotic pitch. 'The moon made a great fuss of her all the way to a place called Great Neck. They had quite a party the moon and Marilyn. I left out had nothing to do but watch.'

That was what they called 'Arlenese.' He did not so much tell a story as embroider one. Fascinated by the world of fashion, he conveyed his sense of wonderment to his readers. Before I began to write this essay I re-read *The Green Hat*. It is a period piece, but though it is dated, it is not *démodé*. The magic is still there.

His first novel was called *Piracy* and his capture of the British and American public was an act of piracy that he carried off flamboyantly.

He wrote exclusively of the upper classes—'I decided,' he said, 'to write about my betters who in England are much easier to approach and understand than labourers' —but he was not in any sense a snob. He was a pirate and his stories are filled with highwaymen. Wilfred Macartney, who served a prison sentence, wrote in *Stone Walls Do Not a Prison Make* that Arlen's books were liked by jailbirds because he had a sympathy for the under-dog.

For me, Arlen had at that time the fascination of a Balzac character. 'What do you want of life?' Vautrin asked Rubempré. 'To be famous and to be loved,' Rubempré answered. Arlen would have given the same reply. Though we did not really become friends till a good deal later, I was constantly running into him during those early years. He was short, he dressed quietly, he never wore loud checks or startling ties, yet he was a prominent figure in any gathering. There was a gloss about him. Years later he was to say in an interview to Geoffrey Hellman, 'My mother taught me to think a distressed area should make the best of itself.' Even when he was poor he never looked poor.

Cocktail parties were not yet in vogue. There were tea parties and after-dinner parties. At evening parties he usually appeared in a white tie. His evening shirts looked as though they were being worn for the first time. He nearly always came alone—an affable, appreciative guest. He would talk a good deal about himself. People would be saying the next day, 'I met Arlen last night at the ——s . . .' and he liked to give them something worth repeating.

But at the same time he was always interested in the other man, what he was doing, what he thought. He always managed to make one feel happier about oneself. Which is a rare thing to do. It springs from a generosity of heart. He never seemed in a hurry. He never abruptly broke off a conversation. He never looked at his watch. Yet he gave the impression always that he was on his way somewhere else, that in the background, somewhere, an exotic woman was awaiting him.

He was the constant object of conjecture. The gossip columns were dotted with references to the table that was reserved for him in the Embassy Club each night; to his yellow Rolls-Royce, which he had had registered in Manchester so that its number plates would carry the letters MA: to the money he had invested in Noel Coward's *The Vortex*. He is the Michaelis of *Lady Chatterley's Lover* and report credited him with a dramatic succession of romances.

He was always laughing, always on his way from something exciting, about to take off for something glamorous. Life seemed to have poured all its treasures into his lap, yet was he happy? Did not his restlessness conceal a loneliness of heart? Had he not once, at the bidding of caprice, driven through the night to Southampton, caught the *Aquitania* for New York, and then on arrival at New York changed his mind and returned in the same cabin? Were not all these love affairs the sign of a central dissatisfaction? His stories contained cryptic clues. 'What is success but solitude made perfect.' 'Freedom is a very lonely thing. It means that no one can be troubled to enslave you.' 'The plotter shall be caught in his own plots'. Was he unhappy in himself? There was a dark secret at his core. It made him the more romantic.

There were those who resented his success. The English are not particularly xenophobic, but certain hidebound tories grumbled against 'this damned foreigner who's persuaded a lot of silly women that he's marvellous'. A jealous fellow novelist labelled him as Turkish propaganda sent over to justify the Armenian massacres. But Arlen had the last word always. He anticipated criticism. He described himself as a case of pernicious aenemia. He said that his success was not a fashion, but an international disease. A quarter of a century later he was to say, 'I was a flash in the pan in my twenties. I had a hell of a lot of fun being flashy and there was by the grace of God a good deal of gold dust in the pan.'

Anything they could say, he could say quicker. I have

seen many kinds of literary success over half a century, but never one that was quite like Arlen's, that was attended with such a flourish, one in which the author and the books were so identified. That is why his consequent story is fascinating. The plotter was caught in his own plot. He could never retire. He had to be Michael Arlen to the chapter's close.

During the period that 'the disease' was infectious, he made a great deal of money at a time when American income-tax was low. He dramatized *The Green Hat* and *These Charming People*; both had long runs and both were filmed. Editors bid against each other for his short stories. For *Lily Christine* he received $50,000 from *Cosmopolitan* for the serial rights, $20,000 advance from Hutchinson on account of the British Empire sales, and $15,000 from Doubleday Doran on account of the American book sales.

Only Arlen himself knows exactly how much he made between 1924 and 1931. He was extremely prudent with it. He turned himself into a limited company which he had registered in South America, where his elder brother lived, with that brother as chairman of the board. When Arlen visited New York he travelled as the company's representative on an expense account. The capital earned during his boom years survived the depreciation of currency to which English writers generally have been exposed.

Lily Christine was published in 1928. In the spring of that year Arlen married. In a recent interview in the *Sunday Times* with Cyril Ray, he said, 'I married and lived happily ever after.' 'Is that really true?' his interviewer asked. Yes, he said, it was.

He was not exaggerating. Atalanta, the daughter of Count Mercate, half-Greek, half-American, was like

Michael a kind of exile. With their background of Eastern Europe they must have understood many things about each other without needing to explain them; they could feel at home with one another, as they could not completely with the island-based English. They matched each other. They were, they stayed, a team. When they were together in a group, he wove her into his conversation. In their first years of marriage she was very silent, but she was always a person of character. I met her for the first time at a small tea party given in her honour shortly after her marriage. William Gerhardi was there. He was a little patronizing, and asked her if she proposed to criticize her husband's novels. 'No,' she said. It was a most eloquent 'No' and made Gerhardi look rather more than foolish.

After his marriage I saw much more of Arlen. We could meet them on equal terms, in a way that we could not when he was unattached and affluent, moving in an atmosphere of yachts and fast cars and fashionable playgrounds.

He bought a villa outside Cannes. The French Riviera was then developing its summer season. Many writers were making their homes along the coast—Maugham, P. G. Wodehouse, H. G. Wells, Aldous Huxley, Gilbert Frankau, Phillips Oppenheim. It was a pleasant world, with its blue skies and blue seas, with its terraced olive groves and flowers, with its healthy, outdoor life of swimming and golf and tennis. Everyone felt well, everyone looked well. The setting for every activity was gracious. A lunch party that might well be ordinary in London becomes idyllic on a balcony shaded by vine leaves, looking over a valley towards a village that is a medieval fortress, with the Mediterranean showing in a gap between the hills, and a liner passing like a toy ship on the horizon.

Arlen was very happy there; happy in his marriage, in his son and daughter, in his way of life. He had many friends; he enjoyed golf and tennis; the climate suited him. In the late autumn he came back to London and was warmly welcomed there. In January he went to Switzerland to ski. He had enough money for his needs. It is very easy in the atmosphere of the Riviera to let days drift into weeks, weeks into months. It is hard to work there unless you are goaded by necessity. Arlen had no such goad. But he went on writing.

In 1931 the serial rights of *Men Dislike Women*—a delightful comedy of manners—were bought at a high price by *Cosmopolitan*. Short stories appeared at regular intervals; they were collected under the title *The Crooked Coronet and Other Misrepresentations of the Real Facts of Life*, and one at least of them, *The Golden Arrow*, was produced by Hollywood. He published two novels, *Man's Mortality*, a story of wars of the future in 1932 and *The Flying Dutchman*, a political allegory in 1939. Both these novels were highly praised by responsible reviewers. 'Does mankind improve? At any rate Mr Arlen improves. He gets better and better as he gets more and more serious.' That was the general tone. J. B. Priestley wrote of *Man's Mortality*: 'I did not think him to be a man of this mettle. Bravo.'

The reviewers were no less enthusiastic over *The Flying Dutchman*. Humbert Wolfe wrote: 'Michael Arlen runs a serious risk of acclaiming himself on the way to becoming a genius. For many years in point of sheer diabolical talent he has been unapproachable.' But in spite of its reviews, this book attracted little public interest. Myself I was unaware of its existence, till I found it in a friend's library several years after the war. The reading of it was a curious experience. It was a good novel, but without the name upon the cover I should never have guessed its authorship.

I realized then that a strange thing had happened

during the 1930s. A divorce had taken place between the Michael Arlen whom the world saw and the Michael Arlen who put his name on covers. In 1924 Michael Arlen was a composite production, the writer and the man were one; in 1939 the Michael Arlen who played golf at Cannes and drank martinis in the Carlton Bar was the author of *The Green Hat* fifteen years farther down the course—but the man who sat at a desk in a study looking out over the Mediterranean had ceased to be that Michael Arlen.

The Flying Dutchman was published six months before the outbreak of the Second World War. That second war, as the first, made Arlen because of his Bulgarian birthplace an odd man out. He was now a British subject but at forty-five he was too old for the armed services. He returned with Atalanta to London in the autumn to look for war work, but it was not easy to find war work during the period of the 'phoney war'. Atalanta joined the Red Cross but Michael played poker at the Savage Club. Then came the fighting war with an opportunity at last for war work: Lord Dudley appointing him Civil Defence Public Relations officer for the East Midlands. Arlen was in Coventry when it was bombed. But with the end of the phoney war, there was a return of xenophobia. Arlen might be a British subject, but he had been born in Bulgaria. Could he be trusted? Might he not be a Fifth Columnist?

Questions were asked in the House and once again Michael Arlen found himself, if not a man without a country, a man without a country that would let him help defend it. He shrugged. It was a situation that amused him. With a domicile in France, he was not normally exposed to British income-tax, but since he was a British subject, the British Treasury considered itself entitled to sequester of all of his and his wife's American possessions with the exception of Michael Arlen Inc., which was registered in South America. He shrugged again. Another Armenian atrocity, he said, and continued to play poker at the Savage.

Early in 1941 his son's school was moved to Canada and Atalanta went with it. Later in the year her husband followed her.

I often thought of him during the next four years. In 1942 I was posted as an intelligence officer to Baghdad, and one of my duties was to keep watch over the Armenian minorities whose subterranean activities the Germans might endeavour to exploit. I many times wished that Arlen were at my elbow to explain to me who stood for what. He at that time ironically enough was working in Hollywood on the film version of a novel of mine that M.G.M. had bought. The story never reached the screen and my report on the Dashnaks remained a draft. If we could have exchanged desks, if I could have worked on my own story, while he interpreted the national aspirations of his compatriots, practical results might have been obtained.

As soon as the war was over, I hurried back to New York and Arlen was one of the first people that I saw there. I met him on a bright September afternoon strolling down Fifth Avenue, spruce, elegant and debonair. In a week or two he informed me he would be fifty, and, 'I don't feel a day under forty-nine,' he added.

He looked very much as he had quarter of a century earlier in W. L. George's drawing-room. He was living now in a small furnished apartment in the Volney Hotel on 74th Street between Park and Madison. His son, Michael John,* was at Groton, on his way to Harvard.

---

* Michael John Arlen has, at the time of writing, a column in the *New Yorker*.

The Arlens planned to stay over in America till their children were settled in the world. They were anxious to revisit London but once again there were problems of nationality. Arlen had come into America on a period permit which he could renew every six months; he wanted to take up a permanent residence, but though he was a British subject, the American immigration laws rate you by the country of your birth, so that in the eyes of Washington he was a Bulgarian and his wife a Greek; the quotas for those countries were filled till the year 2010. He was afraid that if he once left America, he might find it difficult to return. A typical Arlen situation.

I saw him a lot that autumn. We had many friends in common. His flat was small and he had few meals at home. He lunched either at the Colony or at the '21', usually in masculine company. Most evenings he was at a cocktail party; neat, starched, unobtrusively well dressed, his hands folded over his Malacca cane; the centre of the group around him, yet never monopolizing the conversation, bringing others into the talk, making them feel themselves attractive and important, taking genuine pleasure in any piece of good fortune that befell his friends. Then he would leave on a curtain line to take his wife out to dinner.

She too was little changed: her dark hair was flecked with grey, but she was trim and elegant, with the same air of *race*: they were a striking couple. It was very pleasant to see them dining together at the Colony. They were so very obviously enjoying each other's company. They looked a romantic couple on an early date.

He shook his head when I asked him what he was working on. Since his arrival in America he had spent two years in Hollywood, on a contract with M.G.M. but he had written nothing. He had never liked writing, he said. He didn't need to write. Why should he? He preferred reading; all lazy men like to read, he said, and he indulged in this type of sloth seven or eight hours a day. He read the kinds of book he liked, and he was generous in his praise of other writers. It did not worry him that his name no longer stood at the head of the best-seller list. He was getting what he wanted out of life.

'Of course I am happy,' he told an interviewer, 'any man should be happy who enjoys the patience of his wife, the tolerance of his children, and the loyalty of head waiters.'

It was now nine years since I had met him on Fifth Avenue and in a certain sense not much had happened to him since the relaxation of currency restrictions had made it possible for him to move into a large and pleasant Park Avenue department. He had sold his house in Cannes and brought over his furniture and books and pictures. His daughter, Venetia, was now a junior editor at Doubleday's. Michael John had been doing military service after graduating from Harvard, where he was one of the editors of the *Lampoon* and was largely responsible for its very amusing skit on *Punch*; for a year he was in Paris on the *Time-Life* staff. The family immigration problem had at last been settled by means no less august than an Act of Congress, and Michael Arlen had contentedly gone on being Michael Arlen.

The Park Avenue apartment contained a study. 'My wife has taken away my last excuse for not writing novels,' he complained. But he wrote nothing. Sometimes I felt it was a pity that so considerable a gift should have been allowed to wither, but when I read *The Flying Dutchman* I understood why he had let it do so. In the 1930s the following quatrain appeared in a fashionable London weekly:

Mr Arlen
Was formerly Mayfair's darling
But she raised a plucked and supercilious eyebrow
When he went all highbrow.

The side of him that still might have cared to write was no longer Michael Arlen and he had no use for it. He could now be Michael Arlen more effectively by not writing. It was as simple as all that.

He was always a man of gesture, and though the young Armenian who changed his name from Kouyoumdjian could not have foreseen this final chapter of his story, he would have recognized it as being in keeping with the plan of campaign he drew up in the *New Age* offices. He said then of his future and of the novel that he would write, 'The quality I shall desire in it will be fastidiousness.' He showed that quality as consistently in his life as in his writing. He would have been content, while he corrected the proofs of *The London Venture* in 1919, to have foreseen that in 1949 he would be reading the following description of himself in the *New Yorker*: 'Slender of waist, bushy of eyebrow, neatly sideburned, elegantly moustached, poised, urbane, resplendent in a pin-striped blue suit, the flourisher of a gold-banded Malacca cane, possessed by no demon whatever and apparently the world's best adjusted writer.'

It had been a long road from Dvornok, Bulgaria, to that side table in the King Cole Room: a long and a romantic road. Michael Arlen had fulfilled the destiny he chose.

18
W.S.M.: R.I.P.

I saw Somerset Maugham for the last time in Nice, in January 1965. We were strolling in opposite directions along the Promenade des Anglais. It was a warm, sunny day, freshened by a breeze. We paused for a brief gossip. He said to my companion, 'The wind in your cape makes you look like a bird.' He had a quick eye for women's clothes. He was smiling; he looked brisk and cheerful. It was one of his good days. As I watched him walk away, I said, 'I wonder if that's the last time we'll see him.' I hoped for his sake it was. His good days were now rare; his faculties were failing; living had become a burden. Yet in his general appearance, he had changed very little from the distant summer when I had begun to know him well.

That was in 1931, when I was spending a couple of quiet months in Villefranche, working upon a novel, and he invited me to lunch at the Villa Mauresque. But I had met him before, once, briefly in the early spring of 1922 at a lunch organized for the contributors to *Georgian Stories* by its editor Arnold Lunn, the elder brother of Hugh Kingsmill of whom I have written in an earlier chapter. Lunn had no particular qualifications for this self-inflicted chore; when he was knighted in 1952 for his services to British ski-ing, the award made no reference to any services to literature, but he had published in fact in addition to a number of books on mountaineering, a novel about school life *The Harrovians* that in its own field was a classic and that in the summer of 1913 was the centre of considerable controversy; while as a Roman Catholic convert he has been for many years 'a subtle disputant on creeds'. His interest in an anthology that

should be complementary to E. M.'s *Georgian Poetry*, may
be attributed to his having written a story called *A Scrap
of Paper* for which he could devise no other means of
publication. His editorship was not acknowledged,
because I fancy he did not want that story presented as
self-selected.

The lunch was held in a private room in the St Pancras
Station Hotel—a curious venue but the family offices
were conveniently close in Endsleigh Gardens. About a
dozen authors accepted Lunn's invitation.

Maugham who was represented in the anthology by
Rain was one of the first arrivals. Lunn's welcoming of
him was not too happy. 'I can't say I know your short
stories well, but I greatly enjoyed *Of Human Bondage*.'
Maugham made no reply; a wintry smile flickered beneath
his moustache. At lunch he sat next to Violet Hunt—
whom he may have had in mind when he drew the
character of Rose Sparlight in *The Moon and Sixpence*.
They were seated on the same side of the table as myself,
three places away and I had no chance of hearing their
conversation.

He and Violet Hunt left early. The contributors were
paying for their own lunches. As the waiter bustled
forward with their bills, Maugham picked up the two
slips of paper. 'I think I can stand you a lunch, Violet,'
he said. Violet Hunt was in low waters at the moment.
Her private troubles, and they were many, had been
widely publicized. Her soi-disant husband Ford Madox
Hueffer had left her for a very much younger woman
and become the father of a child, and though Violet
still entertained amply at Campden Hill she had ceased
to be a writer of whom anything in particular was
expected. Maugham's gesture re-established her as
regards that gathering. He seemed to be saying to us all
that she was not only an old friend, but the one person

in the room of any consequence to himself. As he was leaving the room, Lunn, from the head of the table, said, 'We don't seem to have decided what is a Georgian story.' Maugham's answer came back pat, 'A story written since George V's accession that we want to re-read today.' The tart retort, the wintry smile, the generous gesture to an old friend made that first meeting symptomatic.

It may seem surprising that Maugham should have bothered to attend the lunch, but that too was in character and keeping. He was always inquisitive about the literary scene, detached though he was from it. He wanted to be in the movement; he was sensitive to criticism. And he was no doubt conscious that his reputation as a novelist did not stand high just then. He was not mentioned once in W. L. George's *A Novelist on Novels* and though it was as a novelist that he began his career, at the turn of the century, it was as a dramatist, a writer of social comedies, that eight years later he achieved his first spectacular success.

His first novel, *Liza of Lambeth*, was a brutal story of low life in Bermondsey for which his experiences as a doctor had given him first-hand information, 'his little black bag protecting him in the foul courts that the police hesitated to enter'. It earned him in royalties during the first year only £20 but it impressed the critics and its reception encouraged him to abandon medicine. He had been left a small sum of money and he decided to invest it in himself. He went abroad and set himself to become a writer. He was then twenty-three.

During the next few years he published several novels including *Mrs Craddock*. They did not earn much money but they were reviewed respectfully. He was also working upon plays, one of which, *A Man of Honour*, was produced by the Stage Society. It was subsequently published in

the *Fortnightly Review*, but it was too sombre and realistic
to attract the commercial theatre. It contained, however,
a scene of comedy, whose reception made Maugham
suspect that he would be wise to exploit this line. He
wrote *Lady Frederick*. In its big scene a woman in her
thirties reveals herself to a young admirer without her
make-up. Managers shook their heads. No leading
actress, they assured him, would display herself at such a
disadvantage. Maugham wrote another comedy, *Mrs
Dot*. This time, managers told him that he was too cynical.
But he persisted and at last had a lucky break. A play at
the Court had to be taken off earlier than had been
expected, and its successor was not yet ready. *Lady
Frederick* was put on as a stop-gap for a six-weeks' run.
The scene in which the leading actress revealed the
intimacies of her toilet 'brought down the house' and the
play ran a year.

Managers now decided that after all he was not too
cynical and sought his wares. He had a number of plays
in the drawer—*Mrs Dot, Jack Straw, The Explorer*. Within
a few weeks his name was on the boards of four simul-
taneous successes, and *Punch* had a cartoon showing
Shakespeare looking enviously at the playbills. That was
in 1908.

Few writers have enjoyed a more sensational success.
But it was not the kind of success to impress the *avant-
garde* criticism of the day. Popularity is always an object
of distrust and 1908 marked the peak of a period that was
in violent reaction against the languid eccentricities of the
'nineties. Art, it was then held, should have a purpose:
and it was to the plays of Shaw and Galsworthy and the
novels of H. G. Wells that the young turned for authority
and guidance. Maugham, in their eyes, had no message.
He did not want to improve people or to expose abuses. It
was held that 'he stood for nothing' and that he was

merely 'an entertainer'. His stock in 1910 stood lower
with the intelligentsia than it had in 1900, and for quite
a while nothing happened to make the intelligentsia
reconsider its verdict.

For the next seven years he wrote exclusively for the
stage. Walking past the Comedy Theatre where the
'House Full' boards were up outside *Mrs Dot*, he thought,
at the sight of a sunset above Panton Street, 'Thank God,
I can look at a sunset now without having to think how to
describe it.' He planned never to write another book. But
he had reckoned without his temperament. He found himself living in his own past. 'It became,' he wrote, 'such a
burden to me that I made up my mind that I could only
regain my peace by writing it all down in the form of a
novel.' That was shortly before World War I and the
novel was *Of Human Bondage*.

It was published in 1915 and in England it made little
stir. It had no bearing on the war and the very qualities
that have given it a capacity to interest the readers of later
generations prevented it from succeeding then. It dealt
with permanent problems at a time when the public was
concerned with the day's events. No, it is not surprising
that W. L. George writing in 1918 should have failed to
realize on the evidence of a single book that the course of
Maugham's career had changed direction. The betting
was a hundred to one against any such occurrence. But
this happened to be the hundredth time.

'Success,' he was to write twenty years later in *The
Summing Up*, 'may well cut the author off from the
material that is its source,' and this might have been his
fate. His plays earned him a great deal of money at a
time when income-tax was low; he bought himself a
house in Mayfair, and soon after married. Had the
marriage proved a happy one he would presumably have

led a fashionable metropolitan life, writing Mayfair comedies, until after a dozen or so years his material wore thin. Luckily for literature that did not happen. His marriage was a failure. Personal unhappiness made him dissatisfied both with the life that he was leading and the work he was producing. 'I was tired of the man I was,' he wrote, 'and it seemed to me that by a long journey to some far country I might renew myself.'

He was over forty, and the exigencies of his war-time duties in Intelligence simplified the cutting of his links with England. They gave him a chance of visiting the South Pacific. As soon as the war was over he went to China. The South Seas gave him *Rain* and *The Moon and Sixpence*, but the Far East was to give him more; it brought him back to the material he understood. He had roots in Malaya to an extent that he had never had in Mayfair.

He had been educated at one of the smaller public schools, and it was from this type of school that were recruited the bank clerks, district officers and planters who people his Malayan stories. The lives that were led in England by the cousins and brothers of his characters, in the prim domesticities of suburbia, would have bored him inexpressibly but their own lives against the background of the East were vivid, violent, and dramatic: or perhaps it would be more true to say that he interpreted their lives in terms of violent and vivid drama.

He wrote always about what are called 'ordinary people', but he showed them under the pressure of unusual circumstance. Many of his Far Eastern stories end with suicide or murder, and adultery is the pivot for a large proportion of them. They are long stories, 15,000 to 20,000 words, roughly the length of a play, and one of them, *The Letter*, like *Rain*, was capable of almost direct transference to the stage. His mind was adjusted to the

types of plot and theme that fitted within this circumference. It is a length that few writers have managed to
employ. But it is a very satisfactory length. It takes an
hour to read, and it gives scope for the introduction of
settings and of minor characters. By writing at this length
Maugham was able to keep the background of the East
constantly before the reader's eye. He rarely attempted
what is called 'fine writing' but his scenic descriptions
are masterpieces of accurate observation. You touch and
smell the East. You can understand how in that atmosphere 'ordinary people' could be driven to desperate reme-
dies.

He re-created himself during a decade of travel and his
output during this period was remarkable: two novels—
The Moon and Sixpence and *The Painted Veil*; two travel
books—*On a Chinese Screen* and *The Gentleman in the
Parlour*; one of his very best plays, *East of Suez*; the
collection of secret service stories which introduced the
character of Ashenden, his *alter ego*; the six South Sea
stories of *The Trembling of a Leaf*; the six Malayan stories
of *The Casuarina Tree* which included *The Letter*; a
number of short stories awaiting publication in book
form. Nineteen-twenty-two also saw the triumphant, prolonged success of *Our Betters*, written in 1915, while *The
Constant Wife* ran for many months in New York though
in London it never recovered from an unlucky first night,
when the pit was allowed into the back two rows of the
stalls and chaos ensued when the owners of the numbered
seats arrived. The pit was asked to move back two rows
and naturally having waited for several hours declined.
I arrived a few minutes before the curtain was due to
rise to find 'God Save the King' being played in order to
get people on their feet, and quiet. The curtain eventually
went up twenty minutes late. Several dramatic critics
were forced to stand throughout and the cast was so upset

that the timing was badly at fault in a play that depended on timing for its success. In New York it was, however, a very great success.

In New York the play of *Rain* ran for two years. In London it was less successful. Tallulah Bankhead had been most anxious to play the lead, but after a few rehearsals the part was given to Olga Lindo. On the other hand the play of *The Letter* with Gladys Cooper as the murderess was a great success in London. By 1930, which saw the publication of *Cakes and Ale* he had become one of the most discussed figures in English letters. Not only was he producing a sequence of exciting and dramatic stories, but he was in tune with the temper of his time. He had had no message for the eager young Fabians of 1908 who had discussed women's suffrage over glasses of Russian tea, but he did have for an exhausted post-war generation that had achieved victory at the cost of immense self-sacrifice only to find that the war that was to end war—H. G. Wells's phrase—was being followed by the peace that would end peace. Maugham was in the same leaking boat. In spite of his wealth and fame he was reputed to be an embittered man. He had won, after long labour, to success, only to find its savour that of dead sea fruit. Disenchanted himself, he offered to his readers the philosophy and pattern of escape. Mystery as well as glamour was about him. There was a sinister undertone to the legend that surrounded him. Where Kipling had presented the British Empire in terms of 'The White Man's Burden', Maugham presented it as a means of cutting free from the Western 'rat-race', from the profit-less amassing of possessions that moth and dust were waiting to corrupt. *The Moon and Sixpence*, *The Casuarina Tree*, and *The Fall of Edward Barnard* coloured the outlook of the disillusioned 1920s just as *Ann Veronica* and *Man and Superman* had fired the optimism of the last

Edwardians. Maugham was the mouthpiece of that decade.

For ten years he lived in suitcases. Then he felt the need of a home, a base, and bought high on Cap Ferrat the villa that can be seen white and rectangular against the pines, along the coast from Antibes, and set on its gatepost the sign against the evil eye that is stamped upon all his books.

A great deal had happened indeed during the nine years between that lunch in the St Pancras Hotel and my first visit to the Villa Mauresque in the spring of 1931.

On that first lunch I was the only guest. There were just the three of us, W. S. M., Gerald Haxton and myself. Much has recently appeared in print about Haxton that could never have been printed in Maugham's lifetime. Maugham had a strong homosexual streak; how strong it is futile to conjecture. Robin Maugham reports his uncle as having confessed that one of his major mistakes was having tried to convince not only others but himself that he was only twenty-five instead of seventy-five per cent homosexual. Haxton, an American, had as a young man been arrested in London on a homosexual offence; he was acquitted, but the Judge was convinced of his guilt and he was registered as an 'undesirable alien' and forced to leave the country. If Maugham wanted to enjoy Haxton's company, he had to enjoy it out of England.

There can be little doubt that Haxton was largely responsible for the break-up of Maugham's marriage. There was a bitter rivalry between him and Syrie Maugham, and Beverley Nichols's *A Case of Human Bondage* has an excruciatingly comic account of an attempt by Syrie Maugham to woo her husband back during a long week-end at St Tropez.

Beverley Nichols regarded Haxton as the evil influence

in Maugham's life. But no matter how reprehensible morally it may all have been, it served the purposes of literature. Haxton may have been a heavy drinker and a reckless gambler, but he was the ideal companion for the travels that were the source of Maugham's development. He was debonair and dashing, good company and a good mixer, everything that Maugham was not. In *The Summing Up* Maugham expresses his debt to him. 'It was a great help when I was travelling to have someone who made friends quickly with the kind of person whom it was important for me to know.' Nearly everyone liked Gerald Haxton, right away. And I have heard more than one man say that his best times with Maugham were in a trio with Gerald Haxton. Cyril Connolly in his review of Beverley Nichols's exposé wrote, 'Haxton was probably a bad hat, but I found him charming.'

From 1931 until the end of his life, I saw Maugham regularly in London and in the South of France. I would hesitate to call myself a close friend of his; disparity of age and of position precluded that; inevitably he meant much more to me than I could ever mean to him. But we had, through my travels, much in common. Myself, I felt always close to him.

He had the reputation of being difficult. Many of his friends complained that they could never feel at ease with him. Certainly his stammer made conversation awkward. He wrote of Arnold Bennett that it must have been infuriating for him to think of a witty interpolation and have to refrain from making it for fear that it would be ruined by his stammer. He was thinking of himself, in early days.

By the time I met him he was treated with deference. The table would wait for what he had to say. He had moreover evolved a conversational style that incorporated his stammer. Even so it was with a sense of conscious effort that a long sentence wound to a full stop. One was left at the end with a feeling both of exhaustion and achievement. One was tempted to applaud as one does when a runner breaks the tape. It was not easy afterwards to pick up the thread of the conversation quickly. There was a danger that each time Maugham began to speak there would be a hiatus when he stopped.

Another reason for uneasiness in his company was the fact that because so many of his stories are told in the first person or through the mouth of his *alter ego* Ashenden, one felt one knew in advance his temperament and tastes. Ashenden was an acute and pitiless observer, judging people by the way they dressed, talked, behaved at table, entertained. It was impossible not to suspect that one was being judged oneself, in just that way; one was on guard.

It was generally held that he did not like to be complimented on his books. In his story, *His Excellency*, he approves the tact of the ambassador who did not mention any of Ashenden's books but indicated by a couple of casual references that he had read them. But I am not certain that he did not appreciate an occasional compliment if it was made at the right time, in the right way. In the spring of 1956, I was escorting along the coast a flamboyant lady of considerable charm but little education. I had qualms about taking her to the Villa, but I wanted to see Maugham, and her feelings would have been deeply hurt had she been left behind. I briefed her carefully. 'Whatever you do,' I warned her, 'don't refer to his books.' She followed my instructions, but on the way back, she said, 'It was ridiculous of you not to let me talk to him about his books. I had something I particularly wanted to say. I know he'd have been pleased. I'm going to write to him.'

She showed me the letter before she posted it. It explained how I had told her that she must not discuss his books with him, but she had to let him know how much his work had meant to her. Mentioning two or three of his short stories, she concluded by saying that she owed her interest in Indian philosophy to him. It seemed to me the kind of routine letter that most professional writers get every now and then. To my astonishment it had on Maugham the effect she had anticipated. Next time I saw Alan Searle, his secretary, almost the first thing he said was, 'What happened to that wild redhead that you brought up here? I've never seen Willie so much touched by anything as by the letter that she wrote him.' Maugham asked after her at once. Repercussions came back to me through Cyril Connolly. 'I couldn't think what Alec was doing with that eccentric creature,' Maugham had said, 'and then from her, of all people, to get that letter.'

Clearly she had been right and I was wrong. Perhaps, in our anxiety to avoid mistakes, to spare him irritation, we all went to the other extreme. Perhaps he missed the homage that we would have paid him so readily, so gladly, from such full hearts.

We accepted, all of us, too easily the picture that he presented of himself as 'I' and 'Ashenden'. The 'I' of *The Moon and Sixpence* and of *The Trembling of a Leaf*, the Ashenden who said, 'You fool, you've murdered the wrong man,' was aloof, detached, sardonic, watching with cynical enjoyment the follies of his fellow mortals. He had a chilling presence. A character in his story *The Pool* quotes Francis Thompson's 'In No Strange Land'. 'I've read "The Hound of Heaven". It's a bit of all right,' he says. 'It is generally thought so,' Maugham's 'I' says. What a freezing remark. What a deterrent to anyone young and enthusiastic meeting Maugham for the first time. Yet behind that mask, there was an affectionate, though watchful person, and it must be remembered that when he was writing *The Moon and Sixpence*, *The Trembling of a Leaf*, and *Ashenden*—the books that first presented his *persona* to the world—he was passing through a series of harrowing domestic crises. The 'I' of *The Razor's Edge* is a very much mellower person than the 'I' of *The Moon and Sixpence*. Ashenden was the screen behind which Maugham protected himself against the facile emotions of a self-deluding world. Some of us are proud enough to feel that at times we broke through that screen, to find on the other side someone whom it was not difficult to love.

Maugham was accused both as a writer and a human being of a lack of sympathy. But he had been trained as a doctor to diagnose complaints and prescribe cures. Michael Arlen's wife said, 'He will listen quietly as though you were in a consulting room. He will ask one or two pointed questions, then he will say, "If you do this, Atalanta, that will happen. If you do that, this will happen. You must decide for yourself." I found great comfort in that,' she said.

A few years ago, an ageing actress came to him in high indignation, because her lover had abandoned her for a younger woman. 'I told her,' he said, 'that she had had nine years of him, and that she should be grateful for what she had had. She thought me very heartless.'

Myself, I always felt that he was the one person in the world who could completely understand me. If I were to go to him in trouble, very little explanation would be required. Like a doctor, he would resolve my perplexities. I always had to resist an impulse to confide in him. I resisted it successfully. But the confidence that I knew I should be understood added a dimension to my deep fondness for him.

In 1936 he published his autobiography *The Summing Up*; it was a kind of leave-taking. A writer set out to create *un œuvre*, he said, and he had finished his. He compared it to a house: in his remaining years he would go on writing; he might add a gable here, a turret there, he might lay out a rose garden, but the main structure was complete. He had reached the tether of his ambition.

He seemed to have everything a man could need. He had made and was making a very great deal of money. In his early sixties, he was active on the tennis court, the golf course, in the swimming pool. He could entertain his friends under the most congenial conditions, looking out from his high terrace, across the sea, to the outline of the Estérels. There were his annual visits to London in the autumn; in the winter there was usually a long trip, to India or the Caribbean. As far as he ever could be happy, I would say he was, in the 1930s. 'All that should accompany old age' was waiting in the wings.

In the preface that he wrote in 1952 to a selected collection of Kipling's stories, he suggested that authors usually reach the full development of their powers between the ages of thirty-five and forty, do their best work for the next fifteen or twenty years then start to decline. He may have thought of himself as being about to enter upon this final stage during those summers of the later 'thirties. But fate once more intervened. In the spring of 1940, the Germans broke through to the channel ports and Maugham in his sixty-sixth year had to make a snap decision. Should he stay on at the Villa Mauresque or risk a return to England in a coal boat through submarine-infested waters? There was another alternative —a phial of sleeping pills in his bathroom drawer. He never considered the possibility of letting himself be taken prisoner, but he must in that hour of indecision have contrasted the dangers and discomforts of that journey with the amount of enjoyment life had still to offer him.

It may not have seemed to offer him so very much. A few years back he had retired from the theatre with his last three plays little more than half successes. He had exhausted his Far East material; the South of France had supplied him with one or two amusing plots, *The Three Fat Women of Antibes* in particular: but the issues in that charming playground were less vital, less dramatic. He had made a disappointing trip to the West Indies. I was to remark to him twelve years later on the eve of sailing for the Leeward Islands that although I had spent many months in the Caribbean I had only found two or three plots there. He had had, he said, a similar experience. Kipling had told him that there were plenty of plots there, 'but that they were mine not his. I went but I found nothing.' The life of the French convicts on Devil's Island gave him two short stories, and a motif in *Christmas Holiday*. But that was all.

In 1937 he had gone to India. He had felt for many years that Kipling had covered the ground too completely for it to be worth his while to go. But Kipling's world no longer existed, and 'I should be trying,' he said, 'to see a different India. I found a lot. As soon as the maharajahs realized that I didn't want to go on tiger hunts but that I was interested in seeing poets and philosophers, they were very helpful. I planned to return there in the autumn of 1939; the war prevented that. I think I should have got a great deal from a second visit.'

As he deliberated the alternative to that phial of sleeping pills, he must have suspected that in the cancelling of that trip to India his last chance of re-creating himself had gone. In *A Personal Record* he tells us that he decided to return because he felt that one or two people in England might still need him. He left the pills in his bathroom. Had he emptied that phial, he would have been spared some bitter hours in his later years, but he would have missed the summit of his career.

In *A Personal Record* he described the discomforts, privations, the farcical situations of that journey back. But he did not tell how a fellow passenger who had deviously acquired an extra ration, offered him a share. Maugham declined. His pride would not allow him, at such a time, to avoid the common lot.

There was nothing for him to do in England. In the First War, he had carried out a number of secret missions but this time he could see no scope for himself. He might as well go to America. Control of currency was strict. He could take no money out of England. His continental income was frozen and he arrived in New York with two dollars in his pocket, to be instructed by the British Treasury authorities in Washington that he must turn over to them all the dollars that he earned, in return for which they would make him what they considered a reasonable allowance. His publisher Nelson Doubleday built him a comfortable eight-room house on his estate in South Carolina, 'in desolate yet oddly beautiful country', and after a visit to Hollywood he moved there in December 1941.

He relished its peace and quiet; but it was too quiet and peaceful for Gerald Haxton, who now that America was in the war, saw an opportunity of becoming something in his own right, not just 'Willie's friend'. He took a clerical job in Washington. While Maugham, in exile, driven back upon himself set to work, once again, upon a major novel.

Through 1942 and the early months of 1943 he worked steadily on *The Razor's Edge*. Never had he written so sunnily, with such serenity. As the narrator he was not Willie Ashenden, but Willie Maugham, speaking in *propria persona* and allowing himself to be teased by a heroine who is no less charming than his own fictional favourite Rosie Gann.

While he was turning his enforced solitude to his own advantage, Haxton, without Maugham's watchful care, was working and drinking himself to death. He died in November 1944.

The serialization of *The Razor's Edge* started in 1943 and the book was published in April 1944. It was as lucky in its timing in the Second War as *Of Human Bondage* had been unlucky in the First. War-time conditions, with the blackout and the curtailment of entertainment, had created a demand for reading matter that the publishers could not satisfy. Old books went out of print, and though new books were issued in rationed quantities the standard of contemporary writing was very low. The young writers were in uniform, the elder ones were either too busy or too harassed to write well or had put aside their pens for war work. It was, in 1944, both for the general reader and the critic, an immense relief to be offered a mature, adult novel, the work of a perfected craftsman, working within his powers, with an exact knowledge of those powers and with the sense of reserves behind him. *The Razor's Edge* is told in the first person and nowhere has Maugham deployed that particular technique with more assurance. Never had he been more mellow.

The timing for the theme, too, was lucky. The plot is that of *The Fall of Edward Barnard*. (How often authors rewrite their old stories after twenty-five years from a different angle: *Theatre* is a retelling of *Mrs Craddock*.) Two friends, Americans, fall in love with the same girl. Their friendship is not ruined by her choice between them. The fiancé goes to Europe to make his fortune; but while away he loses his faith in 'the American way of life', refuses to return to America and stands aside while the girl marries the other man. It is the same plot as *Edward Barnard*, but the theme is different. For whereas Edward Barnard made an escapist's choice, living on in Tahiti, idly, with a pretty Polynesian, the hero of *The Razor's Edge* refused the conventional pattern out of a discovery in himself of a sense of purpose, a working towards the life of a mystic and ascetic. It was a theme appropriate to the hour. Escapism is sympathetic to a decade of disenchanted lassitude, but it is not sympathetic to an hour of strain and action. In *The Razor's Edge* Maugham offered hope; he had got past bitterness. Yet he was not throwing out his solution as a sop. He wrote as a man with faith.

The last time I lunched with him, I asked him whether, when he wrote *The Summing Up*, he suspected that he had another major book inside him. He had written then that he had completed his *œuvre*, but that *œuvre* would have been incomplete without *The Razor's Edge*. He shrugged when I asked him that. He could be exceedingly evasive when he chose. But he did not insist that he had always had *The Razor's Edge* in mind. I like to think of the episode as another working out of that 'divinity that shapes our ends'. Fate had decided to give Maugham the opportunity of expending his talent to the full. He took it with both hands.

In theme and content, *The Razor's Edge* is one of his major books. It is a long novel with a number of secondary stories woven into the central plot. Yet 'the direction of interest', which is his own definition of a plot, is never lost. The book was a great immediate success and it laid the the foundation for the fame he was to enjoy after the war, when he returned to France.

Fame is the proper word to use. During the 1930s he had been sensitive to the lack of recognition that he had received from the intelligentsia. 'When clever young men write essays about contemporary fiction they never think of considering me.' He said more than once that he considered himself unlucky to have begun writing short stories at a time when Chekhov's stock stood so high and Maupassant's so low, and the preface to his collected edition of short stories, *Altogether*, consists in large part of a comparison between Maupassant and Chekhov. He had also mentioned that the French admire order, pattern, and form, and that his reputation stood higher in France than it did in England. More than once he had felt it necessary to defend the magazine short story. But now he had the highbrows on his side. Time had placed him in perspective.

The ten years after the war marked his apotheosis. He was the Grand Old Man of letters. He stood alone. Many of the pre-war writers were exhausted, the young ones had not yet appeared. His stories and novels were reissued in a succession of editions. His plays were revived. TV gave him a new medium. Three selections of his short stories were put upon the screen, with he himself introducing them. Most years he issued a collection of literary reminiscences or critical studies. The Villa Mauresque was still a social centre. He was accorded at last the critical acclaim that he had been denied between the wars. On his eightieth birthday in January 1954, almost every newspaper in the world paid him lengthy tribute. In the birthday honours list, he was made a C.H. (Companion of Honour), the highest award short of the O.M. (Order of Merit) that can be paid to a British man of letters. He was in good health, he was active and alert. He appeared to be thoroughly enjoying his success. In the fall of 1959 he sailed for the Far East to revisit the scenes of his old stories. Thirty years earlier indignant rubber planters in Malaya had sworn that he would never dare return. He could never be forgiven for *The Letter*. But he was received everywhere with honour. It was the climax to an Indian summer. It is a pity that the curtain could not have fallen then.

He lived too long for his own happiness and dignity. His last years were marred by his quarrel with his daughter and the ill-advised publication of the story of his marriage. In *The Summing Up* he wrote, 'Beyond a certain point I do not intend to take the reader into my confidence.' He forgot that promise.

Alan Searle, in an interview, attributed his loss of judgement to the rejuvenation injections that he took in Switzerland. He had three of these operations. He lunched with me in Villefranche on his return from his last visit. It was a mild spring day and we sat in the open at the harbour side. He was allowed to drink only champagne and the gold-foiled bottle in its steaming bucket was an incentive to conviviality. He looked wonderfully well. He had put on weight and the extra flesh on his cheeks had absorbed his wrinkles. It was hard to believe that he was eighty-eight. His appearance seemed to provide an amulet against the approach of age. I asked him about the injections. 'When should I start having them?'

'Before you actually need them. In your case fairly soon.'

But I never shall. His example provides a salutary warning. They gave his body a vigour that at that age his mind could not support.

He announced, when he was working on those final memoirs, that they would not be published in his lifetime. Alan Searle said, 'You had better get yourself buried pretty deep. A lot of people will want to dig you up and hang you.' Maugham knew they should not be published.

But eventually he consented to a serial publication, under the influence of Lord Beaverbrook, so it has been said. The temptation must have been very great. It is difficult for a writer to suppress a piece of work which he believes is good, and *Looking Back* as it appeared in *Show*—in the London *Sunday Express* it was ruthlessly compressed— was a dramatic narrative that could have figured effectively in a fictionalized Willie Ashenden biography. But as a confession purporting to tell the truth, the whole truth, and nothing but the truth about his marriage, it clearly told only half the truth. There was no reference to the part that Gerald Haxton played in its break-up. There was no need for Maugham to take the world into his confidence, but when he once decided to put himself under the microscope, he was beholden to reveal everything that showed upon the slide.

The publication of *Looking Back* roused great indignation among many of his late wife's friends. Nobody particularly minded its being said that fifty years back in the hey-day of Edwardian gallantry a number of rich men had contributed to her support, but the allegation that she sold her jewellery and bric-à-brac and then claimed from the insurance companies was profoundly shocking; a letter of protest to the Press was signed by a group of men and women for whom he could not have failed to feel respect. It was rumoured that when he went into the bar of the Garrick Club, a number of members left the room. That was in the late autumn of 1962. He said that he would never go back to London. As far as I know, he never did.

The last eighteen months of his life were sad. He was unhappy in himself. He had his good days but he was very weak. His memory played him tricks; he had trouble with his eyes; he was very deaf. For a long time he refused to buy a hearing aid—it was too expensive, he said. When at last he agreed to buy one, he lost patience with it and flung it into the sea. Conversation with him was very difficult. One would mention a friend of long standing. 'Ah, yes,' he would say. 'Now I must have met him surely, Alan, thirty or forty years ago.' Searle would reply, 'He spent two weeks here the summer before last.'

Many stories were told about his slips of memory. At a Riviera lunch party he sat next to an old friend, Eric Dunstan. They had a long and cosy talk. Finally Maugham said, 'I was sorry to hear of Eric Dunstan's death. I liked that man.' There was the occasion when his daughter paid him a visit after their reconciliation. He mistook her for her mother. 'Syrie, you bitch,' he shouted. 'You've ruined my whole life. How dare you come into my house? Get out of it at once.'

But I wonder sometimes whether, conscious of his own predicament, he did not often deliberately exploit its possibilities for his own amusement. I recall how at the end of a lunch some months before his death, when I was exhausted by ninety minutes of confusion, a look of schoolboy mischief flickered in his eyes. 'Tell me now,' he said, 'what happened to that fellow who wrote all those stories about Malaya. I thought him rather promising.' Perhaps more often than any of us guessed, the old jester whose sallies from the Edwardian stage sent ripples of laughter through the auditorium, was having a final fling for the sake of his own private chuckle.

At the end of *A Writer's Notebook*, Maugham allows himself to wonder what part, if any, of his work will be read a century hence. He is becomingly modest on the issue, but at the same time he is not unconscious of his unique position. *Of Human Bondage* is the most read of his books and the most generally admired. I asked him once if he considered it his best. He said he had no idea, since he had not read it since he corrected the final proofs. It may seem odd that curiosity should not have sent him back to it, but it is typical of him that he should have resisted the impulse, knowing that he could do nothing now to better it.

In *A Writer's Notebook* he expresses doubt as to whether so long a book can hope to survive the pressure of the future. But it is, it seems to me, on other grounds, that *Of Human Bondage* is less likely to appeal to succeeding generations than many of his short stories. He has said himself that though a writer may set out to draw a picture of life, it can never be more than a partial one, but if he is fortunate he will succeed in doing something else, he will draw a complete picture of himself. And though Maugham has called *Of Human Bondage* an autobiographical novel, there is less of the essential Maugham there than in *Cakes and Ale* and in *The Moon and Sixpence*. Philip in *Of Human Bondage* may have shared many of Maugham's experiences, but he is not Maugham; he is an obscure doctor, not a successful author. A man with Maugham's temperament would never have remained obscure.

In a few years' time, inevitably, Maugham's reputation will undergo a slump. He has been so long supreme, and those who enthrone a new deity will find it necessary to increase the praise of the new god by decrying the qualities of the old. But I cannot believe that the reaction will last for long. Several of his books may go out of print for ever, but there are so few great story-tellers, and few have equalled Maugham's capacity to carry your interest on from one page to the next. You cannot put him down, not only because of the excellence of the plot but for the manner of its telling. It is not chance that led him to put an Arab charm against the evil eye upon the covers of his books. He has a deep affinity with those story-tellers of the market-place who hold their audience with the power of their eye, the intonation of their voice, the movements of their hands. He lays his individual spell upon you, so that in retrospect you remember not only the tale itself, but the teller of it. The story is a medium, a means to an end, and future generations will, I am very sure, be as fascinated as we ourselves have been by this enigmatic man, the object of so much conjecture, a man at the same time so thwarted and so rewarded, a man who has been offered the sampling of every dish the banquet of life has for offering, yet has been denied on his own admission the very consolations that alone make life tolerable for the vast majority of human beings; a man so disillusioned, so unself-deceived, so ruthless towards himself yet to others so invariably helpful; a man who in the last analysis has always been upon the side of what was true and simple, of what the Greeks called 'the beautiful and good'.

19

The MacDowell Colony

(Written in 1965)

D uring the post-war years my links with the U.S.A.
grew closer and stronger. Four-fifths of my
income was earned there and if you work for
magazines, it is as well to be in touch with editors. Moreover I had now more friends in New York than I had in
London. Most of the friends that I had made in 1920 had
been ten to fifteen years older than myself. None of them
had been young enough to serve in the Second War. They
had gone six years in one direction, I in another. Several
of them were on the brink of retirement. We had only the
past in common.

In America, on the other hand, I was meeting my
opposite numbers—either my contemporaries or men
younger than myself, the equivalents to me of what I
had been to my seniors twenty-five years before. You
make friends more quickly and more easily in New York
than you do in London. I was spending five or six months
a year in the U.S.A.

I was happy to be doing so. There was, however, one
major problem connected with my change of base. I have
never been able to work in cities, and I needed in America
some equivalent for the small country inns like the Easton
Court Hotel, at Chagford, where I used to go periodically
for a month's concentrated writing. Carl Brandt shook his
head when I asked him his advice. There was, he said, no
equivalent of Easton Court. There were hotels in the
country and on the sea but they were only open in the
season, when they would be crowded. I would be caught
up into the animation of resort existence. There were

farms that let off rooms to lodgers, but there I should have to join the family at meals. I should not get the seclusion that I needed. 'There is only one kind of place where you could go, one of those artists' colonies. Yaddo or MacDowell.'

The prospect filled me with misgiving. I could not imagine anything worse than the constant company of artists, most of whom presumably would be precious and peevish. Things would have gone wrong with them, personally or professionally, or they would not be at an artists' colony. The old ones would have chips upon their shoulders, the young ones would be superior, disdainful of anyone who wrote for magazines. I should be better off with a family on a farm.

Carl Brandt again shook his head. 'They aren't that kind of place at all. You can tell that from the people who go to them.' He reeled off a list of MacDowell names— De Bose Heyward, Hervey Allen, Elinor Wylie, William Rose Benét, Carl Carmer, Margaret Widdemere, Thornton Wilder . . . the names flowed on. It was an impressive list. I let myself be persuaded. Stanley Young, who was at that time a partner in Farrar Straus, was on the board of directors. He forwarded my application for a two months' residence, and on 1 June 1951 I took the train for Boston, my heart heavy with foreboding. Today, fourteen years later, I wonder how I should have managed without the MacDowell Colony.

The Colony is in New Hampshire, a mile and a half from Peterborough, which claims to be the original of Thornton Wilder's play *Our Town*, and probably it is, since Thornton Wilder has been many times a colonist. Early in the century Edward MacDowell, the composer, bought an estate there; he was in retirement, and he built a log cabin in the woods where he could work; he went off to it every morning after breakfast, and he had his lunch left in a basket outside his door so that the current of his thoughts should not be disturbed. He was visited by a number of his friends, in particular Edward Arlington Robinson. He had studios built for them, and the pattern of the basket outside the studio door was maintained for them. They all agreed that they had never had conditions more congenial for work. When MacDowell died, his widow, in tribute to his memory, decided to enlarge his home, with its log cabins in the woods, into a summer colony for writers, painters and composers.

It opened in 1907, very simply, with three studios; the first colonists were guests, though they contributed a nominal sum to their support. During the winter, Mrs MacDowell was an assiduous fund-raiser; she toured the country, she gave concerts, she organized committees, enrolled benefactors. The funds increased steadily; and as the balance mounted, so did the number of cabins in the woods. There were twenty-four in 1951.

Mrs MacDowell was still alive then, and actively alive. The traditions of her authority were continued. Those traditions have been amusingly described by Margaret Widdermere in *Golden Friends I Had*. Mrs MacDowell was a strict disciplinarian, and she was resolved that the cabins should not be used for any purpose but work. They were unlighted, and there was a rule that no one should go to his or her studio after dinner. A colonist, she explained, might fall and injure himself in the dark and be unable to get assistance; there was also mention of a fire risk. She herself dined with the colonists and expected them to be in attendance until they retired to bed. She did not encourage them to have local friends. The colonist who absented himself with any regularity would not receive a second invitation.

When I paid my first visit to the Colony, Mrs Mac-Dowell was in her late eighties. She played no part in the life of the Colony, but she was alert, behind the scenes. She lived in her own house, Hillcrest, and one by one the colonists would pay their respects to her. It was a little like the ritual that is observed by a British visitor to a British colony; he signs the book at Government House and awaits from His Excellency an invitation appropriate to his social status, the invitation coming through the A.D.C. At the Colony, on one's fourth or fifth day, one would write a little note to Mrs MacDowell, saying that one was now in residence, that one greatly appreciated the amenities and opportunities one was receiving and hoped that one would be given an occasion of expressing one's gratitude in person. A day or so later, there would be a letter from the secretary, asking one to tea at four o'clock on such and such a day.

She was small and slim and very straight. Her hair was brushed back from her forehead. She was in black; I have retained an impression of lace and taffeta and whalebone; of a head held high, above a stiff high collar. There were rings and necklaces. She had great dignity, but she was not stern, which I had expected her to be. She had had herself briefed before the interview. She knew what kinds of book I wrote. She enquired about her English friends, wondering if I knew any of them. She asked, in particular, about Charles Morgan, with whom she was in correspondence and whose wife, Hilda Vaughan, had been a colonist during the war. She asked if T. S. Eliot's reputation stood as high as ever. She was interested in 'the new thing'. She was living in the present and in the future rather than in the past. She asked me if I was finding the conditions at the Colony conducive to steady working. I told her that I had been looking all my life for just those conditions.

I did not exaggerate. The daily routine was this. The men lived in a house, The Lodge, a third of a mile from the central building, Colony Hall. The women lived in two smaller cottages: Pan Cottage and The Eaves, close to Colony Hall. Colony Hall itself was a large, two-storeyed building—it had once been a barn—which contained, in addition to a few bedrooms on the first floor, a dining-room and a large recreation room that housed a small library in addition to billiards and ping-pong tables. There was also, within range of Colony Hall, a very charming library, where in the evenings there would be an occasional concert or poetry reading.

Breakfast was from seven thirty to eight thirty. At seven fifteen a first bell would be rung; at seven thirty a second. The ringing of these bells caused consternation among some of the colonists who wanted to sleep on to the last minute, or even beyond the last minute, who were ready to forego breakfast and heat themselves a cup of tea or coffee in their studios. In every group there is invariably one colonist who will find some original reason for complaint.

Breakfast is usually a gay meal, with a good deal of laughter. But it would be surprising if a group of twenty-four did not contain several who do not feel in the mood for bright conversation early in the day. At one time the experiment was made of having a special 'grumps' table at which conversation was not permitted. But the experiment did not work because the grumps did not like the the sight of each other early in the morning.

By 8.45 the dining-room was empty, and a day of industry, nine and a quarter hours long, until dinner at 6 p.m., stretched ahead of us. Each colonist was promised complete isolation, and the strictest colony rule is that which forbids the visiting of one student by another without an invitation.

Each colonist arranged a different schedule for himself. In the early summer, it is still so cool in the morning that one needs the studio warmed. The first act of the day is the building of a log fire, and the maintenance of that fire through the morning is one of those menial tasks that cradle the creative processes. I am a fast worker and I work to a piece programme of two thousand words a day; that is about four hours' writing; so that by half past eleven I had done three-quarters of my daily stint. It was time for exercise and I would walk into Peterborough to make any purchases I might require and to take a tomato juice at the village pharmacy which is presided over by Myer Goldman, a fervent enthusiast for the arts who has made himself the father confessor to the Colony.

By the time I was back in my studio, my lunch basket would be outside my door. It would contain, in addition to the two statutory sandwiches, and a Thermos of soup and coffee, my morning mail. I kept a bottle of wine in my studio and as I munched my sandwiches and sipped my Californian claret I would read my letters. It is a great advantage to get one's mail with three-quarters of the day's work behind one. One tackles the morning with undivided energy, and with only a quarter of one's work ahead of one, one can take one's problems in one's stride. They seem less important.

Some men who take an afternoon nap prefer to take it directly after lunch. I prefer to wait an hour which gives me just enough time to deal with those last five hundred words. By three o'clock my desk was cleared, and I could, with a clean conscience, lie down for ten minutes' sleep on the bed with which every studio was supplied.

I was fifty-three years old when I first went to the Colony; though I no longer played golf in England, I did when I was abroad; and off the road between the Colony and the town was a nine-hole golf course. The ground had been presented to the community with the stipulation that members of the Colony would be honorary members of the club. During my first two years, this agreement was honoured by the club committee. Later, however, it was not; and colonists had either to join the club or pay a green fee, the secretary arguing that you could not expect an agreement like that to run in perpetuity. I retorted that they had the land in perpetuity. The secretary grinned. 'You can very well afford the subscription, can't you now, and we need money.' Which was a typical example of the modern unilateral dishonouring of agreements; I could, of course, quite easily afford the small subscription and it was an amusing course. I enjoyed my evening round, and I was back at the Lodge in time to take a shower and consume a couple of bourbons before dinner.

Dinner was at six, a barbarously early hour for a hot meal in the summer; and who wants to eat a heavy meal, without wine, at any time? Certainly not me. The dinner hour was the only one in the day that I found difficult. But the evening that followed it was enchanting. There was croquet on an uncertain lawn when the mosquitoes permitted it. There was music, or poetry readings in the library; sometimes we played 'the game', a Colony variation on the traditional guessing game that is played week-ends in the country; there were strolls into the village, to the cinema, or to a tap room where you could get beer without having to eat a meal as well, or the village pharmacy for an ice-cream soda; or you could motor out into the open country and see the sunset from Monadnock. By eleven I was in bed, pleasantly worn out by a day of work and exercise and open air.

I did not exaggerate when I told Mrs MacDowell that these were the working conditions for which I had been looking all my life. There was complete quiet, the freedom from interruption—colonists cannot be reached by telephone during a working day—the solution of all material problems, that you get on shipboard: your ticket is booked, your meals are paid for, you are provided with company and entertainment, you have not to make a single decision for yourself. There was all that at the Colony, but there was in addition the atmosphere of work: which is the very thing I had found lacking in Chagford and in the South of France. There, I had been in touch with holiday makers, with playboys and their companions and with local residents, many of whom were in retirement or were dilettantes, pretending to paint or write. They offered distractions and temptations. 'Oh, come along,' they would say, 'let's make a night of it. Never mind about tomorrow. It'll do you good to take one day off.' And because one is working at high pressure the temptation has an insidious appeal. 'Perhaps I am overworking. Perhaps it would be good for me to knock off for a couple of days. I'll come fresher to it afterwards,' one thinks. There are no such temptations at the Colony. Though there are parties on occasions; though there is private conviviality; though colonists do take their baskets round to each other's studios and share them over a bottle of wine, there is a recognition of the fact that one is there to work, and the colonist who introduced a playground atmosphere would not be encouraged and would have his application to come back refused.

There is also the influence not only of the present but the past. On the mantelpiece of every studio is a collection of wooden boards on which the colonists sign their names and the period of their residence. The studio in which I am writing these pages—The Schelling—is one of the oldest. There are five boards here. And the first entry is for 1909. As I sit at my broad, long desk, looking out across a stretch of grass towards the pines, I think of all the writers who have sat here before me, of all the dreams that have been dreamt, of all the books that have been written here.

Many of the names on these boards are now long forgotten; but on the first board, against the date 1921, is Hervey Allen's name. He had inscribed himself as a poet, as had Du Bose Heyward, the next name upon the board, an inch lower down is Luis Munoz Marin, who was to figure so prominently in the world's affairs as Governor of Puerto Rico, but in 1924 thought of himself as a writer; and below his name is that of William Rose Benét.

On other boards there are other names familiar to me —Theodore Maynard in 1931, Carl Carmer in 1934, Rumer Godden and Marjorie Fischer in 1949, Peter Viereck in 1954, Louise Bogan in 1957, and in more recent days Kathrin Perutz and Lael Tucker Wertenbaker. They are friendly ghosts at my elbow, looking over my shoulder, wishing me well.

My first studio was The Cheyney. On one of its boards was the name Tess Slessinger. I had never met her. But I had been very struck by the collection of her short stories that I had read in the 1930s. She died young; she came to very little; I believe that she went to Hollywood, and that things went unluckily. But she had a genuine talent, and more than that, her stories gave the impression that she was in herself a rare and precious person.

She was very real to me during the time, six months in all, spread over three visits, that I spent in the Cheyney studio. As I paced its length, I would picture her pacing it in just that way, relieving the tension in her limbs and nerves; and in the afternoons when I would lie out on the hammock settee on the balcony, looking across the trees, to the majestic mountains, my mind abroad, I would think how she must have lain there, looking out towards Monadnock, while the characters in her stories talked to her, and their ideas took shape in action.

I have never seen a photograph of her, only a head and

shoulders snapshot on the cover of one of her books. She was in her late twenties when she was at MacDowell. I pictured her as tall and slim, with long, straight legs; dark-haired, pale skinned, with eyes that often looked very tired, with a deep contralto voice. She would stride up and down the studio like a restless panther. When she lay out on the hammock settee she would be completely immobile. Hour after hour, day after day, I was conscious of her presence there. Why should I not have been? One day perhaps my ghost will loiter there.

I had been apprehensive, before my first visit to the Colony, lest I should find many of the colonists precious or peevish. I need have had no such fears. The list of colonists that I have set down is proof enough of that. Moreover, the fact that the group was equally divided between composers, painters and writers, removed the danger of professional jealousy. The writers did not expect the composers to know anything about their work, nor did the composers expect adulation from the painters. Very little 'shop' was talked because there was no common ground for 'shop'. Talk was general, as it would be in a drawing-room, and friendships were not determined by a community of professional interests.

Inevitably there were likes and dislikes, but it was easy to avoid, certainly in the summer, anyone whom you found irritating. You could synchronize your exits with their entrances, and vice versa; for the most part we lived in amity. Inevitably there were one or two quarrelsome colonists, but they were so few that each in his or her different way became part of a legend. There was the lady who was always putting everyone right, who threatened to leave when anyone contradicted her. Finally she did leave. A fellow colonist expostulated, 'Now surely, May, that is a rather foolish point of view.' She retorted, 'I am not going to stay here and be called a fool.' She left the table, breakfasted next morning in the kitchen and was gone by ten o'clock.

One year when I was on the house committee, I made the experiment of having a wine evening twice a week; the colonists each contributed their thirty cents and received with their dinner two glasses of Californian red. This mild libation proved fatal to one frail colonist who, with the ramparts of her restraint undermined, polished off a bottle of bourbon in her bedroom, took off all her clothes, went into the telephone booth and proceeded to abuse a male admirer in New York. She might have escaped detection had not another colonist wanted to ring up her husband. The fact that another colonist had a legitimate consort with whom she wished to speak enraged the occupant of the booth. She refused to give up her post and punctuated her vituperations to New York with shouts of 'I won't let that bitch Marigold in here'. She, too, left next morning.

Occasionally a colonist would be unable to tolerate the loneliness and isolation of the life; this particularly affected those who had not already come to terms with their project, or who came up, their minds blank, believing that they would get ideas once they were on their own. If ideas did not come, they found themselves in a fury of frustration. More than one colonist during my visits has left suddenly before his time was up.

One case was a pathetic one; a young painter from California who had never seen snow before and could not come to terms with it. He felt himself in an alien world. He could not concentrate on his canvases; instead he began to write poems to another colonist; rather good poems. He was tall and blonde and gentle. Everybody liked him, but the loneliness of the long, empty hours got upon his nerves. He decided that he had to leave.

He kept this decision secret. I happened to know because I was chairman of the house committee and the manager of the Colony had told me. There was a curious quality of dramatic irony about his last evening. He sat down to dinner as though it were any ordinary evening. He took his usual part in the conversation. He was not very talkative. After dinner he took his place at the Scrabble table. Half past seven became half past eight. I began to wonder whether he had changed his mind. Shortly before nine, he stood up after playing his hand. 'I won't be a minute,' he said. We went on with the game. It was assumed that he had gone to the lavatory. Five minutes passed. It was his turn again. We waited. We looked at one another. 'Perhaps we should go on,' I said. Presently the friend who had driven him to the bus station returned with the news that he would not be coming back. Two weeks later we each received from him a gracious friendly letter, saying how much he had enjoyed meeting us, thanking us for our kindness to him and hoping that we should be meeting again soon.

Enmities at the Colony are very rare, but a number of deep, warm friendships have been started there. There have been also a number of Colony romances, some of which ended in successful marriages, some in disastrous ones. It is inevitable that there should have been. There was a community of interests; there was also a similarity of status, since all colonists are partially displaced persons, otherwise they would not be at the Colony. Mrs Mac-Dowell was very much on her guard against such frailties. Margaret Widdermere stated in her autobiography that Mrs MacDowell had her spies who reported on the nocturnal movements of her guests, and she had part of the porch of the Eaves cut away so that members of the opposite sex could not sit out there in the evenings.

There was no such scrutiny when I went there first. Yet the studios were theoretically out of bounds after dinner, and there was an exciting sense of truancy about going there in the dusk and shading one's fire and one's candle so that the light should not be reflected on the windows. I do not think that Mrs MacDowell was a prude. She thought gallantry interfered with work. And she had had a wistful example in Edward Arlington Robinson of the deleterious effect of alcohol on poetry. She is reported to have said when a particularly dramatic encounter was brought to her attention, 'Well, if this is the great love affair of the century, I've no right to interfere with it.' In this case she felt that the purposes of literature were being served.

In Mrs MacDowell's lifetime, the Colony was only open during the summer, from the middle of May until the end of September, and two months was the maximum period of a single stay. In 1957, however, the experiment of opening a winter Colony was made: all the studios were fitted with electric light, and in a certain number of them oil stoves were installed. During the winter a colonist could remain in residence for four months. From this point on, all my visits were made during the winter, partly because those months were for me the most difficult to fit into my programme. The climate of the South of France was capricious. It could rain a lot in Tangier. The West Indies were at their best, but they were also at their most crowded and expensive. On the other hand, the New Hampshire climate was very pleasant. Four days a week the sun was shining and the sky was blue. Snow would be on the ground. Clean, dry snow. The air would be keen and fresh, like that of Switzerland: for someone bronchial like myself it was as healthy as the dry air of Arizona. There would be a day and a half of blizzard; thirty hours of grey skies, then once again the sun should be shining. I would as soon be in Peterborough between Christmas and the first of April as anywhere.

That was the first reason why I went there in the winter.

The other reason was a sense of duty. I was free to go anywhere, at any time. The average colonist was not. He could only come up in the summer. Many of the composers were teachers. Their long summer vacation was their only opportunity in the year to get their own work done. I did not feel that I was justified in applying for a studio when it was badly needed by someone else. As long as I got my two or three clear months, it did not matter when they came.

Only fifteen studios were heated in the winter, and the atmosphere was very different. We were a smaller group and we lived under confined conditions. In the summer, on most evenings there was a cocktail party in one or another of the studios. But in winter no one who had fought his way back through the snow to the central Colony buildings wanted to go out again, after they had tidied up. There was, in consequence, less conviviality. The females in the Eaves had a drawing-room and a fireplace; they also had a refrigerator in their kitchen. They would invite males down before dinner for a drink or cocktail. And their male guests every so often would contribute a fifth of bourbon. It was also the custom for one of the colonists, on an occasion, to put wine upon the table. It was scarcely a practical proposition when there were twenty-six colonists. It was easier when there were a dozen.

There are two bad hours in every day. They come at a different time according to the place and time and one's own metabolism. I made once a long, slow sea-trip westwards from Marseilles to Tahiti in a second-class French ship. Lunch was at eleven thirty; at twelve twenty, just about the time when the meal was ending, the midday bell would clang, and the minute hand would go back to twelve. That twenty minutes to be lived through again symbolized the dreariness of the long hot afternoon that stretched ahead. I had been up since dawn. I had written three-quarters of my daily stint. I would not start again till the day had cooled. How could I survive till four o'clock?

In the MacDowell Colony in the winter, the bad period for me comes between quarter past seven and nine. For me dinner without wine is something of a purgatory, but if I have a couple of strong bourbons in my room I reach the table in sufficiently high spirits to find the first half-hour tolerable; but the exhilaration subsides, and one by one the colonists drift away to the billiard table, the Scrabble board, the TV set. I find an hour of TV adequate. I like to wait till nine, so that I shall be ready to go straight to bed when the show is over. By ten o'clock I shall be drowsy. But if I watch an early programme, I shall not be sufficiently drowsy by half past eight. There is a bottle of bourbon in my room. It would be a pleasant companion for at least fifty of those hundred minutes, but I do not wake fresh if I take alcohol after dinner. I do not want to read. My eyes have been occupied with print all day. There are the alternatives of pool and Scrabble and desultory conversation. I play out time as best I can till nine o'clock, consoling myself with the knowledge of how good the world will seem when I wake up, fresh at five, with the prospect of a long day's work ahead.

20

Self-Portrait—
Nearing Sixty

(Written in 1955)

The least occurrence when we are nearing sixty launches us on a stream of reverie, and a few weeks ago, when my publishers sent me a questionnaire about my habits, plans, tastes and friends, I found myself looking back to 1930, when I was first importuned with such inquiries, a travel book of mine having been a Literary Guild selection. A great deal has happened in the world in general and to myself in particular during the interval and it surprised me that I should be giving practically the same answers that I had a quarter of a century before.

In 1943, as I organized a section of military intelligence in Baghdad, I told myself that 'the old world' had gone forever and that on my eventual return to professional authorship I should have to adjust myself to an entirely new way of living. Yet here I am fourteen years later with my routine fixed within a familiar quadrilateral of travel between London, New York, the Mediterranean, the West Indies—with an occasional trip farther afield to the Seychelles or the China Seas—and the issue regulated by what has become for me, as it has I suspect for many of my colleagues, the basic problem of how I am to organize my routine so that it combines the search for subjects with the leisure and tranquillity in which to write, and how that routine is to be reconciled with the needs of those whose lives are involved with mine and with my own personal feelings in regard to them.

As it was in 1930, so is it in 1955. And if in 1930 I could have been shown a picture of my life as it is today, there would have been little in it to surprise me, in spite of the vast changes that the war is supposed to have wrought in all of us; the essential difference being that I am now nearing sixty whereas then I was in the early thirties. But that was a difference which I had foreseen and, could I have been shown that picture in 1930, my chief surprise would have been in the little difference that twenty-five years have made.

Cyril Connolly was recently asked to contribute to a symposium in the *Daily Express* on what made life worth living. 'There are,' he said, 'only three things which make life worth living: to be writing a tolerably good book, to be in a dinner party for six, and to be travelling south with someone whom your conscience permits you to love.'

I could not have been so admirably succinct, but at any point in the last thirty years I would have given the same answer, but with cricket added, and that addition pinpoints the difference between being in the thirties and in the fifties. I watch cricket now instead of playing it. Yet even so cricket means very little less to me as I sit in the top gallery at Lord's. Bill Hitch, the old England and Surrey cricketer, told me that he had not realized how much there was to cricket till he became an umpire.

Travel is as much an adventure to me as it ever was. I love the South and grey skies sadden me. A liner draws away from the docks, a plane lifts from the ground, a train sets out across a continent and there is a sense of an old self discarded. A little later there is the first sight on the horizon of a shadowy shape. Is it a cloud or an island? I lean against the taffrail, with straining eyes and the sense of a new life beginning.

In *Where The Clocks Strike Twice* I wrote of my first evening in the Seychelles Islands:

'I sauntered that evening along the water front. It looked like a hundred other places. They are all the same, at a first glance, these tropic islands. The one main shopping thoroughfare; the wooden stores with corrugated-iron roofs; the honking horns, the rattling rickshaws; the natives in their Sunday finery; the government buildings, rectangular, two-storeyed, weatherworn; the mango trees that flank the football field; coconut palms aslant over the lagoon; streets that climb back into the hills, losing themselves in greenery; isolated white-verandahed bungalows; the crotons and the bougainvillea; the brilliant scarlet of the tulip tree; the mountains towering behind. I had seen it all before, in the Pacific, in the Caribbean, in the China Seas; and yet I knew very well that I was to find something here that I had found nowhere else, something unique and personal to this colony that existed nowhere else. What was it to be? I asked myself. My nerves were alert and quivering; the old excitement was upon me. New places and new people, new ways of thought and living, new landscapes, new friendships: that for me is adventure.'

I had the same feeling five years later when a B.O.A.C. aircraft circled over Aden. Those of us who are bitten by the wanderlust are always fretting to get our trunk packed again.

During the last decade, New York has become increasingly my base. For me it is the most exciting city in the world.

Ford Madox Ford entitled a book *New York is Not America*. I have seen enough of America to know that that is true, but I have also seen enough of America to know that Boston is not either, nor is Chicago, nor New Orleans, nor even the Western prairies. America is a composite entity to which fifty states, two hundred cities, two thousand townships, and innumerable farms have made their individual contribution so that each man and woman who has put down roots within its frontiers is aware of kinship. To those who assert that New York is not America, I reply that it provides a home for eight million Americans.

Twenty-six years ago Charles Hanson Towne called his reminiscences *This New York of Mine*. A petulant critic said, 'It may be his; thank God it isn't mine.' It was a foolish complaint for it is the charm of all great cities that its citizens can lead private lives of their own choosing and it is the special charm of New York that it should offer such an infinite variety of choice.

During my first long stay in New York I rented a furnished apartment on 36th and Lexington, but for over twenty years I have been staying at the Algonquin, a hotel that is a home for its old friends. In America, where the rooms are much warmer than in England, I wear unlined coats, and the valet stores four suits for me. 'Brownie', the head porter, keeps in the basement a kitbag of books and a trunk with a few pictures, an electric kettle, a tea service and a cocktail set. A few personal possessions convert an impersonal hotel lodging into a home. When I am in funds I take a suite, when I am out of funds, a one-room apartment.

The Algonquin is on 44th Street between Fifth and Sixth. My two clubs, the Century and the Coffee House, lie on 43rd and 45th respectively, a stone's throw distant. My bank is on Park and 42nd. The office of my agent, Carl Brandt, is on Park and 40th. The New York Public Library is two blocks away. My world has a circumference of half a mile.

It is usually in the autumn or the winter that I am in New York. October and November are my favourite months. I spend about a month each visit. I can never work in cities. Too much is going on. I talk my work over with Carl Brandt and with my editors. I do research in the New York Library. But I regard my visits as holidays.

My morning routine is very simple: getting up around six and writing letters; watching the 'Today' programme while I shave, breakfasting at a coffee shop twenty-four doors away; reading the morning papers at the Century while 'Bridie', my maid at the Algonquin, does up my room; returning to make a call or two; then settling down to a holiday equivalent of a morning's work, the revising of a manuscript, a visit to the library; sometimes I take in a cinema.

It is soon time for a pre-lunch walk. Walking is the one way of keeping fit for one who is past squash racquets and I walk at least six miles a day. Often on sunny mornings I lunch in the cafeteria at Central Park Zoo. It is pleasant sitting on the terrace with a hamburger and a glass of beer, watching the seals fed. I am told that during World War II many expatriate Europeans frequented it, imagining themselves in Prague and Paris.

In the afternoon I read and rest. Most evenings I have some engagement: a dinner, a theatre or a cocktail party.

London is a man's city, New York a woman's city, but in spite of St James's and Savile Row I believe that a man has a better time in New York, simply because it is a woman's city. There is greater immediate warmth and friendliness; there is also greater intimacy. You get to know men quicker in New York, also you get to know them better, because you know their wives. In London I have no idea whether the majority of my friends at the Athenæum, the Savage and the Beefsteak are married, divorced or involved in an obscure liaison. I do in New York. At the Coffee House there is an admirable system by which, on Saturdays at lunch time, members and their feminine guests sit together for cocktails around the raised octagonal table. Since the war I have made more men friends in New York than I have in London, largely, I feel, because I know the womenfolk who have enriched or complicated their existence.

Cocktail parties in New York have no fixed closing hour. Much nourishment is served and the last group does not leave till ten. On evenings when I have no definite commitment afterward, I buy during the afternoon a single ticket for a theatre. I am thus spared the letdown feeling that can come at a cocktail party around eight o'clock, when you feel that there is no point in staying. When I do feel there is a point, it is not without a sense of gesture that I tear up that stub. On days when I tear up the stub, I am unlikely to get back to the Algonquin before half past one: I bring the *Daily Mirror* with me and study Li'l Abner, Walter Winchell and Sheilah Graham before I fall asleep.

That is the way it is day after day, except that on Sundays I usually motor out into the country for lunch, and I can well imagine a Londoner impatiently demanding what I mean by describing New York as the most dramatic and exciting city in the world. What else is it for you, he will ask, but a round of cocktail parties? Well, perhaps that is a fair complaint if you see New York in terms of London, but that is something which you cannot do. No two cities could be more different.

New York is built on a rock, whereas London is built upon a swamp. That is a basic difference. Where London is spread over a wide area, New York rises fifty storeys high. Everything in New York is very close. A Londoner living in Swiss Cottage meeting at a Bloomsbury lunch party somebody who lives in Kensington might well feel that she lived so far away that it was scarcely worth while following up the acquaintanceship. In New York I am within walking distance of everyone I know.

The tempo is faster in New York because so much more

can happen there. Social life is fluid. Acquaintances ripen quickly into friendships. Many Londoners are shy of ringing up someone they have met the night before. They are inclined to ask their hostess to arrange another meeting some time. New Yorkers have not the time for that. New York is a port. There is a long tradition of welcoming ships and waving them Godspeed. If you want to see somebody again you must move fast; she may be gone tomorrow. In a few days your whole life can be reorientated by one new friend who opens a series of new doors for you.

There is also the climate. London is in a temperate zone. New York swings in a few weeks from arctic cold to tropic heat. These changes acerbate the nerves. There is a quality in the air in spring and autumn that makes it possible for you to do more there than in any other city.

But I think what makes New York so dramatic for many of us, certainly for me, is the immediate importance that one's work acquires there. New York is a market where you buy and sell and, though I do little writing there, I arrive as someone who has just finished a piece of work or is half-way through or about to start one. One's friends are interested in one's work. For a writer who spends so much of his life alone, that is an exciting change of climate. There is challenge there and a spur to victory —a sense of having one's batteries recharged.

I can imagine myself living very happily in London as a retired man, pottering round my clubs, going to galleries and exhibitions, watching cricket in the summer, exchanging gossip with old friends. But I should not care to live in retirement in New York; I should feel out of things. You need to be in the swim.

That is what is essential: being in the swim. New York is one of the most expensive cities in the world and I have heard it said that unless you are spending money fast you get no fun there. That is true, but as a corollary, not as a principle. For if you are in the swim you are making money in terms of your opposite numbers and that is what matters: being able to meet your opposite numbers on equal terms. If you cannot, then you are the spectre at the feast. You are better off somewhere else.

Perhaps it is the knowledge that I am a sojourner on 44th Street which makes me love New York so dearly. Sooner or later the bell will toll for me, as it has for others; the rat race will become too fierce and I shall look for a quiet harbour in the sun.

As I re-read this last section, I remember my old friend's advice, 'Never choose a novelist as your hero.' It is a playboy's life that I have described and it would be difficult to show in a novel how those five or six weeks in New York each year are the reward for months of secluded writing, of living alone with my characters and stories. The discovery of retreats where I can do this is one of my chief concerns. Before the war I went to Villefranche and the Easton Court Hotel at Chagford on whose 'stout tables' Elizabeth Eliot, Pamela Hansford Johnson, Patrick Kinross, C. P. Snow and Evelyn Waugh have written novels, but Villefranche with its row of cafés along the water front has become a *boîte* and I need to spend in London and with my family the few weeks each year that are allotted to me in England as a foreign resident.

My retreats today are as scattered as my life is. In Duarte, California, the late Rollin Kirby's daughter, Janet Banning, has a guesthouse across the lawn from her ranch where I can cook my own breakfast and work through the morning until it is time to join her at the swimming pool. I have spent three summers at the Mac-Dowell Colony in Peterborough, New Hampshire, where each of the twenty-four colonists has a separate studio in the woods outside whose door a lunch basket is left so that the current of the day's thought is undisturbed. One winter that excellent regional novelist and one of my dearest friends, Virginia Sorensen, went to Denmark on a Guggenheim. Why not? I thought and half a book was written in Copenhagen, in a room looking on the sound. But, by and large, Nice out of the season has been my most constant perch.

For several years now I have based myself in the Escurial, a second-grade residential hotel which lies half a mile back from the sea, in the Avenue Georges Clemenceau. I have a corner room on the fourth floor. One window faces east and I can see on the skyline Vauban's fortress towering above Villefranche; the other window faces south and looks down on a side street cut by roads running into the Avenue de la Victoire.

I have never worked in a more congenial room. I like to be high up. I need to see something happening: a sailor painting a boat, a small boy selling newspapers, a farmer ploughing a field. The manuscript on my desk then becomes a part of the manifold activities of man. My corner windows in the Escurial present and explain the heart of Provincial France: teen-age girls hurry with slung satchels to their convent school; servants return from market with long rolls protruding from their baskets; modish young women walk their poodles; retired bureaucrats move stiffly and slowly to the Promenade des Anglais.

Nothing could be more placid than my existence there. I wake between half past five and six. The Brasserie du Lyon opens at seven thirty, but its coffee is not hot till a quarter to eight; that gives me ninety minutes at my desk before I go out to breakfast. On my way to the café I buy a paper from a diminutive and shuffling crone.

Nice-Matin is excellent on foreign news, it recounts local peccadilloes with an engaging Latin levity, and the half-hour I spend over my rolls and coffee is one of the pleasantest of the day. On the way back to the Escurial I do my minor marketing—fruit and cheese and yogurt and the cutlet or the slice of steak that I shall cook on my gas ring.

I write 2000 words a day. I may or may not have reached that point by half past eleven. I do not hurry. I am uninterrupted. There are no room telephones and the difficulty of reaching me via the desk and the maid upon the landing is so great that my friends save time by writing. The post arrives shortly before ten. For one who lives abroad the arrival of the post is the day's big event, and it is for that reason that I resist the temptation to collect my letters when they arrive. Good news might elate me, bad news might depress me, the waving of a friendly signal might send me into a nostalgic reverie; or there might be no mail at all, which would rob the day of half its savour. Anyhow, the current of composition would be broken, so I wait till I have finished my morning's work and then take out my letters to a seat on the Promenade des Anglais or in the Jardin Albert Premier, or on inclement days to a table in the Café Monnot.

I have friends in Nice, Mougins, Antibes, and about once a week I go out to lunch or dinner or somebody motors over to take a meal with me. And in Cimiez lives Cecile who once ran a bar in Villefranche and of whom I have written in *Where the Clocks Strike Twice*. Often in the late afternoon I take the trolley bus up the hill, gossip with her for half an hour and walk back as the lights are waking.

I keep a store of red Burgundy in my cupboard and before I go down to collect my mail I open a bottle, so that the wine may breathe and be ready to welcome my return. I sip it slowly, munching a hard dry cheese, brooding over my story, living with my characters, talking out their speeches. It is the most creative period of my day. An hour becomes ninety minutes and in the street below the noontide siesta is broken by the Vespas and motor-cycles of people going back to work.

By two the bottle is three-quarters finished. I cork it up, tidy away the plates and if I am short of my daily quota I make it up. If I am not, I answer letters till it is time for my siesta.

When I wake it is close on four and by four o'clock the London newspapers will be on the kiosks. The Promenade des Anglais will be crowded and it is very pleasant strolling along the water front in the declining sunlight, when the sea on windless days takes on the glazed mauve sheen that made Homer call it wine-coloured, pausing now and then to read the paper and to watch the passers-by, with the agreeable sense of fatigue and of fulfilment that follows a hard day's work. Pleasant though it is, however, when the light fades there comes that melancholy which George Moore described in 'Bring in the Lamp', the loneliness endemic to those who work alone. Evening is at hand and it is easy to be self-pitying, thinking of all those for whom the recompense of the long day is being paid: work is finished; pleasure and relaxation are opening their doors; the sidewalk tables beckon.

Between six and seven there is a steady parade back and forth down the Avenue de la Victoire. It is pleasant to sit over a Pernod watching it. One Pernod becomes two. And after two Pernods one finds oneself saying to oneself, 'Why not a proper meal in a restaurant for a change?' But that would involve wine and after a good dinner in a restaurant it is a temptation to linger over a liqueur, and I know that after a heavy meal and spirits I should not wake so fresh. So I go to a cinema instead.

By the time I come out, evening has given way to night, my mood of melancholy has passed. I return to the Escurial, heat some soup and finish the wine. Maybe I write a letter or two. Maybe I read for half an hour. Usually I am in bed by ten, with *The Oxford Book of English Verse*: within a quarter-hour, I have switched off the light.

That is my real life and nothing could be less dramatic: you could not make a novel out of the interior problems presented by a routine like that. It is when I am living like that, that I am most myself.

'The pleasure of writing a tolerably good book.' Who is to say what is 'tolerably good'? By what standard is one to judge oneself? By ultimate standards or by the more modest and more human, 'Well, I don't think this is too bad for me'? So much highfalutin nonsense was written once about the agonies of composition and the high fever of imagination that it is now fashionable to be low brow, with novelists talking about themselves as, though they were hard-boiled businessmen 'out to make the most of it'. That is not really the way it is. It may seem presumptuous for a very minor writer to talk of the excitement that his work brings him. It lays him open to the obvious retort: 'It is a relief to know it excites *him*. It leaves us calm enough.' But the best periods of my life have been those when I have been working on a congenial theme.

I have no illusions about my status as a writer. A writer is tried before a high tribunal. Not only the present sits in judgement on him, but the past as well. A field-marshal's stature is not diminished by the victories of Condé, Marlborough and Napoleon. But a modern novel is made puny by the continuing challenge of *War and Peace, David Copperfield* and *The Brothers Karamazov*.

I started with very high ambitions and if in 1917 I could have foreseen myself as I am in 1955, with so little done, I should have been humiliatingly disappointed. That is a usual experience; it is the common lot. The contrast between the promise of life and its fulfilment is a familiar theme. On the other hand, had I at eighteen foreseen what my personal life was to be I should have been astounded. I had no idea then that life could be so full, so varied, that its gifts could be so abundant. I did not know life had so much for giving. Yet the things that have made my life a continuing adventure—sport and gallantry, soldiering and travel—have been side shows in the last analysis. Though my achievement is so minute, I have always put writing first. I have been most alive seated at a table in a hotel bedroom facing a solitary day.

Writers have their ups and downs and in January 1953, my fortunes had struck an all-time low. For eighteen months I had been concentrating on short stories, and had sold only one story in America, to *Esquire*. I had not an idea left. I was wondering where I went from there, and then that one *Esquire* story was bought by Hollywood.

My first thought, naturally for me, was, 'I'll take a long trip, find new subjects, renew myself.' But on the crossing back to England on the *Ile de France* I got the idea for a West Indian novel. I did not guess then that it would be a quarter of a million words in length, but I knew that it would be long and I was grateful to Twentieth Century-Fox's pennies for allowing me to devote my entire energies to it for twenty months.

That was as good a moment as life has given me and I have never been more excited than I was fifteen months later when, with the book half written, I flew up from the West Indies, where I had obtained the final material, to a quiet ten weeks in the MacDowell Colony where, with every facility provided for concentration, I could write the rest of it.

If a genie were to offer me a final wish, it would be this—that I might meet an equivalent excitement once more before the curtain falls.

21
Island in the Sun

In the previous chapter I described how in January 1953 my fortunes sank to an all-time low, how I was reprieved 'in the nick of time' by the sale to Twentieth Century-Fox of a short story and how on the journey back to England, I got the idea for a West Indian novel. The writing and publication of a novel is usually undramatic and the biography or autobiography of a novelist which deals with his novels one by one, in detail, is tedious. Yet even so, for those who are interested in authorship and authors, the story of certain books has its fascination. And in my own case two books fill their own small niche in literary history: my first novel, *The Loom of Youth*, and my eighteenth, *Island in the Sun*.

I got the idea of the book in a flash as I was pacing the decks of the *Ile de France*, but the idea was the sudden fusing of four different plots that had been turning ineffectively in my mind. Shortly after the end of the war I had begun a novel about a woman who had killed a man by mistake—in the course of an argument she struck at him; in stepping back he slipped on a rug and as he fell, hit his head against the edge of a table. She decided not to tell the police; she was later blackmailed. I set the plot in Baghdad and called it 'Murder at the Alwiyah Club'. I wrote 25,000 words and then broke down.

I also had had the idea for a short story turning on colour. A young American from the South falls in love with the daughter of a West Indian planter. She discovers that she has coloured blood through her father; she feels that she has no right to marry a Southerner; their children will be outcasts. Her mother puts her mind at rest by telling her that she is not her father's daughter.

I had another embryo plot. I got it from the highly respectable and punctilious wife of a neighbouring vicar. She said that when her husband went to preach in another parish and spent the night away from home, she raised the seat of the downstairs lavatory so that if a burglar broke in he would believe that there was a man in the house and would not come upstairs. I thought that a raised lavatory seat could fan a husband's jealousy. He could return home to recognize the smell of an unusual cigarette. The lavatory seat was raised. A strange man must have been in the house.

In 1948, the Labour Government appointed Lord Baldwin to the governorship of the Leeward Islands. They wanted a Socialist and a peer, a man who had ample private means, and would not be made pusillanimous by the career-official's resolve to avoid trouble at the end of his career and finish up as a knight. Baldwin's appointment was the subject of fierce criticism in the House of Commons, and his conduct in the Islands was melodramatic. I wondered what kind of dramatic commotion would have arisen had a Conservative Government appointed a peer who was a first-class cricketer: I had Lionel Tennyson in mind.

For these four different ideas, a fifth new idea acted as a catalyst. A planter of the old school, in order to discredit a young coloured rabble-rouser and the democratic, in his eyes subversive, ideas that the rabble-rouser stood for, incites a riot in which he himself is killed; a riot which will convince the authorities in England that the West Indians are not yet ready for self-rule. With these various themes at work on my imagination, I set off early in March for Nice to get the back of the book broken.

Of course I did not. It has been my invariable experience to open a novel with enthusiasm, to write at a steady pace for three weeks or a month, and then suddenly run dry. I have to wait at least a month, usually longer, before I can get started again. This time I wrote solidly for a month. I took a month's holiday in England, then set out again for Nice. On the way down, by air, I read the typescript of the first section. I realized that it would not do at all. Something was badly wrong.

During the next month I came to realize what that something was.

The novel in this first draft opened with a husband— the old-time planter—returning to his house shortly before lunch to detect the smell of an unusual cigarette. He does not smoke himself and as a result is particularly sensitive to the smell of smoke. He goes into the lavatory. The smell is stronger there. The seat is raised. A man has been smoking that cigarette. At lunch his wife makes no reference to a visitor. He gives her an opportunity to describe her morning. She does not refer to any visitor. His suspicions are roused. It is a quick six-page scene.

The second scene described a cocktail party at Government House. It is a long forty-page scene; it introduces all the chief characters and sets out the main problems of their lives. It was a very intricate piece of writing. I thought I had got it right, but the narrative dragged. At last I realized why it did. The reader had not been sufficiently alerted by the opening scene to feel inquisitive about the various people who were going to influence the course of the action that had opened in that first scene. And they had not been sufficiently alerted because the husband and wife were in their middle fifties. A middle-aged husband married to a young wife could be acutely, physically jealous. But he would not be jealous in that way about the companion of thirty years who has borne him three children. He might be worried and concerned, largely on her account, feeling that she was on the brink of a great mistake; he might be distressed on his own account because the security of his home and family were imperilled; there are a number of emotions that he might experience, but there was one very certainly that he would not feel: the wild uncontrollable jealousy that Othello felt for Desdemona. And that was the kind of jealousy that was needed to keep the reader on his toes during a forty-page description of a cocktail party. It had to be a young husband who was uncertain of his wife. So I made it the son of the old-time planter who returned to the smell of an unusual cigarette. The reader's curiosity was set alight.

I worked on the novel intermittently through the summer. Then in September I went to Nice, to 'the small hotel bedroom' that has solved so many problems for the novelist. By Christmas half the novel was finished—about 120,000 words. After Christmas I went to New York. Carl Brandt was very anxious to see what I had written. But I declined. I felt that there was something wrong with the book, but I wanted to find out what it was myself. I was afraid of being side-tracked. Carl would sense that there was something wrong. He might prescribe, I will not say the wrong medicine, but a medicine that was not the one most in tune with my own subconscious conception of the plot. A novelist always knows inside himself what his story needs. If he gives himself time he will find out for himself. And luckily I had time, thanks to my Hollywood dollars.

I had an invitation to spend two weeks in Duarte and I spotted my mistake. One of my characters, the son of the Governor, and a future peer, was, in a sense, the hero. He was the man for whom the reader was expected to be 'rooting'. He was a thoroughly sound, wholesome fellow and it is very hard not to make that kind of character a prig. Yet if one tries to humanize him, by putting into his mind, or by expressing in a subjunctive soliloquy, devious intentions, the reader is put off. 'That's wrong for him.' It was essential that I should get him right. But how to do it?

The device I chose may seem a very simple one, but it is one that would only occur to an experienced novelist unless, by chance, he had got it right from the beginning. After writing twenty novels, one knows the various techniques and I realized that to make this character, Euan, a sympathetic, warm human being, I must never let the action appear through his eyes. He must always be presented to the reader through the eyes of other characters. He must be described and talked about; but his own thoughts must never be put on paper except in as far as they emerged in conversation; in the way, in fact, that Galsworthy presented Irene Forsyte. I left Duarte knowing that I had solved my problem.

I finished the novel at the end of July, and in August I took the typescript down with me to Villefranche to revise. I was accompanied by my second son, Peter, then a schoolboy in his sixteenth year. I would join him on the beach shortly before lunch, with three hours' work behind me. He told me afterwards that he had never seen so much excitement on a face before. 'I think it's all right, Peter,' I would say, and my eyes were glowing. I had no doubt about the book at all. I was confident that it was good. I was wondering how good. My surprise and consternation could not have been more complete than when I received, four weeks later, a chilling reception from my London agent.

It was in his opinion much too long. Pruning was not enough; it needed a major operation. He suggested the removal of the murder which was the backbone of the book. Even if I retained the murder, the funeral scene that followed it must go. The chief character did not convince him. He made a number of additional objections. He found nothing to praise, though he concluded his letter with the hope that he had not discouraged me. 'There is a good book here,' he wrote. He invited me to call and discuss it with him.

It was the biggest shock that I had received not only in my professional career, but in my personal life. Virginia Sorensen has kept the letter that I wrote her the next day. 'If this man's right,' I said, 'I do not know where I go from here.' I put myself in the confessional. I was fifty-six years old; I had been writing for nearly forty years. That was a long time. I might have lost my critical capacity. I had already lost the knack of the short story, which needed conciseness and taut treatment; within the broad limits of the novel I might have become garrulous and flabby. I did not, however, lose my head. 'You may be right,' I told my agent. 'But before I hear what you have to say, I want to re-read the book, in the light of your letter.' I was bound for Copenhagen. I took the MS. with me.

I read it slowly. It was nine hundred pages long. It held no surprises for me. When I had sent off the revised script, I had thought, 'I shan't ever have to read that again. I'll only glance through it in covers.' Yet, even so, I did not find the re-reading tiresome. The narrative moved fast. It was easy reading. The murder came half-way through the book. It was an extension of the original 'Murder at the Alwiyah Club'. It was melodramatic certainly, but most long novels need violence at a certain point. The novelist arranges a setting of normal people leading their customary lives, then something unusual happens. You recognize their true natures by seeing how they behave under unusual circumstances. That is an axiom of the craft of the fiction. The murder in my novel fulfilled a necessary function, as did the funeral scene to which my agent had objected.

In most detective novels, certainly in Agatha Christie's,

there is a scene about half-way through where the detective
recapitulates the evidence so as to remind the reader of
what has passed and put him in full possession of all the
facts before the second lap begins. That was what the
funeral scene did here. It gave each character a chance to
indulge in a subjective soliloquy. It was a gathering up of
all the previous threads. It was an essential scene, but it
was four pages too long. My agent, because he had been
bored, thought the whole scene should go. Not being a
novelist himself, he did not realize how much difference
can be made by the cutting of four pages. With those
pages removed, the funeral scene played its part effectively
in the development of the drama. I felt as confident about
it now as I had in Villefranche, but I thought I would
take a second opinion.

Virginia Sorensen, whom I had met the previous
summer in MacDowell, had come to Copenhagen on a
Guggenheim. It was, indeed, her presence there that was
responsible for my desertion of Nice. I asked her if she
would read it. She did not see my agent's letter. I did not
want her to start with a preconceived idea. I only told
her that he had thought it overlong, that he had told one
of his staff that I had bitten off more than I could chew.
She herself tended to write too lengthily at the beginning
of her novels. The drama did not develop for a hundred
pages or so. She had usually had to cut her opening
chapters; and I imagine that she began to read it with the
thought, 'How can I explain to him most tactfully that,
excellent though this is, in the interests of the whole it
should be cut?' But on the contrary she, as its first reader,
was its first enthusiast. That decided me. I instructed
'my man in London' to send at once one copy to Cassell's,
and another to Carl Brandt in America.

He replied, 'So be it. No one will be more pleased
than I if Carl approves of it,' rather in the tone of the

headmaster who says, 'No one will be more pleased than I, Waugh, if you have passed your exam,' knowing full well that you have not. Luckily, however, Carl Brandt did approve. He wrote:

Your novel got here and I had myself a fine time with it. I read every word although I was rather sure from the first hundred or so pages that magazine use would be very unlikely. The reasons for this I am sure are as clear to you as they are to me.

Not only the colour question but the frankness of some of the relations of sex. I am, however, letting Hugh Kahler of Ladies' Home Journal see it. Miracles do happen!

But I want to tell you that to me, this is your best novel. I could give you a list of reasons but I'll spare you. Primarily I'm for it because of your characters and their interplay.

The story is brilliantly steered through its intricacies of plot. Your balances of interest are always even. It seems to march inexorably to its goal.

And the characters! H. E., Archer, the Police Chief (what a ducky he is!), the man who got murdered, H. E.'s son, the American reporter. The women—Olivia, Sylvia, the brazen hussy who was made into a woman by the negro Attorney General, the mother—the whole works! 1000 congratulations. If the book does not sell, I'll not know what's wrong with the public.

No book is a best-seller unless it has a lot of luck and the fairy godmother in the case of *Island in the Sun* was unquestionably Carl Brandt. It owed everything to him. If he had reacted as my London agent had, I doubt if Farrar and Straus would have bothered to read it. They would have wondered how best they could cut their losses on it. Roger Straus is, indeed, fond of telling of the dismay with which he viewed the bulk of this new MS. He had been losing money on me steadily for seven years. This seemed the last straw. At Christmas a Press reporter in Copenhagen had photographed me holding between both hands my bulky manuscript. I sent the photograph to John Farrar. I wrote, 'Look what Santa Claus is sending you for Christmas.' John did not think it funny. He made no reply. Roger Straus had the manuscript sitting on his desk for ten days, trying to work up the courage to tackle it. It was only Carl Brandt's incessant badgering that forced him eventually to take it home with him. Once he had started reading, he went on reading. 'This, clearly,' he wrote to Carl, 'is the book we have been waiting for. We will print a first edition of ten thousand copies.'

A copy of this letter was sent to London. I awaited my agent's comment with curiosity. As I received no letter from him I assumed that he was on a holiday, and when I wrote to him on another matter, a month or so later, I asked him where he had been for his holiday. 'Why do you think I have been away?' he wrote. 'I have been dutifully at my desk since Christmas.' Neither then nor later did he refer to the different reception the book had received from that which he had anticipated. He did, however, make a contribution to the book's success. He was responsible for the title. I had originally called it *The Sugar Barons*. That was a big contribution.

Thirty years earlier, when I had watched the success of novels like *If Winter Comes*, *The Green Hat*, *Anthony Adverse*, I had observed a familiar pattern to the process. A book was published, it received good reviews, it was talked about, then suddenly it 'caught on', and the printers could not turn out copies fast enough. Curtis Brown, the agent, once said to me, 'There is a turning point at which the avalanche begins. It might be the weight of a single copy that turns the scale.' That is not the way it is today. A book becomes a best-seller eight months before it has been published, before a single copy has been bound, before it has been read by a single critic.

Virginia Sorensen had decided to finish off her Guggenheim with a trip to the South of France. I acted as her guide. We made our base in Nice, at the Hotel Escurial, where I had written the first half of *Island in the Sun*. It was early April. One afternoon we returned from an excursion in the mountains to find a message that New York had been trying to reach me on the telephone. It was the first time that I had been telephoned from New York. I had a twinge of anxiety. Could anything be wrong? But there was nothing that could be wrong. It was eight months since I had been there. No member of my family was in New York. It had to be good news. My heart was beating as I waited in the telephone box. There was a succession of voices, first French and then American; finally there was a familiar voice, Carl Brandt's. '*Ladies' Home Journal* has bought your novel. Twenty-two thousand, five hundred.'

It was completely unexpected. I did not know what was happening. Carl Brandt tells me that I asked if it was dollars or francs and then said, 'I'm going out to stand a drink to everyone on the Promenade des Anglais.' But I do not remember; I was in a daze. I sat on the hotel stairs, my elbows on my knees, my chin supported by my fists. 'If this has happened,' I thought, 'anything can happen.'

I sat there for several minutes. The plump manageress of the hotel walked across the hall. I jumped up. I ran towards her. I flung my arms round her neck and kissed her on both cheeks.

'If this could happen, anything could happen.' Three days later there was a cable, saying, 'Literary Guild Selection January'. The following day there was another cable: 'Reader's Digest Condensed Book Club'. There was a letter from Roger Straus: 'I can picture you driving up the Promenade des Anglais in a yellow Jaguar.' Every day that week we were having celebrations. Eliza Parkinson, one of my best friends, a director of the Museum of Modern Art, was down there, and with her another dear friend of mine, the painter Lily Cushing. It was one party after another.

From Nice Virginia and I were going to Geneva by
bus, where our ways were dividing, temporarily. We had
to make an early start; as we waited for our taxi on the
hotel steps the night porter came up with the news that
New York had tried to get me on the telephone last night,
but that he had not been able to find me. Virginia and I
were celebrating in her room with a final bottle of champagne. We looked at one another. New York on the telephone again. That could only mean one thing: Hollywood. On the way to Grenoble I cabled Brandt the name
of the hotel in Geneva where I would be staying. On our
first afternoon there, the call came through. '20th
Century Fox. A hundred and forty thousand dollars.'
Virginia Sorensen tells me that I said, 'I didn't know there
was so much money in the world.'

In the course of four weeks I had earned nearly a
quarter of a million dollars. At the age of fifty-six I had
become overnight a different person, with a different
future and different problems. Yet the strange thing
about this metamorphosis was that to my friends I was
exactly the same person. None of my friends in London
were aware that anything had happened. When *If
Winter Comes*, *The Green Hat* and *Anthony Adverse* were
booming, A. S. M. Hutchinson, Michael Arlen and
Hervey Allen were obviously the spoiled children of good
luck. They did not have to tell anyone how many editions
had been exhausted. Everybody knew. But nobody knew
that I had hit the New York jackpot. And I could not
very well announce it in the sandpit at the Savile. It was
a very curious sensation. I had a sense of masquerading,
of pretending to be someone that I had ceased to be.

The news of my good luck trickled slowly through. In
June I went to the P.E.N. Club Congress in Vienna.
Harold Rubinstein's nephew, who was a partner in
Gollancz's firm, was there. He had heard a rumour and

asked me if it was true. Cecil Roberts wrote me a letter from Alassio: 'I have just heard that you have made 500,000 dollars. I am sure that there must be an extra nought slipped on, but 50,000 is a lot of money. I am delighted.' At the Authors and Booksellers Cricket Match, Billy Collins congratulated me on my good luck. And in the Savile, Nigel Balchin came across to me with a 'They're talking about you in Hollywood these days.' But otherwise that summer was no different from any other summer except that I had more money. I fancy that Farrar and Straus were holding back the story until nearer publication, which had been fixed for January so as to allow for the serial version to run in the *Ladies' Home Journal*. It was not till September that the story broke, with a paragraph in *Time*.

In the same week, I started out on a trip to Hong Kong, pausing at Aden, Rangoon, Singapore and Borneo. In none of these places could I expect anyone to have heard of *Island in the Sun*. At Aden a man said to me at dinner, 'I have read all your brother's books and your one book.' I thought to myself, 'That's probably the last time I shall have that said to me.'

I returned to England shortly before Christmas to find a number of press cuttings from America. In the *New York Times* Book Review, Harvey Breit had written:

The story of Evelyn Waugh's brother Alec—as a writer we mean—is a story to hearten all writers. Five years older than the cigar smoking satirist, he has in a sense lived in the large and provocative shadow of his brother's renown. Still Mr Waugh—our Mr Waugh—went along publishing his novels and doing quite all right. He seemed to fit the niche of the solid professional who lived in relative comfort. When his new manuscript came along a little while back, we should be willing to bet Farrar Straus and Cudahy were pleased in a routine kind of way. At least that's how *we* would have responded, we confess.

But then something happened. We don't know what exactly. Maybe

334

Mr Waugh put a little extra something into his novel titled 'Island in the Sun'. Maybe Farrar, Straus and Cudahy, or one of the editors there, found a way to put it over. At any rate Mr Waugh's newest fiction has gone over with an allergaroo, as they say in college. *Instance* the Reader's Digest Book Club has taken it for its mid-winter issue. *Instance* the Ladies' Home Journal is serialising it in five instalments. *Instance* the Literary Guild has made it their January selection. *Instance* Twentieth-Century Fox has bought it and the film will be produced by Darryl Zanuck.

Mr Straus, we understand, wrote Mr Waugh the tidings and at the end added 'I suppose you will be shopping for a yellow Jaguar'. Mr Waugh replied no, he didn't even hold a driver's licence. Jaguar or not, licence or not, Mr Waugh will roll into New York in time for culminating celebrations January next.

There was a letter from Roger Straus listing some of the parties and publicity that he was planning for my arrival in the week after publication. He himself was giving me an evening party at his house: there was to be a cocktail party on one of the Grace Line ships on the eve of its sailing on a luxury Caribbean cruise. I was to appear on the 'Today' show. I was clearly going to be fêted, yet as the day approached I became increasingly apprehensive. It still seemed to be fantastic that a novel should be a best-seller before a single critic had pronounced judgement on it. What an opening it gave for an irritated reviewer. I reminded myself that 'my man in London', who had thought so poorly of the book, was an exceptionally sound critic. The failings in the book might well be more marked than its merits. I could imagine a disgruntled envious reviewer writing: 'The contemporary literary market has reached an all-time low when a novel can gross very nearly half a million dollars before a single qualified critic has given his opinion and before the public has had an opportunity of deciding whether it is to its taste. The arbiters of popular taste are a small panel of interested persons who sit on editorial boards and book club committees; a dozen people at the most decide what the public is to read, and dictate the public taste. Let us, therefore, examine at length, carefully and judicially, the book that has been accepted for this fantastic acclamation.'

He would then proceed to pull the book to pieces as 'my man in London' had. 'And this is the book,' he would conclude, 'that has been accorded this ridiculous financial accolade, when books of genuine quality sell their few thousand copies and their authors are driven to hack work of various kinds to provide them with the leisure in which to write them. To what a parlous state have the standards of critical taste descended?'

A certain type of critic would be sorely tempted. He would believe himself to be performing a high service to literature. And perhaps he might be. It was, after all, ridiculous that one book should earn so much, when better books earned so little. And it might not be only one ill-tempered critic who wrote in that tone. The majority might well agree with my London agent. I might be made a laughing stock. I tried to console myself with the thought that even if I were, I should have my share of a considerable bulk of bullion stacked away. That was well worth a blush. But all the same, I was apprehensive.

I was due to dock in New York on the first Saturday in January. The book was published on the Tuesday. On that evening I received in mid-Atlantic a cable from Roger Straus congratulating me on my birthday press. The ship stopped at Halifax. I searched the shops for New York papers. I found a copy of the *Herald Tribune*'s Sunday Book Supplement. It contained a long review by Virgilia Petersen. There was hardly a single 'but' in a page of praise. I re-read and re-re-read it. The sentences so imprinted themselves on my mind that I quoted them in my dreams. I woke up repeating them. That showed me how apprehensive I had been. I need not have been. It was roses, roses all the way.

Success is a heady wine. For a man who had never in his most prosperous period earned fifteen thousand dollars in a year, and usually thought himself lucky to get away with ten, the sudden earning in four weeks of more than he had made in forty years, at the age of fifty-six, may well appear a shattering experience. So many things that had been out of reach all my life and that I had ceased to expect to come within it were now accessible. There was a parallel with Jurgen's recovering of his youth in middle age. Yet actually the very fact that I was fifty-six made the experience unexplosive. I knew that I had only a brief summer to enjoy. I could not at my age, with nearly forty books already written, expect to follow up this success. I had neither the energy nor the material. Moreover, I was a man who had built his life the way he wanted and had no wish to alter it. I liked its rootless, semi-bachelor pattern. I liked living in hotels. I loved the sun, and the grey skies of an English winter saddened me. I loved to travel, to be a part of a dozen different worlds. I was a scattered person. I liked my life the way it was. I had no wish to have it any different. *Island in the Sun* made it possible for me to continue to lead the same life a little longer, a bit more amply.

Micawber said that to have an annual income of twenty pounds, and spend twenty pounds and sixpence was misery, but to have twenty pounds a year and spend nineteen pounds, nineteen shillings and sixpence was happiness. Up to the summer of 1955 I had always been slightly, though not dangerously, in the red. Now I was comfortably in the black. I committed no rash extravagances. I travelled more often and I travelled farther. I went round the world. I went to Japan and Brazil for the P.E.N. Club Congresses. I spent a winter in Siam. Once or twice I flew first class by Pan American for the experience, but for the most part I continued to fly tourist. I was on my guard against the

337

humiliation I might feel when I could no longer afford to travel first, and had to confess to my travel agent that I must travel cheaply.

I did not patronize *de luxe* hotels. In New York I did not want to live anywhere but at the Algonquin. I took a suite, though, instead of a one-room studio apartment. When I entertained I still went to the Chateaubriand, but I ordered better wines and I entertained more often. In London, by throwing a few parties, I was able to re-establish contact with old friends I had lost touch with.

I was also able to take over a number of expenses connected with my children. I stocked up on my wardrobe. I acquired enough clothes to last me for six years and the Brandt office's secretary Frieda Lubelle cunningly converted a proportion of my royalties into 'stocks and bonds'.

From the outside, I continued to live precisely the same life that I had two years before and I had the consoling knowledge that when the inevitable slump arrived the signs of it would not be apparent to my friends; they would scarcely be apparent to me. I should be doing the same things, only on a smaller scale, less frequently. And by then I should be ten years older. I should have less energy. I should be content with less. In *The Forsyte Saga* Galsworthy refers to Soames's parents as having ceased to give big parties. They had reached the point when the servants realize that 'the master and the mistress are no longer up to it'.

In 1917 *The Loom of Youth* had been published in the same week that I went to France as a machine-gun subaltern; so that my head did not get turned with flattery and parties. Now in 1956, the postman had knocked a second time. I was protected by my age and tastes from establishing a changed way of living that I could not maintain.

338

Had I been told in the summer of 1954 that a novel of mine was going to enjoy such an astonishing success as *Island* did, I should have imagined that my whole life would be reorientated. It is surprising how little difference it has made in the long run. Early in November 1964, I went down to Nice to write the last half of a novel whose back I had broken in the MacDowell Colony in the preceding spring. I hoped to finish it by the middle of January when I planned to return to England. I should be following precisely the same routine that I had eleven years earlier when I was writing the first half of *Island*. I was not staying in the same hotel, the Escurial, but the Windsor in the Rue Dalpozzo was in the same area, and I passed the Escurial every morning on my way to the same Brasserie for breakfast. The Brasserie de Lyons in the Avenue de la Victoire had now become the Grande Café de Lyons, but several of the same waiters were at work. It was smarter, but I looked out on precisely the same view, as I drank my morning coffee over the *Nice-Matin*.

My routine was still the same with one of my two main meals a picnic in my austere hotel bedroom. There would be the same afternoon siesta with the day's work finished and the sunset stroll along the Promenade des Anglais before the arrival of the London papers and the reading of them in Café Monnot over a coffee, where there was music and singing in the afternoon; and now, as then, would be the problem of the two hours to be filled in between six and eight, when shops and offices were closing, and men and women, boys and girls, were hurrying back to their homes and families; and loneliness would descend, and I would combat the impulse to sit in a café over a beer, by spending two hours in a cinema. It was all exactly as it had been eleven years before. Nice looked the same, in spite of all the new apartment buildings along the road to Cimiez and the Promenade des Anglais. The football that I watched every Sunday, with the same Australian painter, looked just the same although Nice had temporarily slipped from the first into the second division, and I felt the same, although I was eleven years older.

There was only one difference: my retirement from the literary arena, which could not be many months distant now, was protected behind a bastion of blue chips; and that did make a difference.